I0084719

GLOBALIZATION AND RESPONSIBILITY

Challenges and Opportunities

Edited by
Stefan Litz

Globalization and Responsibility

Challenges and Opportunities

Edited by
Stefan Litz

Common Ground Publishing 2015

First published in 2015 in Champaign, Illinois, USA
by Common Ground Publishing LLC
as part of Global Studies books

Library of Congress Cataloging-in-Publication Data

Globalization and responsibility : challenges and opportunities / Stefan Litz (ed.).
pages cm
Includes bibliographical references.
ISBN 978-1-61229-793-4 (pbk : alk. paper) -- ISBN 978-1-61229-794-1 (pdf)
1. Globalization--Economic aspects. 2. Globalization. 3. International relations. 4. International economic relations. I. Litz, Stefan.
HF1365.G5776 2015
303.48'2--dc23
2015023060

Cover Photo Credit: Phillip Kalantzis-Cope

Table of Contents

CHAPTER 1

Globalization and Responsibility: Challenges and Opportunities

Stefan Litz

The on-going globalization processes poses unique challenges to as well as ample opportunities for socially and environmentally responsible business and management. It is imperative for present and future leaders in business to investigate the challenges and opportunities if they wish to thrive in their field. This reader is designed to help students, scholars and practitioners to (further) familiarize themselves with the contentious issues in the area of business and globalization. The collection contains many thought-provoking papers that can also be used as reading materials for university courses, seminars and colloquia dealing with the nexus of globalization, business, management, responsibility, and ethics. Discussing the issues presented in the reader can be very useful for developing a critical understanding of the challenges and opportunities of globalization for business and management.

Teodor Negru's article will highlight that globalization processes are not a recent phenomenon but have been around for centuries, beginning with the conceptualization of the world as a globe. He points out that economically motivated explorations and trade, aided by scientific discoveries, political expansionism and colonialism, have created hybrid cultures around the world. Notably, the globalization processes engender socio-economic forces for the homogenization of culture and economic system. In this regard, societal changes can be perceived as being driven by a dialectical process of hybridization and homogenization. In the next article, Pedro Geiger analyzes globalization processes from a geo-historical perspective discussing theorists such as Marx, Lenin, Hegel, Kautsky and others. He differentiates the globalization process into three distinct historical economic stages, i.e. Mercantilism, Capitalism and contemporary Globalization. Geiger stresses that the needs of business and the economic sphere propel economic globalization and consequently cultural and social globalization. If globalization is a century long process primarily driven by business and economic forces, it is important to consider the role of the (nation)-

state. Alessandra Sarquis challenges in this context the notion of the demise of the nation-state becoming a puppet of the economic forces. Sarquis points out that, as a consequence of the globalization process, the nation-state though needs to cooperate more than ever with other states and other political actors in order to resolve economic or other social conflicts arising in the global economy.

Next in line, my own paper discusses *grobalization* and *glocalization* processes in multinational corporations (MNCs) by employing George Ritzer's (2003) four different types of globalization processes. Drawing on the macro level analysis of globalization developed by Ritzer (2003), my paper adds a meso-level dimension and pays attention to the different types of globalization processes unfolding *within* organizations. Given that modern societies are "organizational societies" (Presthus 1962) it stresses that an analysis of the various key organizational elements (management, production process, products etc.) reveals the different importance of the various intertwined sub-processes of globalization within MNCs. Arguably, corporate globalization processes are ultimately driven by the economic imperatives of capitalism: maximize profit. In this sense, globalization means simply making the capitalist mode of production and consumption ubiquitous around the globe. Capitalist globalization, therefore, leads to the "end of history" (Fukuyama 2006). Hosseini's article in the reader discusses how the perception of corporate driven injustice and increasing inequality triggers individuals and organizations to resist the current mode of capitalist globalization and consequently to challenge the system. Hosseini suggests an integrative theory of justice that could serve as a new foundation on which to build upon ultimately a more just economic system and business practices. He highlights the emergence of a "transversalist notion of justice" while outlining some basic principles required to deal with the universalisms and particularities of (in)justice.

But as history shows, notions of (in)justice are continuously changing. Randall Horton argues in his contribution that what is morally acceptable for conducting business and trade has significantly changed over time. For example, while slave trade was once a widely accepted, legitimate business activity, today slave trade is not only immoral but also illegal. Horton stresses that the changes in notions about morally appropriate behavior does not automatically come about. He argues that the development of humanities (philosophy and literature) and exposure to the humanities in education have played and continue to play an important role in changing moral attitudes and behavior of the population and political and business leaders. Perhaps in the near future, given the virulent climate change problem, the exploitation and pollution of natural resources by businesses and corporations will be increasingly regarded as criminal offences.

In this respect, Elizabeth Edmondson's article grapples with the changing notion of social responsibility with regard to global problems and risks such as climate change. Moving away from the current focus on individual responsibility, she stresses the notion of collective responsibility and relating liability issues. Edmondson argues that not only individual actors but also collective actors may be jointly held responsible for their (non)activities. In this context, she stresses the role of nation-states in protecting societies from human-made climate change. John Janzekovic's paper further elaborates on the notion of collective responsibility. He argues that the very core of collective responsibility (so far mainly related to humanitarian protection from war and genocide) is changing. The responsibility of states and international organizations is shifting from the duty to protect humans from violations of their human rights to *preventing* them to occur in the first instance. Janzekovic discusses this shift in the context of concerted efforts to protect and prevent genocides. This shift also applies to corporations and businesses of all types. Managers and business leaders must take appropriate steps to protect employees and the wider communities from incidents of human right violations.

In the following article, Raymond Izarali suggests that in order to mitigate the negative effects of globalization processes, politicians and leaders of business communities around the world should especially take measures to ensure that states and corporations respect basic human rights. Not only should a global minimum moral standard be established and enforced but corporate activities and human right violations need to be monitored and reported in a transparent and reliable manner by corporate agencies. Consequently, the role of accounting in general may have to change significantly. From being primarily financial bookkeepers focusing on reporting corporate financial conduct, accountants will have to need to also report corporate social responsibility (CSR) conduct. Susan Wild and Edwin Mares illustrate in their paper that the role of accountants in New Zealand has already changed significantly. In consequence, a solid command of globally standardized CSR reporting frameworks including the UN Global Compact and the GRI Reporting Framework is likely to become one of the key professional requirements and occupational skills of accountants and general managers alike.

But what kind of Ethics should be the basis of socially responsible business that successfully balances profit making with social commitments? Lydia Amir grapples with this question in her contribution. She highlights that Spinoza's ethics can provide the theoretical underpinning of Business Ethics as it is, in contrast to many other virtue ethics, not demonizing the profit seeking motive. For Spinoza, the act of money making is wrong only if the reason lies in seeking pride in itself and demonstrating superiority. But if the act is driven by the need to satisfy certain basic human needs (e.g. food, housing etc.), it is not an indecent act.

Henry Venter and Elaine Venter's paper also concerns the idea that profit making is acceptable, if it is driven by the search to fulfill basic human needs and that it may serve the wider community as profits are used in a socially responsible way. In this respect, the authors discuss the well-known pyramid of "human needs" proposed by Abraham Maslow. According to Maslow's concept of a "need hierarchy", the attempt to fulfill perceived needs is the main driving force or motivator in life. As lower level needs categories, such as "safety" and "security", are satisfied to a certain degree, higher level needs, like "social belonging" and "self-actualization", become driving forces. The standard business textbook outlines that the needs in the category of "self-actualization" are the highest in the hierarchy but since it is a "growth need", it may never been fully satisfied. Venter and Venter hold the view that Maslow has actually proposed another level of human needs, the need for "self-transcendence". Individuals at the level of "self-actualization" are still primarily concerned about themselves rather than others. The behavior of people at the level of "self-transcendence" is, however, motivated by something "beyond themselves". This includes and requires taking the perspective of Others and the need to help others to fulfill their needs. Few individuals actually may ever reach the "self-actualization" level in the needs hierarchy and even fewer may ever reach the "self-transcendence" level. Yet, the capability of "perspective taking" and considering the needs of Others may be the *sine qua non* for responsible action.

But even for an individual who reached the need-category of "self-transcendence", another difficult psychological step has to be made in order to include distant Others beyond their immediate local neighborhood or their own in-group (e.g. country, nation, ethnicity etc.). In fact, as Charles Wright points out in this essay, psychological and evolutionary studies demonstrated that taking the perspective of Others is quite a difficult challenge. It reinforces the view that most people are quite unlikely to ever reach the "self-transcend" level to take the perspectives of distant Others into account. In the last paper, however, I argue that "self-transcendence" may not be needed for individuals to behave in a responsible manner. Egoistic "self-centrism" and "self-love" may in fact be the key to ensuring responsible behaviour. Drawing on Erich Fromm, I argue that as some dangers and risks are global and imminently threaten ourselves, we have the motivation to behave responsibly and to reduce the harms to distant Others, while primarily motivated by the desire to protect oneself. Ironically, selfish attitude may lead to unselfish and even responsible behavior and positive outcomes at the end. In other words: fostering "self-love" (i.e. egoism) rather than the "self-transcendence" (i.e. altruism) may lead humans to behave in a responsible manner.

I hope that the papers collected in this book will help students and scholars interested in Business Ethics, Corporate Social Responsibility and International Business to further enhance their background knowledge in this field. It features a range of contributions which are focusing on various facets of responsibility primarily related to business activities and ethical management within the context of globalization. Even though the selection of the contributions in this book has been primarily made for scholars and students in the area of business, it may serve as a good starting point for students and scholars in other disciplines who are interested in exploring issues of globalization and business responsibility.

Needless to say that there are other readers available also presenting collections of papers on globalization. For example, Steger's (2010) "*Globalization: The Greatest Hits, A Global Studies Reader*" presents a collection of some of the most prominent contributions in the field of global studies. George Ritzer's and Zeynep Atalay's (2009) *Readings in Globalization: Key Concepts and Major Debates* also provides a whole range of key contributions, particularly discussing globalization processes in relation to culture and political economy. David Held and Anthony McGrew's (2003) T*he Global Transformations Reader: An Introduction to the Globalization Debate* and Frank Lechner and John Boli's (2011) *The Globalization Reader* as well as David Held, Anthony McGrew, and Gareth Schott's (2007): *Globalization Theory: Approaches and Controversies*, are also offering a stack of collected key papers. Most of the texts included in the mentioned readers are especially from the fields of political sociology, cultural studies, politics, and sociology. They are providing a great resource for additional reading.

References

Fukuyama, Francis. 2006. *The End of Historyand the Last Man*. New York: Avon Books.

Held, David and Anthony McGrew. 2003. *The Global Transformation Reader: An Introduction to the Globalization Debate*. Cambridge: Polity Press.

Held, David, Anthony McGrew, and Garreth Schott. 2007. *Globalization Theory: Approaches and Controversies.*Cambridge: Polity Press.

Lechner, Frank and John Boli. 2011. *The Globalization Reader*. Chichester: Wiley & Blackwell.

Presthus, Robert. 1962. *The Organizational Society. An Analysis and a Theory*. New York: Alfred A. Knopf.

Ritzer, George and Zeynep Atalay. 2009. *Readings in Globalization: Key Concepts and Major Debates*. Chichester: Wiley & Blackwell.

Ritzer, George. 2003. *The Globalization of Nothing*. Thousand Oaks: Sage.

Steger, Martin. 2010. *Globalization: The Greatest Hits, A Global Studies Reader*. Oxford: Oxford University Press.

CHAPTER 2

The Production of Hybrid Cultural Space

Teodor Negru

INTRODUCTION

We are used to thinking that globalization is a contemporary process that emerged during the second half of the twentieth century, owing to economic, technological, political, or cultural transformations worldwide. The causes usually associated to this phenomenon are: the expansion of capitalism, which has had as a consequence the creation of new world market, the intensification of the relationships between states with a view to removing trade barriers and formulating some global strategies to fight against certain phenomena affecting all the actors on the world stage, proliferation of information technologies and communication systems, having effect on the growth of data processing and transmission speed, the formation of a culture resulted from the development of communication media, which served to promoting the principles of the capitalist market relationships at the expense of traditional values.

The idea of the contemporary origin of globalization was held by the value postmodernism put on the categories of space to explain reality to the detriment of the temporal categories the modernists called for. In this context, the introduction of the idea of globalization came to being as a consequence of the approaches that gave up regarding progress as important, as the main drive of civilization, while preferring to focus on how the world is configured, considering the existing power relationships within the world political framework, positioning capital in the world, the capacities of technology to surpass the spatial barriers, etc. Such an approach that only stresses the current manifestations of globalization does not consider that the origin and constituting the idea of globalization have emerged long before the awareness of it. Regarded from this perspective, modeling the consciousness of human beings, by means of the shape and extent of the space where beings live their live, has been possible ever since the modern period.

The first encounter with the world as a sphere happened at the beginnings of the modern period, when, for the first time, the Earth was empirically proved to be round. This incontestable proof was provided by the first voyage around the world, started by Magellan with five ships, in 1519, and ended by his skipper, Il Cano, who reaches Spain only by one ship in 1521. This was the first global view of the Earth, the first proof of the extent of the space we live in, which ceases to be an exterior under the sign of unreality. Even if many of these geographical discoveries of the modern era were conducted with a view to annex territories and to find easier routes to procure certain resources, their effects was not reduced merely to proliferating capitalism as a new form of organizing the economy. Becoming aware of the spherical shape of the planet represented mainly a new sensitivity of the space which modified the way man's role in the world was understood, the understanding of nature and of the living creatures, and last but not least, which imposed other principles of acquiring the knowledge of the world. Thus, globalization represents not only a consequence of the expansion of capitalism, but a set of consequences generated by the way the terrestrial space was thought of and used over the millennia. Therefore, globalization will not be considered as a contemporary phenomenon but as one connected to man's spatial imaginary, namely to the how the conditions of belonging to this space affect the conception of the human being.

What happened at the beginning of the modern era, alongside the first expedition around the earth, represented the process of transforming the ideal and unreal space into a real one. The idea that the Earth is round had existed ever since the Ancient times, the image of the sphere paying an important role in understanding the universe. This is twofold understanding: on the one hand, we speak about the concept of sphere as an ontological one, which lay at the base of a certain way of understanding the being. This is about a "morphological globalization (or rather onto morphological)" (Sloterdijk 2005, 33) operating on some ideal spheres, the sign of perfection existing in the universe.

On the other hand, modern science aimed at supplying some evidence that the Earth is round, consistent with the new cosmology that placed the Sun in the middle of the universe and transformed the Earth in a moving planet, just like the others. To Copernicus, this new position of the Earth resulted in rethinking the status of man as the world was meant to him and that he has the necessary means to know it. As Hans Blumenberg remarked, Copernicus, by the anthropocentric position he adopted, does not reach the theorization of "self-assertation" of man as during the Enlightenment, but it represents a moment of discontinuity with the medieval view by placing man at the centre of the universe, meaning by man's occupying the position assigned, in the preceding era, to God. But all these changes do not have a direct connection with conceiving the spherical shape of the Earth, which is seen as a consequence of the planet's capacity to move.

> With Copernicus, the Earth's spherical form cannot be the result of imagined physical processes. Instead, it is already a precondition of essential characteristics of this heavenly body, especially of its natural mobility. (Blumenberg 1989, 491)

Theorizations of the spherical shape of the Earth expressed by the Ancient and Renaissance science did nothing but built, based on some metaphysical assumptions, at best, based on some indirect, empirical proof an ideal space with no connection with reality. Therefore, one cannot talk, in this case, about a modelling of thinking starting from the awareness of the Earth's spherical shape. The awareness of the terrestrial space became effective only after the spatial limits of the Earth were discovered. Hence, the Earth ceased to be an idealized sphere and turned into a finite and real space, which determined the replacement of the metaphysical assumptions of understanding reality with the need to use other assumptions that could explain the concrete reality. In lieu of the infinite reality ordered and homogenized by the will of divinity, there emerges a finite but diversified reality, which needs exploring and explaining.

What happened after the provision of the first proof that the Earth is a sphere represented a proliferation of the Earth's globalization modalities. The scientific expeditions, setting forth commercial traffic networks, the discovery and mapping of each geographical area, the expansion of the conquest of the aerial space, photographing the Earth from satellites have modified the perspective on globalization, bringing new elements which have transformed permanently the image of the global space. This does not mean that we should see all these events as connected in a unitary history, unfolded with a view to reaching a certain degree of globalization. The conception of globalization is not subjected to a unitary understanding, but it is guided by the sensitivities and events that marked each stage.

These events can certainly by subordination to some general principles creating the impression of some distinct stages in the creation of globalization. Peter Sloterdijk completes the first stage of globalization, called morphological, with an intermediate stage, from 1492 to 1945, characterized by the era of the European expansion, to reach, in the end, the stage of electronic globalization, characteristic of today's world. Such a division into periods highlights the existence of certain dominant trends in building the space we live in. For example, the idea of globalization cannot be separated from the capitalist expansionist tendencies or by the proliferation of communication technologies and mass media, which modeled a certain perception of the space. But, beyond these generalizations, the representation of the terrestrial space was marked by a plethora of events which led to the understanding of the new dimensions of globalization. From the first voyage around the earth to the First World War, from the first world economic crisis to the first photograph of the Earth taken from space, all these globalizing events, to which many others have been added, have produced new meanings of globalization. Therefore, instead of talking about stages, we prefer talking about waves of globalization, which means that the Earth globalization has been constantly produced by offering new perspectives on the representation of the space we live in.

Producing the Global World

The first voyage around the world revealed the fact that the space we live in is limited; it is nonetheless diversified, which make it impossible to contain in a single incursion. Therefore, the specificity of the modern era is given by the construction of spatial barriers as humans explore and take possession of the terrestrial space open to them. Until the complete representation of the terrestrial space, it is divided in the West and the East, in an extended space and a conquered and possessed space. In its beginnings, the image of globalization is colonialism that consisted of the concrete export of the Western culture and civilization to the new territories, while the knowledge of the world was increasingly enriched via the contact with the new spaces. Thus, the need for better and better theoretical and technological tools became apparent in order to encompass the diversity characterizing the world. In other words, similarly to the previous stage, the exchanges between the metropolis and peripheral territories, between the West and the adjacent civilizations (which, according to the era, were the Phoenicians, the Egyptians, the Arabs, etc.) have determined the consolidation of the first global "product," i.e. science. Man's status in this world, which, on the one hand, is destructured in its hierarchical order, and, on the other hand, becomes finite in terms of extent, is given by man's capacity of "self-assertation", which is materialized in their capacity to choose solutions to their problems and to configure their destiny, independently from the divine will.

> Self-assertation "represents an existential program, according to which man posits his existence in historical situation and indicates to himself how he is going to deal with the reality surrounding him and what use he will make of possibilities that are open to him. In man's understanding of the world, and in the expectations, assessments, and significations that are bound up with that understanding, a fundamental change takes place,

> which represents not a summation of facts of experience but rather a summary of things taken for granted in advance [Präsumptionen], which in their turn determine the horizon of possible experiences and their interpretation and embody the 'a priori' of the world's significance for man. (Blumenberg 1983, 138)

Proclaiming independence from divinity has also determined the rethinking of the way the world functions. Thus, idea of the mechanism of the image governed by divine principles emerges and becomes a means of "self-asserting" man's capacities which allow him to know and subject the natural laws, which are independent from the divine will. Man's "self-assertation" involves the development of the means to conquer and dominate the space, which also means the objective representation of the space according to the mathematical principles that are the basis of any scientific research. The rational representation of the space is materialized in its mapping, by which modern science creates an abstract space which allows for the rigorous delimiting of territories and the precise location of the so diverse cultures and customs. Associating the subject to a certain space characterized by a specific culture becomes an essential requirement of the modern subject's stability, besides their focusing on reason.

Moreover, the requirement of man's self-assertation becomes the possibility of travelling faster and faster within this space, which, by representation, becomes more and more compact and familiar. Speed makes possible a new representation of the global world, which, owing to the means of transportation that do not provide speed only, but greater safety as well, by sea and by land, and to the transfer of information from the centre to the periphery and the other way round, produces a space more and more accessible to mobility. The idea of mobility is also included in the modern concept of progress, which heralded the continuous development that would mark the global world in the context of the more and more accelerated transformations in all the fields of knowledge. If continuous movement becomes the essence of modern civilization, then it will affect human nature as well. The inclination towards action, the proliferation of inventions, and the search for novelty are the new coordinates of the modern man, whose role is to find new ways of accelerating movement. The idea of progress becomes thus:

> the center of what modern philosophy calls subjectivity. Its essence is inseparable from the mysterious initial force that expresses itself as the ability to ignite new chains of movement, which we call "actions." If something like progress does exist as a matter of fact it is because movements originating from subjectivity do undeniably take place. Kinetically they are the material that modernity is made of. When a

> subject gets to the point of carrying out the thought "progress," then within him a self-igniter introduces progress-like self-movements. Whoever really knows what progress is already is moving toward what has been conceived; he knows it because he has progressed and is progressing further. Those who understand what modernity is can only understand it based on the self-igniting self-movement without which modernity would not exist. He must have made a step forward in his self-creation—the step that remains the kinetic element of further progress. Progress is initiated by this step toward the step that at first introduces itself, by itself, in order to run over itself. Therefore, the term "progress" does not mean a simple change of position where an agent advances from A to B. In its essence, the only "step" that is progressive is the one that leads to an increase in the "ability to step." Thus, the formula of modernizing processes is as follows: Progress is movement toward movement, movement toward increased movement, movement toward an increased mobility. (Sloterdijk 2006, 37)

Transforming progress into the main aim of the modern society heralds the beginning of the space compression process by increasing the speed of vehicles, information, etc., that is exceeding global distances by means of mechanized technologies.

The image of the space saturated by faster and faster vehicles is illustrated in Jules Verne's novel "Around the World in Eighty Days," whose very title anticipates the performances of modern technology. If the first voyage around the world took three years, filled with tragic moments (and culminating with the demise of its initiator), the voyage imagined by Jules Verne takes less than three months, and is rather filled with exciting adventures, where the hero criss-crosses the world like a tourist. Using the main means of transportation provided by the industrial revolution, the train and the steamer, and even anticipating the assault of the aerial space, which would represent the next stage in the space compression, the hero, Phileas Fogg, shows another facet of globalization. To modernity, global space means incorporating the West and the East in traffic networks, supported by the discoveries of the technical civilization[1].

---

[1] Sloterdijk (2005, 62) highlighted in German: „Es illustriert die quasi-geschichtsphilosophische These, es sei der Sinn modernen Verhältnisse, den Verkehr im Weltmaßstab zu trivialilisieren. Nur in einem globalisierten Ortsraum lassen sich die neuen Mobilitätsbedürfnisse organisieren, die den Personentransport ebenso wie den Warenverkehr auf die Basis von ruhigen Routinen stellen wollen. Verkehr ist die Inbegriff reversibler Bewegungen."

Modernism does not pose the issue of discovering the space but of covering it at the highest speed. Hence, Jules Verne's hero symbolizes the modern man in a permanent movement, to whom covering distances as fast as possible, or even removing them, is at stake. Not as a last point, we should point out that within the new global space, marked by the accelerating possibilities of modernity, the media play an increasingly important role. Fogg's presence amidst every instance of the voyage is closely monitored from the centre, owing to the telegraph which allows for the transmission of information in a very short time. The media herald thus their future role as the main means of compressing the space.

The conquest of the aerial space and the possibility of travelling in the outer space have determined not only a new mobility of information but also a new perspective on the terrestrial space, which have contributed to changing the way space is constructed. Increasing the speed of travelling in space has been facilitated by the advent of computers, whose network surrounding the entire world, have virtualized the space, making its compression even more accelerated[2].

The discovery of the natural space in the modern times and its research by building artificial spaces used by the means of locomotion and communication is followed by the discovery of the global space via producing the virtual one. Transforming space into a virtual one involves the interconnection of all the points on the globe with a view to creating a space that lack traditionally territorial tensions. The new space created by the information and communication technologies, the media included, is described as a space freed from any barriers, which facilitates the acceleration of information or of the capital speed aiming at instantaneity. Parallel to this virtual space, which simulates reality up to the point where it becomes a simulacrum, the perception of space is affected by the circulation of capital. In the post-fordist era of flexible accumulation, space is created according to the way capital finds possibilities of multiplying itself.

---

[2] Sloterdijk (2005, 217) continued to outline: „Virtuelle Schalen haben den imaginierten Ätherhimmel ersetzt; durch funk-elektronische Systeme ist das Wegdenken der Entfernungen in den Macht- und Konsumzentren effektiv implementiert. Die global players leben in einer Welt ohne Abstände. In aeronautischer Hinsicht ist die Erde auf eine Jet-Flugstrecke von höchstens fünfzig Stunden reduziert; bei Satelliten-Umrundungen und Mir – Umläufen, neuerdings in Umläufen der Internationalen Raumstation ISS, haben sich Einheiten von circa neunzig Minuten eingespielt; für Radio und Lichtbotschaften ist die Erde nahezu auf einen stehenden Punkt geschrumpft – sie rotiert, als zeitkompakte Kugel, in einem electronischen Filz, der sie wie eine zweite Atmosphäre umgibt.“.

> But the collapse of spatial barriers does not mean that the significance of space is decreasing. Not for the first time in capitalism's history, we find the evidence pointing to the converse thesis. Heightened competition under condition of crisis has coerced capitalists into paying much closer attention to relative locational advantages, precisely because diminishing capital barriers give capitalist the power to exploit minute spatial differentiations to good effect. Small differences in what the space contains in the way of labour supplies, resources, infrastructures, and the like become of increased significance. Superior command over space becomes an even more important weapon in class struggle. It becomes one of the means to enforce speed-up and the redefinition of skills on recalcitrant work forces. (Harvey 1989, 294)

The latest wave of globalization is under the sign of virtuality, involved by the digital revolution and by the increasingly volatile feature brought about by the acceleration of capital. Hence, if in the modern era space was produced by tracing spatial borders, and during modernism, space has been homogenized via speed, in postmodernism, space is being produced by virtualization. It does not involve homogenizing space but enhanced possibilities of interaction among all such areas so that „what happens in a local neighbourhood is likely to be influenced by factors such as world money and commodity markets operating at a indefinite distance away from that neighbourhood itself' (Giddens 1990, 64). Modernist tendencies of capital expansion, of differentiating and surpassing distances have determined the creation of an ultra-connected space, which would provide for the multiple contextualization of the self.

Hybridization of the Global Cultural Space

The idea of compressing space owing to some forces which tend to escape man's control (such as capital, technology, etc.) has led to the collapse of the modern spatial categories. This means that the implosion of the local within the global, the removal of the distinction between the centre and the periphery, as well as of the tensions between centralization and decentralization with a view to creating a hybrid space produced at the intersection of various cultural traditions and civilizations, of the information flows or of the influence of the capital concentration centres, which are now closer than ever. The hyper-mobility of the contemporary world has determined its conception as a "world of disjunctive flows," which means that „the paths or vectors taken by the kinds of things have different speeds, axes, points of origin and termination, and varied relationships to institutional structures in different regions, nations, and societies." (Appadurai

2001, 5-6) Any local manifestation cannot escape the disjunctive flows criss-crossing the contemporary world, hence manifesting itself as a global event and acquiring new meanings, by displacement from the original framework where it was created.

The new condition of producing the space is implied by the concept of glocalization (Ronald Robertson), which defines the hybrid space where what is local and what is global make each other and interpenetrate. The newly created space is a space of fragmentations where local elements translated in global codes, cut out the discontinuity areas. Hence, the cancellation of the idea of a homogenous globalization, which would standardize all local manifestations and would reduce them to some mere clichés – universally accepted due to the fact that they have been sustained by shallow consumerist rhetoric.

> In other words, much of the promotion of locality is in fact done from above and outside. Much what is often declared to be local is in fact the local expressed in terms of generalized recipes of locality. Even in the cases where there is apparently no concrete recipe at work – as in the case of some of the more aggressive forms of contemporary nationalism there is still, or so I would claim, a translocal factor at work. Here I am simply maintaining that the contemporary assertion of ethnicity and/or nationality is made within the global terms of identity and particularity. (Robertson 1995, 26)

Furthermore, the globalization idea leaves behind the tensions between the centre and periphery, specific to colonialism. On the one hand, the compressed space lacks a unique centre, which would radiate power and would assimilate the areas around it, turning them into adjacent spaces. We speak about a "Thirdspace" (Soja) or an "in-between space" (Bhabha), which represents a new understanding of the space situated beyond the materiality of the spatial forms (Firstspace) or the transcendent structures that make space representation (Secondspace) possible). In this way, one aims at overcoming the constraining dichotomies of the oppressive modernity[3] and opening toward a "other-than" or "additional otherness," which involves exploring and proliferating new cultural identities. On the other hand, within the compressed space, the reactionary force of the local is

---

[3] "*Everythings* comes together in Thirdspace: subjectivity and objectivity, the abstract and the concrete, the real and the imagined, the knowable and the unimaginable, the repetitive and the differential, structure and agency, mind and body, consciousness and unconscious, the disciplined and the transdisciplinary, everyday life and unending history." (Soja 1996, 56.)

lessened as compared to the previous periods when it would manifest itself as resilience to the dominant trends of the centre. What is local is now seen as being inevitably built up on what is global. Despite the differences expressed by local forces, turning them into enclaves and isolating them from the rest of the world is no longer possible.

Glocalisation implies deterritorialisation and reterritorialization of culture, as its constitutive processes. Deterritorialization of culture refers to „this general weakening of the ties between culture and place, to the dislodging of cultural subjects and objects from particular or fixed locations in space and time." (Inda 2008, 11.) Detaching cultural products from the environment where they were created is followed by their re-territorialization in other cultural spaces and using other cultural codes in order to understand them. Deterritorialization of culture has occurred due to the exacerbation of the forms of capitalism of modernity, which, one should admit, have configured the global post-modernism we live in. Mass media and communication technologies have allowed transmission of images and messages beyond national borders, creating thus the possibility of universal cultural forms, addressed to masses of people, to exist, which would further allow the exploration of some new identities, different from those existing in the traditional spaces. Circulation of goods and capitals, encouraging any kind of consumption have led to adopting new life styles where the mix of trans-cultural elements would promise the way to reach a happy and fulfilled life[4]. Moreover, people migration either in search for new jobs or due to on-going wars has determined the formation of some new diasporic cultures which combine elements of the original culture with cultural elements of the transited countries. And it is not last to mention, the circulation of political ideas has determined the creation of "concatenation of ideas, terms and images, including 'freedom', 'welfare' ,'rights' , 'sovereignty' , 'representation' and the master-term 'democracy'" (Appadurai 1997, 299) whose content generates multiple locally-tinted speeches.

The postmodern globalization creates thus a hybrid culture which is situated beyond the modernist distinction high culture – popular culture. The search for a pure, genuine cultural form is denounced in postmodernism as a totalitarian endeavour, which tries to reduce the cultural field to a dominant cultural code that cancels the plurality of artistic expression. Hybridisation represents precisely the acceptance of the multiplicity of styles characterizing the global world and which is expressed by means of the mélange, collage, or montage.

---

[4] "We exalt in our ability to confound the high priests of modernity by changing our identities on a whim precisely by changing the forms of difference we consume, even by playfully consuming more than one identity at any one time." (Kahn 1995, 125).

> The overall tendency towards increasing global density and interdependence, or globalization, translates, then, into the, pluralisation of organizational forms. Structural hybridization and the mélange of diverse modes of organization give rise to a pluralisation of forms of co-operation and competitions as well as to novel mixed forms of co-operations. This is the structural corollary to flexible specialization and just-in-time capitalism and, on the other hand, to cultural hybridization and multiple identities. Multiple identities and the decentring of the social subject are grounded in the ability of individuals to avail themselves of several organizational options at the same time. Thus globalization is the framework for the amplification and diversification of „sources of the self." (Pieterse 1995, 52)

Just as the idea of glocalization denounces the arbitrariness of the traditionally spatial categories, the idea of hybridization gives up the conservation of traditional forms, decontextualizing them and combining them with a view to displaying this diversity of styles which characterises the contemporary world. The mix of cultural practices has led to approaching the global culture in terms of 'creolisation' (Hannerz), 'orientalization of culture' (Featherstone), 'the hegemony of rewriting the Eurocentre' (H. Bhaba) or 'translocated culture' (J. N. Pieterse).The global cultural space in the contemporary world is a hybrid space where perfection, authenticity, and genuineness are no longer sought, but the interaction among the cultural forms undergoing continuous change.

Globalization/homogenization	*Globalization/diversification*
cultural imperialism	cultural planetarization
cultural dependence	cultural interdependence
cultural hegemony	cultural interpenetration
autonomy	syncretism, synthesis, hybridity
modernization	modernization
Westernation	global mélange
cultural synchronization	creolisation, crossover
world civilization	global ecumene

(Pieterse, 1995, p. 62)

Hybridization becomes a hallmark of the contemporary world in its wholeness, representing the new reality of a contingent world where nothing is stable any longer. Whether it is about the imaginary of hybridization taken from man's interaction with technology (e.g. cyborg, virtual multi-sensory stimulation), whether we discuss the imaginary of hybridization created by biotechnologies (under the guise of improving man's natural abilities), or about the imaginary of hybridization of the different cultural forms (e.g. new artistic expressions, new life styles), all these are the expression of the contemporary man's hybrid cultural identity. The consequence of compressing the global space and of the implosion of the global within the local has meant the generalization of the experience of hybridization, meaning the hybridization of man's cultural manifestation forms alongside their affirmation within the global space.

REFERENCES

Appardurai, Arjun. 2001. "Disjuncture and Difference in the Global Cultural Economy" In *Global Culture: Nationalism, Globalization and Modernity*, edited by Mike Featherstone, 295-310. London: Sage.

Appadurai, Arjun. 2001. "Grassroots Globalization and the Research Imagination" In *Globalization*, edited by Arjun Appadurai, 1-20. Durham: Duke University Press.

Baker, Chris. 1999. *Television, Globalisation and Cultural Identities*. Buckingham and Philadelphia: Open University Press.

Blumenberg, Hans. 1983. *The Legitimacy of the Modern Age*. Cambridge: MIT Press.

Blumenberg, Hans. 1989. *The Genesis of the Copernican World*. Cambridge: MIT Press.

Giddens, Anthony. 1990. *Consequences of Modernity*. Cambridge: Polity.

Harvey, David. 1989. *The Condition of Postmodernity*. Cambridge: Blackwell.

Inda, Jonathan Xavier, and Renato Rosaldo, eds. 2008. *The Anthropology of Globalisation. A Reader*. Malden: Blackwell, 2008

Kahn, Joel S. 1995. *Culture, Multiculture, Postculture*. London: Sage.

Pieterse, Jan Nederveen. 1995. "Globalization as Hybridization" In *Global Modernities*, edited by Mike Featherstone, Scott Lash, and Ronald Robertson, 45-68. London: Sage.

Robertson, Ronald. 1995. "Glocalization: Time-Space and Homogeneity – Heterogeneity" In *Global Modernities*, edited by Mike Featherstone, Scott Lash, and Ronald Robertson, 25-44. London: Sage.

Sloterdijk, Peter. 2005. *Im Weltinnenraum des Kapitals: für eine philosophische Theorie der Globalisierung*. Frankfurt am Main: Suhrkamp.

Sloterdijk, Peter. 2006. "Mobilization of the Planet from the Spirit of Self-Intensification" *The Drama Review* 50: 36-43.

Soja, Edward W. 1996. *Thirdspace: Journeys to Los Angeles and Other Real-and-Imagined Places*. Cambridge: Blackwell.

CHAPTER 3

Globalization Geographies

Pedro Geiger

INTRODUCTION

The expression "globalization" contains in itself a spatial concept. Every historical phase presents its particular social geographical world designs. However, the term globalization emphasizes the bright role of the geographical connections and of the geographical spatial forms and dimensions in the courant world economic and social developments. Parallel movements between geographical changes and social changes appear clearly, as for instance, in the moving of the world hegemony pattern, from a mono or a bi-State center, to plural State centers. It appears also in the present locations took by workers manifestations, which moved from factories to the Metropolis streets. A choice that expresses the new characteristics of the labor class and of the societies, and the new policy strategies undertook by the labor class in a new world conjuncture.

Globalization means a new geography. A geography characterized, not only by the size and the densities of the connecting linkages between the places, but, mainly by the instantaneity of the current communications between the World places, provided by the Informational means. The electronic developments since the last quarter of the past Century inspired the idea of a historical Informational Age (Castells 1989). However, in face of the continuous strong changes observed in every social instance, or system of practices, of all the World societies, Globalization overlaid all other suggested names to express the nowadays historical phase.

However, the restricted applying of the term Globalization to define the present times, receives objections from currants of historians. They argue that the connections between the places of the whole world were being established all the times. Some of the historians concede globalization starting only by the 1500, after the discovery of America, unknown to Europe before this time (Bentley 1996, 749–770). I support the use of globalization to define the present historical phase, considering the recent diffusion of the term, frequently repeated by the media, internalized and pronounced by common people everywhere. Differently, the term Geography has a long existence. It appeared during the Antiquity, together with History, inside the Greek Philosophy. Herodotus's classical statement, "Egypt is a donation of the Nile river" is a first statement about the interactions between the different geographical entities.

New social sciences appeared during the modernity and they started to deal with the spatial and temporal dimensions of their objects. They also started to enlarge the theoretical thinking in social science, while Geography and History remained, practically, for a long time, as descriptive knowledge. This picture reduced the former academic positions occupied by History and, mainly, by Geography. In the case of Geography, inclusively, when some of past authors tried to theorize, they blunder with ideas about a determinism of the physical geography on the human behaving, and on the social inequalities (Semple and Ratzel 1911).

The appearance of Marxian theory, since the 19th Century, introduced the concepts of Historical Materialism and of the historical periodization related to the succession of different modes of production. It also brought the proposal of a build history by an intentioned way. These theses, based on theoretical formulations, together with the academic reactions against them, promoted intense debates, resulting in a recovery of prestige and interest by the History. In the case of Geography, the recovery of it started later, by the last decades, influenced by the postmodern culture and by the globalization.

The culture of Modernity exposed the ideals for more homogeneity, as by demanding the end of classes, the diffusion of the Western civilization, or the replacement of the States by internationalism. While the contemporary postmodern culture emphasized the simultaneity of homogenization and diversification inside the social development, and established the known sentence of "diversity in the unity". As Geography deals with the natural and social diversity of the Earth's surface, this science received a strong philosophical and practical stimulus for reassertion. On the other side, globalization, with its dense nets of geographical connections, emphasized the needs of geographical knowledge. A knowledge in the interests of the capitalist accumulation, but, also in the interest of the social critical theory, as globalization brought new large geographical patterns of inequalities. Thus while during the modernity, and with Marxian influence, the time was emphasized, during the post modernity the space is receiving a same value (Soja 1989). Another source of Geography's recovery in times of globalization lies in the enormous space being occupied by the environmental issue, which comprehends large geographical knowledge.

Following this Introduction, that exposed the current reassertion of the discipline, the paper continues with a first section in which further ideas about the nature of Geography are presented, in light of recent cultural developments. It also deals with the place Geography may occupy in the Marxian view of the social structure. A second section describes the geographical spatial composition of the current globalize world. Then, the geographical space appears as one of a three legged composition that moves history. The third section observes the relations between the current world conjuncture and the current political map. The paper finishes dealing with the main preoccupations of the future, offered by the current geographical map.

Geographical Entities and the Economic Social Formation

It is common to hear that Geography is the science that deals with spatiality. However, as mentioned above, all sciences deal with the spatiality of their built objects of knowledge. On the other hand, in the Introduction above, it was said that culture as a strategy of late capitalism. That helps to solve the posed contradiction.

The postmodern culture brought larger interdisciplinary practices, not only inside each field of activities, as in science, arts, or philosophy, but also between these different fields (Deleuze and Guattari 1992). Philosophy returns occupying a larger space in the production of all other activities. Based on Martin Heidegger's considerations on the issue of beings and entities (Heidegger 1962), I suggest, first, the recognition of a category of geographical entities as rivers, forests, climates, cities, regions, states, etc. They are the components of a geographical space. The explanation on how one defines the geographical entities will not be realized in this paper; the interested reader can find sources in Camille Vallaux's Les Sciences Geographiques (Vallaux 1929). Secondly, I propose defining Geography as the science which has as its object of built knowledge the geographical entities and the spaces they compose. This built knowledge comprehends the interactions of these entities with all the other entities, to give place to the broad meaning of space in the social science, or to the meaning of world-space, in Braudel's (1996) terminology. Therefore it makes Geography being involved in all the social instances.

While time is an abstract reality, the materialized space of the geographical entities may be considered as part of the economic social structure. Any changes in the economic social structure comprehend changes of the geographical space and any change in the built geographical space brings changes in the economic social structure. In Brazil, for instance, the new federal capital, Brasília, 1,200 kilometers from the coast, built during the end of the fifties, facilitated the opening of new roads to the Amazon region, influencing new aspects of the country's development.

The issue of the geographical space appears in Marxian literature (as in the Communist Manifesto proposal of control of cities growth), theoretically in the concept of the economic social formation (Luporini and Sereni 1973). The term formation has one root in the term form, which refers to space, and another root in the term action, which refers to time. Therefore the concept of economic social formation comprehends a geographical location and a historical temporal moment. Therefore, Marxian theory gives room to consider that the geographic space plays roles in the succeeding of the modes of production. As every entity contains a spatial and a temporal dimension, every part of the social structure, its base, or its top, have their spatial or temporal dimensions. As a result, any changing occurring in the economic base, reverberate on the geographic space and vice-versa. In the case of the city of Rio de Janeiro for instance, urban improvement in some slum areas are provoking flows of populations in these areas. One observes the entrance of people from the low middle class and the exit of poorer people.

In conclusion, one may conceive the economic base of a mode of production as being three legged, composed by the means of production, by the social relations of production and by the materialized geographical space composed by them.

The Economic Base and its Three Legged Movements

The social structure is a whole, containing all the social levels and their movements: the economic level, the cultural level, the ideological level and the political level. All these instances or levels interact between themselves, each one with each one of the others, and with the totality. Therefore the movement of each instance, or system of practices, is influenced by the total structure. However each instance disposes of a relative degrees of freedom and history is made by this integration of all these composed and autonomous movements

Geography may also be seen as a totality, composed by diverse geographies that are treated by disciplines as Economic Geography, Political Geography, Cultural Geography and so on. The different geographies will compose a composite geographical environment, or the space of each historical moment. The works of Braudel (1996), as in "La Mediterranée", detach the role of the geographical social space in history. Thus one considers the economic base a three legged system composed by the means of production, by the social relations of production and by their built geographical space.

Some examples are presented, in very brief terms, about the relationship between the movements of the three legged economic base and the changing of modes of production. The movements of the means of production are represented by the technological innovations.

Mercantilism

The invention of the triangular canvas and of the caravel by the Portuguese allowed the use of sea routes in long distance commerce. The intensification of the European commercial activities brought the definitive imposition of the mercantile economy over the feudal agriculture economy.

Merchants and bankers had existed for long, before the mercantile age, but their nearer approaching to the ruling power started with the mercantilism. As described by Shakespeare's "The Merchant of Venice". The build-up of the geographic environment showed the creation of the Hanseatic League during the 13th century. It was an economic and political alliance of merchant cities that brought new rights and new political power to the ascendant class. The mercantile economy represented the major development of the sea and river ports, such as Hamburg, Amsterdam, London, Venice, Boston, among others. The inducer of the invention of the probabilistic mathematics was the intensification of the oceanic commerce and the needs of related insurance practices (Hogben 1939, 595-598).

Capitalism

This paper considers separately the capitalist phases developed until the 80's, and the recent phases known as times of globalization. Actually the changes observed in the economic social and geographical structure are so large that some authors are in doubt about considering the world still being modeled by capitalism as we knew it (Graham and Gibson 2006). The invention of the machine was the basis for the development of industrialization and of capitalism. Socially, capitalism has been characterized by a class structure composed of owners of capital, or of the material means of production, in one side, and workers operating those means of production, in exchange for wages, in the other side.

The geography of capitalism brought in the dominating role of the urbanization. In general, the industrialized countries have from 75% or more of their population living in cities. Dense urban nets with numerous levels of urban hierarchy contain a variety of urban entities as industrial centers, conurbations, metro poles, suburban cities, satellite cities, metropolitan areas, megalopolis and others. Historically capitalism developed is center in countries on the border of the North Atlantic Ocean and of its seas. This ocean did become a sea space with a very high density of navigations. NATO is a military political heritage of capitalism.

Globalization

The continuous enlarging of a virtual world, based on the informational means, is one of the main features of the globalization to a point that in the economic field one created a called virtual economy, distinguished from the called real economy. The virtual and the real economies are led by the corporations. On the base of the informational means of communication a dense net of big transnational corporations dominates the world economic scene. Corporations are present in any of the economic activities.

In a counterpoint, globalization presents the appearance and diffusion of the so called 'creative industries', in which the capitalist relations are minimized. In the creative industries many of their entrepreneurs take part also as workers in the production operations. As known, one Marxian principle characterizes capitalism as a process that dispossessed the artisans from their work instruments. Now the development of the creative industries comprehends a growing picture of workers utilizing their own instruments of production.

The personal computer may be chosen as the symbol of the economic base of the globalization. A multitude of corporation offices furnished with computers for the work of their employees is a common landscape of nowadays and it is also impressive the number of people owing their personal computer for working proposals. In the economic social field one emphasizes also the growing role of the executives, the actual managers of the world economy. They are present in the private sector of the economy, but they also dominate increasingly the public sectors and the governments. In general terms one may consider the Universities as the pool from where this category comes out. Considering a Kalecki's nomenclature, one may think about a three class formation for the present times, consisting of capitalists, wage capitalists and wage owners (Kalecki, 1954). The executives, the managers of capital would be part of the components of the wage capitalists.

Another aspect of the social field refers to the world diffusion of cognitive cultural societies, in which the past division of the working class, between white and blue collars, is being replaced by a division between qualified and non-qualified sectors (Scott 2007, 1465–1482). The development of the so-called 'creative industries' is strongly related to both, to the cognitive cultural society and to the growing economic role played by the cultural instances (Jameson 1996).

With regard to the built environments, globalization presents many of new features. They can be recognized, 1, on the political economic world map; 2, on the social economic world urbanization and regionalization, and 3, on the economic infrastructure world map.

1. At the first capitalist phases in Europe, when the train of coal was the most advanced mean of interurban transportation, countries like England or France were considered big, compared to a small Belgium, or Holland Historically the USA (today a GDP of about 15 trillion dollars, area of about 9.650 million square kilometers and population of about 315 million people) was the first country to establish a national developed capitalist industrial economy in a continental size. After, the former USSR also emerged as a second powerful State in a continental size (Geiger 2010, 75–90).The current geographical political economic map shows the ascension of emergent countries that are also characterized by their continental or sub-continental size to the first rank of the world powers by GDP.

The BRIC, that comprehends the leading emergent, presents China (with about 7 trillion dollars GDP, 9.6 million square kilometers and 1, 4 billion population) now occupying the second world place, having over passed Japan. Brazil (with about 2.5 trillion dollars of GDP, 8.5 million square kilometers of area and a population of 200 million people) that is over passing UK, in GDP, to assume a fifth world position; Russia (with 1.8, 17 and 145, respectively) and India (with 1, 9, 3.2 and 1,200, respectively). The building of the European Union contains the strategy of a similar idea, the creation of an economic entities of a continental scale (about 500 million population, about 5 million square kilometers of area and a GDP of about 15 trillion) The current EU difficulties derive in a large measure from the fact that the EU countries were not capable yet to impose a united centralized management policy on this geographical entity as a whole.

While these large geographical political entities are responsible for a large part of the world production of goods and services, simultaneity a number of small inherited political unities is receiving other economic functions. As for instance the so called ‘fiscal paradises’, small islands distributed around the Oceans, like the Cayman Islands in the Atlantic, or some autonomous cities, devoted particularly to operate financial businesses for capitals streaming from all around the world.

One of the present world economic dilemmas lies in the increasing or not increasing the States controls over the market, particularly over the financial and banking system. These financial centers, called as fiscal paradises, appear precisely as refuges for capitals that intent to escape from the observance of the governments of their countries of origin. At the present times, due to the deep capitalist crisis, loud voices of the public opinion is calling for an international agreement to impose controls and fiscal rules on these fiscal paradises. Another geographical deep change related to the globalization is the economic rise of regions of the Pacific Rim and the high densities reached by shipping in the North Pacific Ocean. Several economic political entities were established during the last decade assembling States of the Pacific Ocean shores, one during this year of 2012 joining Canada, the USA, Mexico, Costa Rica, Colombia, Peru and Chile.

While during the previous capitalist phases, the North Atlantic became as a lake of intense shipping, now it is the North Pacific that is taking such a landscape. The Economist edition of April 4th 2002 showed already higher vessel cargo transportation in the North Pacific, in comparison to the North Atlantic. 2.1 million TEU were moved westbound, and 1.6 million TEU eastbound, between Europe and North America during 2001. While in the Pacific Ocean the figures were, respectively, 3.7 million eastbound and 7.3 westbound

2. The spreading of urbanization over all the continents is a general feature of globalization. However it's a regional selective process which enlarges selected cities, multiplies metropolitan areas, and creates global city regions. While other regions and cities are left aside of the globalization flows and become stagnant. By 2000, beside Tokyo, the first larger urban area, with 27.9 million people, according to UN estimated data, the three following largest were already metropoles of the BRIC, Bombay in India, with a population of 18.1 million, São Paulo, Brazil, with 17.8 and Shanghai, China, with 17.2.

The global city regions "range from familiar metropolitan agglomerations dominated by a strongly developed core, such as the London area (…) to more polycentric geographic units as in the cases of the urban networks of the Randstad or Emilia-Romagna".[The city-regions] "increasingly function as essential spatial nodes of the global economy and as distinctive political actors on the world stage (...) the city in the narrow sense is less an appropriate or viable unit of local social organization than city regions or regional networks of cities" (Scott et al. 2001, 11).

3. As a counter point to the increasing of the metropolitan multitudes and of their new political potentials (Hardt and Negri 2004), another kind of space is being built. It is a space dominated by large transnational corporations where they locate specialized activities, as for instance the specialized port terminals, the hubs, the specialized railways, etc. During the past one saw sea cities holding ports; now, one sees ports on the sea holding cities. Thus, while in the past, by absorbing transfer costs, the common port stimulated the appearance of new entrepreneurs and the city's general development, now, in these spaces controlled by the corporations, the linked cities are reduced to a limited growth. One has a

separation between urban spaces, particularly the metropolitan spaces, that assemble all kind of entrepreneurship and geographical spaces that are occupied by big transnational corporations. Urbanization expands in the metropolitan areas, where still one finds the assembling of a Pleiades of activities and entrepreneurs. In the spaces controlled by the large corporation the urban growth is content. It appears clearly in Brazil, in the case of the hub built on the side of the city of Itaguaí, in the Rio de Janeiro state.

Determinant and Dominant Levels and the New Geographies

Marxian theory defines the social structure as being constituted by a deterministic economic base covered by diverse other levels of social systems of practices, or instances. At any moment, one of these other levels, as the cultural, or the ideological, or the political, or a group of levels, takes a guiding role of the social movement. One calls dominant the level that guides the social movement from the surface. Its action, however, is always influenced by the stimulus or the permanent impulses steaming from the economic base. This economic base acts as a deterministic force, from the bottom (Badiou 1979, 20–23).

A dominant social level defines a conjuncture. When Galileo, utilizing the lunette, discovered and stated that it is the Earth which moves around the sun, a new conjuncture was established. The place occupied by Religion started to be reduced. And because Galileo's statement was introducing this new conjuncture, it raised the strong Church reaction that almost sent him to the bonfire. The new conjuncture was giving the upper hand to scientific experiments in face of religious traditional narratives. It suggested that like the Earth, all the earthly entities may move, including the social structure.

A more recent example can be given by the 1930's conjuncture when the ideological political level reached a maximum charge. And one may say that the economic crises after the First World War stayed behind the spread of the fascist and Nazi ideologies among the Italian and German populations during the 20's and 30's of the last century. Also, the articulation of this ideological level with the political level guided to the outbreak of the Second World War. In spite of the appeasement policies managed by Chamberlain, the high aggressive nature of the Nazis conduced to the War.

A Controversy between Lenin and Kautsky

By 1914, in a sharp attack against Karl Kautsky, W. Lenin, in calling him the "German Marxist", denied his ideas about the possibility of peaceful deals between the democratic capitalist States. In agreement with the ideas of Ralph

Angell, a British economist winner of the 1933 Nobel Prize (Angell, The Great Illusion), Kautsky sustained that, as the wars did become too costly to solve opposite interests, at the end, the democratic capitalist States could reach a situation of a collective deal to control the capitalist system (Kautsky 2008). For Lenin, wars would be inevitable inside the capitalist system. (Lenin, L Ímperialisme). Kautsky, also, did not adhere to the Spartacus's revolution in Germany, and was finally expelled from the Marxist establishment and nicknamed the "renegade Kautsky".

Leninists still sustain an inescapable violence between capitalist States. They argue with the occurrence of the two World Wars, and with the invasions of Iraq or Afghanistan, (omitting the non-declared wars in Korea and between China and Vietnam, started by non-capitalist countries). However, one can reply that the First World War occurred when the influence of the aristocratic class on the European State's affairs was still very high and played a major role on the outbreak of the War. Illustrated in Jean Renoir's classical movie La Grande Illusion (Renoir 1937). About the Second World War, one can remember the appeasement policy of Chamberlain during the 30's in face to the Nazi violent aggressions; or the USA positions, staying out of the European war and trying to negotiate a deal with Japan over the Asian politics. They represented the already searched peaceful solutions by, at this time, the two leading democratic capitalist powers. About the recent wars in Iraq or Afghanistan, they cannot be considered as occurring between capitalist powers. They express more a resistance in peripheries of traditional cultures to the world order imposed by the capitalist system.

These signaled facts, apparently, are giving credit, at the moment, to Kautsky's thesis. However, one may concede that the atomic weapon played a major role in removing, until now, the war between the leading world States.

The Economy as a Determinant and Dominant Level

The diffusion of economic growth among the big world countries induced their governments to what John Friedmann once called, applying to cities, as a "competitive cooperation" (in an oral presentation at the 1999 Conference of the American Association of Geographers). The competitive cooperation between States of different ideological and political orientations, is made by accorded policies between them, which express their common interest in the maintenance of the world economic system. It superposes openly the economic level, as a dominant level, over other levels. It is a diverse situation compared to when the former Soviet Union existed, Communist China appears today as a fundamental pillar of the world capitalist system. In Brazil, the anti-American ideological movements led by leftist parties, which were very strong by the nineties, are appeasing, as a government guided by a leftist party aims to occupy higher economic and political positions in the global system. As if following the Italian Marxist Domenico Losurdo thesis, the emergent powers realized their economic advantages as they were becoming leading partners of the world economic system. Self-esteem increased among them as the crisis which started in 2008 exposed that a dominant role is played by the emergent countries in the efforts for a global solution.

The exception to joining political collaboration in favor of the global system appears in countries of Islamic fundamentalist governments and in North Korea. In the case of Cuba, it stays out of the system by impositions from the USA and related to particular American national interest.

The cultural environment of the cognitive-cultural societies is bombarded every day by the media with numbers related to the economic, financial and social conditions of each country and of the world. More and more people relate their satisfactions to the management quality of the economy and of the public affaires, executed by the private and government executives to a point that it is raising the critics of philosophers, as of the American Michael J. Sandel.

The economic instance is being elevated to a dominant level in the major developed and emergent countries. This fact contributes to a common effort of countries in solving the current crises of the world capitalist system. The current crisis which started in the USA at the end of 2008, spread quickly around the whole world. The reactions of the leading States of the capitalist system did present a picture very different from what happened during the 30's. At that time each State tried its particular solution, as the USA did with the "New Deal" or Germany with its rearmament and conquests. Now one sees an orchestrated action to reverse the recession by States with extreme social political differences, as between the USA and China, or the UK and Brazil. A group of the 20 most developed States, the G-20, meets regularly to reach coordinated economic measures.

The present economic crisis is stronger inside the old historical capitalist center than inside the BRIC countries. China still grows at an annual rate of 8% and it is also increasing sharply its military power. Brazil was also capable to maintain a relative high continuous growth, based on social inclusions that elevated domestic consumption. Therefore, the idea that one moves from a 'mono pole world' led by the USA to a 'multi poles world', with a larger equilibrium of forces, is being reinforced. However, all the candidate countries to become world economic poles, are considering now that their fate of growing is tied to the health of the entire capitalist system.

HEGEL, MARX AND ENGELS, AND THE STATE

In Hegel's views, at the end, history will reach the Universal State. For Marx and Engels, on the contrary, history will return to its beginnings, but in a higher level, by the establishment of societies without classes and States, the Communism. For Marx and Engels the State appeared as a class instrument, took after the industrial revolution by the capitalists of each country.

What one sees at the present moment is that, in general terms, everywhere in the world, the State is enlarging is presence in the social life, although losing spaces in some particular instances. The out stepping from the present world crisis cannot be conceived without the State actions. The globalization expansion is referred to the neo liberalism policies introduced by Thatcher and by Reagan, by reducing the presence of their States in the economy. However, these actions were centered on domestic markets. Decisions such as the creation of Common Markets, the opening of country borders to free economic and financial flows, the common fiscal legislations, depended on the decisions and the further control of many States. The States play a major role in the globalization process.

When the current crisis broke out in the USA, some blamed the State, for not controlling the financial market enough, while other blamed the State for interfering in the housing business. The controversy about the State presence in the economy is enlarging continuously all around the world. The present crisis contributes to emphasizing a debate .that divides executives and scholars. The popular and lefty parties favor the higher presence of the State. In the States where they are in power, they try to give an impression as if socialism is being established, although class structure is maintained. In the European Union, left oriented parties, supported by popular masses, consider the recovery, from the present crisis, dependent on larger state expenditures. They oppose the current dominant policies of austerity, of cutting debts and of diminishing the role of the state as a wealth provider. They propose more consumption, to stimulate production, even at the costs of enlarging the public debt and producing inflation.

The emergent countries, such as Brazil, and especially China, did develop recently, and are developing currently, in conjunctures of high involvements of their States in the economic and social activities. Bureaucracy has been one of the high prices paid by the model in case of Brazil. On the other side, the USA appears as the model of a country that since its foundation aimed to have and actually presents, in comparison to other countries, a State with minor roles in the activities related to the market and to the social instances.

In the current world economic conjuncture, the USA faces now the dilemmas of moving or not moving to a larger interference of the State in the economic and social activities. A dilemma of leaving or maintaining traditional ideologies and their model of a minimalist State. Often one sees President Barak Obama being called "socialist", as a strategy of the traditionalists, to prevent any move directed to enlarge the role of the State. For instance, on his moves to provide a larger Medicare population cover, while proposing raising the income tax of the richer, when the inequality of the income distribution is reaching the highest historical levels. One may think that the future of the USA as a number one Nation of the world lies in its choices about the role of the State in economic and social practices.

CONCLUSION

After the Second World War, one saw the development of the Providence State and of an affluent society, mainly in Western Europe. In part the government measures taken in this sense were defensive, against the growth of the left parties. This cycle was closed by a crisis that brought a stronger development of the market forces since the 70's and that installed the so called neo-liberalism. A new class enlarged enormously its size inside the new conjuncture, the class of executives, or worker capitalists. The new class increased also its insertions in the state boards, inclusive in the electoral sector.

The neo-liberal cycle brought the expansion of globalization, with the States/Nations playing an important role. However, since 2009 a deep crisis affects the world economy. Considering the recent history of successive cycles, it seems that time is now in favor of the increasing of the States presence in the world economic and social affairs. As the cycles were succeeding, permanent transformations were occurring in all social levels, such as in the fantastic technological evolution, in the appearance of the cognitive-cultural society, in the enlarging of the executive class and a in new world political map.

The executives, or the labor capitalist, come out from the new cognitive cultural society. The executives appear like hybrids, with capitalist and worker consciousness. They are divided about a desirable format of relations between state and market. The size of the cognitive cultural society, in each country is related to its economic and social degree of development. The ideologies of universal peace and of sustaining development are carried inside these cognitive cultural sectors of the societies.

The new world political map shows a new geographical distribution of the economic and political State powers. A distribution related to the distributions of the variables mentioned on the paragraph above. This geography plays a decisive role in nowadays economic and political evolution.

World history since the end of the Second World War presents a period of time in which the threats of a new World War were continuously removed. Two main sources sustained this tendency. One was the evolution of capitalism inside the developed and the majority of the developing countries. The presence of the aristocratic class and the influence of the national industrial bourgeoisies were diminishing. While the role of the transnational corporations and of the class of executives, or labor capitalists were growing. It is this class of executives that guided the movement to globalization and currently manages States and big enterprises. The other source lies in the development of the cognitive cultural societies. Increasing masses of population become aware that international wars between State/Nations are not a solution for their problems. And that at each time it becomes more difficult to mobilize citizens to war when the survival of their State/Nation is not in risk.

However, one cannot and one does not desire to give the impression of a rosy picture of the present economic and social picture of the world globalization. The crucial enlarging of the income inequalities during the last decades is well known. As are well known the high levels of the unemployment accompanying the present economic crisis. The critics to the economic system and to their ideological contents never stopped. They were covered by a fantastic material growth, but now, with the crises, one see the return of the strength of the ideologies aimed to deep structural changes.

Some scholars see in the present evolution a transitional movement, to a new mode of production. The machine that brought capitalism was invented during the 18th century, but the definition of a new mode of production was established only by the mid-19th century. One needs what is called a 'critical distance', to observe an object as a whole. Certainly one needs more time to better understand what is happening with the current mode of production.

Dangers of disruption of the present landscape exist, however, for instance, in the failing to reverse stagnation by some States. As it occurs in Europe where the dominant policies centered on austerity are criticized by diverse Nobel Prize winners, as Stiglitz or Krugman, who favor like-Keynesian policies. A derailing of a convoy of states in one region may produce a domino effect, each country returning to their own policies. Another danger, in a larger term of time, lies in the world environmental issue. But a greatest immediate danger lies in the possibility of use of nuclear weapon in a war between regional powers, and capable to involve the world powers.

References

Angell Lane, and Ralph Norman. 1910. *The Great Illusion*. London: Wilhram Heimemann.

Badiou, Alain. 1979. "O (re) começo do materialismo dialético" In *Materialismo Histórico e Materialismo Dialético*, edited by Alain Badiou and Louis Althusser, translated from French by Elisabete A. Pereira dos Santos. São Paulo: Global Editora e Distribuidora.

Bentley, Jerry H. 1996. "AHR forum–Cross cultural interactions and periodization in world history" *American Historical Review* 101: 749–770.

Braudel, Ferdinand. 1996. "Civilização Material. Economia e Capitalismo" *Séculos XV-XVIII*, Volume 3, O Tempo do Mundo, translated from French by Telma Costa. São Paulo: Martins Fontes.

Castells, Manuel. 1989. *The Informational City, Information. Technology, Economic Restructuring and the Urban Regional Process*. London: Blackwell.

Deleuze, Gilles, and Felix Guattari. 1992. *O que é a Filosofia?* Translated by Bento Prado Jr., and Alberto Alonzo Munoz. São Paulo: Editora 34.

Geiger, Pedro. 2010. "Capitalism, Internationalism and Socialism in A Time of Globalization" *Comparative Civilization Review* 62: 75–90.

Graham, Julie, and Katherine Gibson. 2006. *The End of Capitalism (as we knew it)*. Minneapolis: University of Minnesota Press.

Hardt, Michael and Antonio Negri. 2004. *Multitude*. New York: The Penguin Press.

Heidegger, Martin. 1962. *Being and Time*. New York: Harper-Collins Publishers.

Hogben, Lancelot. 1939. *Les Mathematiques pour Tous*, translated by F.H. Larroy. Paris: Payot.

Jameson, Frederic. 1996. *Postmodernism or The Cultural Logic of Late Capitalism*. Durham, NC: Duke University Press.

Kalecki, Michael. 1954. "Teoria da Dinâmica Econômica, Ensaio Sobre As Mudanças Cíclicas A Longo Prazo Da Economia Capitalista", translated from Theory of Economic Dynamics-An Essay on Ciclical Long Run Changes in Capitalist Economy, 1954, by Paulo de Almeida, in Os Economistas, São Paulo: Editora Nova Cultural Ltda. 1977.

Kautsky, Karl. 2008. "O Imperialismo e a Guerra" In *História e Luta de Classes*, Ano 4, n°6:921, São Paulo, 2008.

La Meditirranée, Paris: Champs Flammarion, 1985.

Lênin, Wladimir L. 1975. *L'Imperialisme. Stade Suprême du Capitalisme*, Paris : Éditions Sociales.

Luporini, Cesare, and Emilio Sereni. 1973. El Concepto de "Formacion Econômico-Social", Cuadernos de Passafo y Presente 39. Córdoba:: Siglo XXI Argentina Editores S.A.

Renoir, Jean. 1937. *La Grande Ilusion*, Paris: Les Realisations d'Árt Cinematographiques.

Soja, Edward W.. 1989. *Post Modern Geographies: The Reassertion of Space in Critical Social Theory*. London: Verso.

Scott, Allen J. 2007. "Capitalism and Urbanization in a New Key? The Cognitive-Cultural Dimension" *Social Forces* 85: 1465–1482.

Scott, Allen et al. 2001. "Global City-Regions" In *Global City-Regions, Trends, Theory, Policy* edited by Allen J. Scott, 11–32. Oxford, New York: Oxford University Press.

Semple, Ellen C. and Ratzel, Friedrich. 1911. *Influences of Geographic Environment on the Basis of Ratzel's System of Anthropo-Geography*. New York: H. Holt and Company.

Vallaux, Camille 1929. *Les Sciences Geographiques, Nouvelle Édition*. Paris: Librairie Fèlix Alcan.

CHAPTER 4

Global Governance and the Demise of the Nation State

Alessandra Sarquis

INTRODUCTION

In the literature of global governance, the state is far from being regarded as a key factor in creating and sustaining the process of globalization (Hay and March 2010, 258). In this literature, two schools of thought illustrate such a perception: the 'hyperglobalists' and the 'transformationalists' (Jones 2010, 72). The 'hyperglobalists' represents the radical view. They defend the demise of the state in face of the increasing dynamic of international society. Rosenau, for example, argues for the disintegration of political authority (Rosenau 2006, 22). For him, "the states-are-forever habit" may have to be supplanted by a looser approach when thinking about rebuilding the state in war-torn societies nowadays. It could be positive to allow history to follow its fragmenting path, leaving it to the different groups of war-torn societies to decide how they should cooperate.

Transformationalists, such as Held and his collaborators, offer a more nuanced approach, arguing for a reevaluation of state's traditional roles. For them, the tension between the remaining state system and an active civil society leads to a contestation of the state's authority, but it does not undermine the state's instrumental role in regulating the environment where individuals can exercise their global citizenship. It is rather seen as an opportunity to empower the voices of a global civil society through mechanisms that bring transparency and accountability to the overall system of states (Held 1991, 197; Archibugi 1998, 198; Held 2010, 143).

In my viewpoint, these two approaches oversimplify the role that the state can actually perform nowadays. For them, the state only acts reactively to the hyperactivity of international civil society. They fail to understand that the state can have a more encompassing and determinant role in actively supporting the formation of independent and responsible moral agents in a globalized world. Individuals' possibility of making use of multiple and transnational networks to express their identities and demands does not secure their ability to manage these resources in a coherent and accountable manner vis-à-vis one another. The state remains fundamental in helping the individual to find a fine tune between his independence, critically reflecting on his choices and habits, and respect for others, accepting their inalienable dignity as human beings (Honderich 1995, 586).

The state helps individuals to formulate their perception of themselves and others through the incitement of a structured way of exercising public reasoning in the construction of a historically situated system of right. This state's constitutive role has nonetheless to be rethought considering the place of diversity nowadays. The states are supposed to reciprocally interact with each other in a more critical and self-revealing way to put into place more efficient institutions and procedures able to secure that this referred exercise of public reasoning be widespread in a globalized world. They should also work together with representatives of international civil society, offering them a more active role in the definition and provision of traditional public goods.

The paper is divided into four sections. Section one critically analyses how studies on multi-level governance, particularly Rosenau, perceive the decrease of the state's importance given the emergence of more active and demanding transnational players. I claim that Rosenau dangerously overlooks the constitutive role the state can perform in individuals' moral formation, inconsequently defending the market forces of transnational society. Section two discusses studies on cosmopolitan democracy. I claim that Held and his collaborators presuppose but are not willing to analyze in depth the ethical role the state has in the formation of morally driven individuals in a globalized world. Their unwillingness leads them to misconceive the place of diversity in the construction of cosmopolitan democracy, rendering their arguments open to old kind of criticisms. They can still be accused of formulating new forms of discourses to continue defending a biased neo-liberal model. Section three re-assesses the terms by which the state remains fundamental in this increasingly globalized world. The final section presents some conclusive remarks.

Rosenau and His Arguments for Multi-level Governance

Studies on multi-level governance, particularly the one carried by Rosenau, challenge the assumptions of international relations as an academic discipline. This discipline is much defined by the existence of territorial sovereign states, seen as terminal entities for loyalties, policy decisions and moral authority. Its specialists, however, fail to ask whether changes derived from globalization might lead to the emergence of newly emerging entities (Rosenau 2006, 19–30).

The links and overlaps between a localizing and globalizing dynamic (the forces of fragmentation and integration, named "fragmegration" by the author) are evolving and rendering the global stage denser with SOAs (Spheres of Authority). Once seen as anomalies, these new spheres are soon becoming patterned regularities.

For Rosenau, world affairs are currently governed through a bifurcated system: 1) the system of states; 2) a multi-centric system of diverse types of other collectivities, emerging as rival sources of authority. These new collectivities, or SOAs, respond to the strong demand for governance in this era of economic interdependence and fast communication. They proliferate and governance assumes a multi-level dimension–top-down governance, network governance, bottom-up governance, side-by-side governance, market governance and mobius-web governance. Consequently, the state has its authority contested. Its legitimacy has from now on to be constructed through the critical assessment of citizens who have at their disposal other memberships to fall back on (Rosenau 2004, 35; Rosenau 2006, 117).

Despite its fragility, the state is still responsible for the preservation of a formal and widespread normativity in today's globalizing environment. No matter how independent the SOAs become in their ability to congregate efforts, achieve their objectives and even put pressure on the state system to change the norms that frame international relations, they still have to rely on such a system to regulate their relations. But it is worth pointing that this state's regulatory role is circumstantial and can eventually be performed by other forms of institutional arrangements in the near future (Rosenau 2004, 24).

The fragmentation of governance has positive side-effects according to Rosenau. First, the advent of pluralism avoids dominance by one institution and amplifies the players' influence, making possible to them to check the authority of each other. Second, it enhances individuals' reflexivity given that their exposition to the new dynamics leads them to a growing understanding of the necessity of change. Third, the advent of networks and flow of horizontal communication brings many people to dialogue, broadening the spectrum of viewpoints and confrontation among them. Fourth, the growing presence of SOAs based on mobius-web governance bring creative solutions to both local and global problems (Rosenau 2004, 35–37 ; Rosenau 2006, 100).

Rosenau's analysis is based on the presupposition that individuals' potentially autonomous abilities will have a great chance of flourishing in a dynamically transnational environment. The possibility that individuals develop critical thinking (reflexivity), establish dialogue among them and define common action is directly linked to their participation in groups or movements of a globalized civil society. In great part, this participation contributes to the construction of persons, the perception they have of others and even to the kind of moral obligation they could eventually develop towards each other. As Rosenau further argues, individuals would tend to intensify bonds among themselves and form a sense of international community when participating in a globalized civil society (Rosenau 2006, 100).

But the simple acceptance of the above presupposition without further arguments weakens his analysis. He fails to understand that the above positive outcomes of fragmentation he optimistically enumerates end up not necessarily being realized. More importantly, he fails to understand that the new dynamics of civil society will not necessarily contribute to the formation of individuals who can comfortably manage multiple identities and act independently while respecting others as ends.

Rosenau, for example, fails to acknowledge the fact that the plurality of new actors is still accompanied by differences in the political and socio-economic power of them. Few of them are really prominent and capable of directing the kind of debate that frames the rules of international civil society. In many ways, inequality among these associations reflects the structural inequalities of the present world economic order, which still separates developed and underdeveloped societies. The majority of prominent non-governmental organizations (NGOs) specialized in human rights, such as Amnesty International and Human Rights Watch, are based on a liberal perspective of society, sharing with it a specific perception of these rights and the legitimate ways to pursue them. There is no guarantee that their aims and methods take into consideration dissonant voices.

Even if individuals are equally able to develop their independent capacities, there is no guarantee that they will make use of these capacities in a fair way. The events surrounding the terrorist attacks in New York (2001), Madrid (2004) and London (2005) support the im- plausibility of this supposition. These attacks were perpetrated by individuals who make use neither of their reflective capacities nor of the kind of mobilization suggested by Rosenau. Their radicalism reflected the understanding that it was fundamental to share the plight of their Islamic brothers living around the world and to voice their respective demands though violent acts responsible for taking innocent lives. Religion is here used as an ideological and political tool, fomenting discrimination and hatred feeling towards non-members.

In my viewpoint, Rosenau overestimates the role international civil society can play in helping individuals to make use of their potential capacities of independently critical thinking. It is not because individuals are exposed to a new dynamic civil society that they will be able to critically judge the situation that surrounds them and join efforts to fairly act on the basis of this constructed judgment. In this sense, it can be problematic to discard the role political communities could eventually play in securing an environment where individuals can equally and systematically learn to reciprocate commitments on a fair basis. To do so is to implicitly accept a free market logic to the constitutive (ethical) relations arising in the heart of international civil society with no guarantee that imbalances in power or in the use of individuals' abilities would be addressed. At the extreme, it is implicitly to accept that there would not be necessarily sustainable reasons to treat individuals as ends and not means in themselves.

In the next section, I analyze the arguments of Held and his collaborators, which represent the other spectrum of the globalization debate. They stress the dynamism of international civil society and its potential ability to bring more accountability and transparency to governments. At the same time, they attribute to the democratic state a fundamental role in sustaining institutions and procedures of this new world order. Implicitly, they assign to the state a preponderant ethical role in the construction of this order but fail to analyse the implications such an assignment.

HELD AND THE NOTION OF COSMOPOLITAN DEMOCRACY

For the last 10 years, Held has been consistently developing a theoretical approach to globalization focusing on its singularity as a phenomenon. For him, globalization has to be understood as the widening, deepening and speeding up of social interactions in all aspects of contemporary life, creating new flows and networks of activities, relations and the exercise of power worldwide (Jones 2010, 75–80; Held 1999, 16). It necessarily leads to a transformation of the relationship between sovereignty, territoriality and state power.

In an environment where political problems, such as national security and environment, gain a transnational dimension and can only be partially addressed by intergovernmental organizations, a democratic state becomes an imperfect political entity to sustain the citizenship rights of its members (Held 1996, 223) (Archibugi and Held 1995, 156). States would have to be considered in parallel to sub-national or supra-national spheres of competences as centers of legitimate power. State sovereignty could be stripped away from the idea of fixed borders and territories and deemed, in principle, as malleable time-space clusters. Policy issues would then be allocated to different levels of governance following the tests of extensiveness, intensity and comparative efficiency (Held 1996, 236).

For Held, democratic cosmopolitanism imposes itself in this logic. It is conceived as "the ethical and political space which sets out the term of reference for the recognition of people's equal moral worth, their active agency and what is required for their autonomy and development" (Held 2010, 49). Its founding principles are egalitarian individualism (individuals as ultimate units of moral concern), reciprocal recognition (individuals' equal worth recognized by all) and impartial reasoning in public deliberation and argument. Then, these principles give rise to universal duties that establish the avoidance of harm and the amelioration of urgent need. (Held 2010, 15).

From this viewpoint, the institutionalization of cosmopolitan democracy would offer political representation to citizens in the world community, bringing more transparency and accountability to the state system. Democratic public law would be supported by cosmopolitan democratic law, which is founded on universal hospitality. Such a law would extend itself to a universal community where individuals have the "right to present oneself and to be heard" while equally enjoying their autonomous status, independently of their membership in a nation-state (Held 1996, 228). Moreover, legal pacifism would prevail and become the rationale to support institutional reforms of multilateral organizations. As Archibugi suggests, this underlying rationale could eventually lead to a reform of the UN that takes into account the creation of an Assembly of Peoples and the reinforcement of independent judicial power of the International Court of Justice (Archibugi and Held 1995, 140; Held 2010, 103).

Contrary to Rosenau, the most relevant ethical locus for individuals in Held's scheme continues to be the states and the multilateral structures sustained by them. But it is worth observing that the states and the multilateral structures sustained by them are primary defended in instrumental terms. Following the cosmopolitan tradition of thought, the moral substance of the individual is defined by a universally inherited reason. It is from the reasonable derivation of the elements sustaining this inherited reason that the background conditions for a cosmopolitan order should be understood, encompassing principles defining the common structure for individual action and social activity (Held 2010, 76–77). In this understanding, states are merely seen as facilitators, helping to put in place socio-political structures through which individuals can actually make use of their applied reason and manage their interactions in this new world order (Held 2010, 84–85).

In order to not suffer from recurrently communitarian critiques, Held reconsiders Rawls' arguments on political liberalism. His notion of cosmopolitanism is permeated by the understanding of autonomous individuals as citizens of democratic societies. This "layered cosmopolitanism" insists that the interpretation of cosmopolitan principles and therefore their significance are partly localized, depending on situated interpretations (Held 2010, 79–81). Western democracies can be said to provide the most encompassing discourse that protects and nurtures the human standpoint. Their democratic institutions and procedures sustain the notion of equal worth of autonomous individuals (Held 2010, 85). Though encompassing, such a discourse still respects difference in terms of the possibility of other discourses and focus of authority so far as it does not question the basic elements (equal freedom) that define this human standpoint. That is precisely why it is possible to talk about a cosmopolitan democratic order sustained by a concept of world citizenship.

Held's perspicacious defense of democratic cosmopolitanism does not however offset the main weakness of his arguments. The conditions for taking cultural diversity seriously are not laid down in the structure of the argument. Individuals` ability to meaningfully exercise his autonomy is preconceived from a liberal viewpoint and it is that pre-conceived notion that gives rise to democratically cosmopolitan structures. Diversity is only introduced when analyzing the actual functioning of these structures. It is only as a second thought, already imbedded in a pre-formed way of deliberation, that interaction with difference is really considered.

Two problems emerge from this weakness. First, the constitutive role of historically situated political structures is not discussed in the formation of an autonomous individual. It is at best assumed when presenting the advantages of a liberal democratic way of organizing society. There is therefore no analysis of the extent to which public reasoning is being supported or even incited by procedures and institutions defined by democratic states in a changing world order. By failing to analyze this issue, Held ends by discarding offhand the possibility that the state becomes a prominent shaper of this new world order by developing its ethical dimension.

Second, as diversity comes as post-thinking in his theoretical scheme, the liberal justification for a democratically cosmopolitan order is not really open to contestation. Other viewpoints must be respected but they do not have any input in the definition of the parameters that establish the principles of this order. The tragic consequence is that the perception of otherness as being someone who actually differentiates from me and helps define who I am because questioning my values is not taking seriously in individuals' moral construction. In this sense, Held could still be accused of defending a status quo by offering biased terms of dialogue among cultures in supra-national structures. He could still be seen as rearticulating an old neo-liberal discourse that hides patronizing kind of attitudes.

In my viewpoint, the problems facing Held's scheme ends by limiting the understanding of the challengingly environment we live in. In a highly changing environment marked by new centers of power and modes of authority, old socio-economic structures are being questioned. A cosmopolitan model of democracy based on a historically biased notion of individual autonomy will necessarily be put to test not only by the emergence of new interpretations of this notion but also by the denial of the terms by which this notion assumed preponderance. If this model does not seriously consider the issue of diversity, being open enough to re-evaluate the proper terms of its liberal discourse through active interaction with these challenging interpretations and conceptions, its capacity of suggesting functional arrangements to this new world orders will be dangerously restricted.

In the next section, I discuss the continuingly moral relevance of the political community (state) to an increasingly globalized individual in face of my criticisms against Held's conception of democratic cosmopolitanism. Although I also ground my analysis on a liberal tradition of political thought, I re-interpret it so to incorporate diversity as a foundational element in the understanding of the emerging world order.

BRINGING THE STATE BACK IN THE INTERNATIONAL SCENARIO AS AN ETHICAL ENTITY

In my interpretation, the state can still be considered a fundamental shaper of the new global environment we live in. The state does not play just an instrumental role in providing for regulatory institutions and procedures or for channels of communication by means of which individuals can safely interact in this global environment. It also helps to shape such an environment. The state id still the most adequate entity to incite the formation of autonomous individuals who can make use of their capacity of public reasoning in a responsible way. This exercise of public reasoning is based on the reciprocal recognition of free claimants kept on an equal standing when actively participating in the definition of historically situated system of rights.

Let me develop the argument. An individual is autonomous when he is able to critically reflect on his free will by considering to what extent others are conjointly helping him to define this will. It is a reflection on the social construction of his will and its worth. In this sense, an individual is autonomous not just when he has the capacity to act autonomously in the Kantian sense, acting rationally by taking others as ends, but when he actually exercises this autonomy in a situated, concrete living social environment (Kant, 1996; Wood, 1995, p. 23–37). It is self-mastering the elements of his identity, including more importantly the conscious understanding and acceptance of the social roles he performs with others in a specific historically constructed environment. By being able to assess the shortcomings of social interactions and to identify ultimately with their foundational elements, they become more inclined to bear the public responsibilities imposed on them.

This conception of autonomous individual is based on the Hegelian idea that self-consciousness can only be developed when individuals are actively involved in the construction of social wholes, being the political regarded as fundamental in this development (Hegel, 1996; Wood, 1995, p. 195). The political community here mentioned is not an abstraction but a body (the state) that exists through individuals as concrete subjects deliberating on a specifically defined system of laws (the structural basis on which lies this socio-political order). It fundamentally derives from the fact that individuals mutually recognize each other as sources of independent valid claims when participating in the formulation and implementation of collective decisions. Its structure can, in this sense, be consciously known. Moreover, it can be willed for the sake of its own rationality–a rationality embodied in the common decisions taken together.

It is fundamental to notice that the referred exercise of mutual recognition is dynamic. It does not merely imply recognizing a pair in a *strictus sensus*. It refers to the fact that individualities are revealed through the constant construction of points of identification (commonalities) and dissonances (differences) among themselves in the process of public deliberation. In this sense, the proper exercise of public reasoning is constitutively marked by moments of contradictions and incoherence.

Moreover, the exercise of mutual recognition among citizens should be seen as widespread. Considerations on openness to diversity at both national and international levels are essential to the proper definition of this exercise. Nationally, it is fundamental to consider, for example, the social inclusion of citizens with discrepant socio-economic backgrounds and the place of immigrants and their offspring in the actual definition and implementation of public policies. Certainly, this kind of inclusion puts pressure on the exercise of reciprocity, revealing accentuated differences among citizens and raising new questions about the focus of identification among them. But, at the same time, it renders this exercise more dynamic and makes possible a better understanding of the ways the interrelation between national and international dimensions helps to construct global individualities.

Internationally, a consideration on openness is based on a deeper understanding of states' interactions in terms of their ethical need to mutually recognize their self-determining capacity and to use this recognition to construct more workable international institutions and procedures at a global level. Such a deeper (ethical) understanding of state interactions involves a better appreciation of the place of diversity in international relations. If an individual's essential capacity of rational thinking is universally given, its elaboration in a set of particular ethical principles of conduct is contingent on space and time. It is dependent on the participation of individuals in the actual construction of a state structure (a system of rights). The plurality of states at a time, when qualified in terms of states' ability to recognize each other as unique ethical locus to their citizens' moral development while being open to each others' claims and to inputs of international civil society, provides for a broad spectrum of experiments through which it is possible to have a clear grasp of the common conditions necessary for the moral development of global individualities.

Let me analyze more precisely the state' distinguished ability in supporting the widespread exercise of public reasoning nowadays. In my viewpoint, it is precisely the uniqueness of this ability that allows the state to distance itself from other authoritative organizations present in transnational society, and to reinstate its significance in the new globalized era.

First, the state guarantees the inclusiveness of the exercise of reciprocity developed inside its structure. This exercise involves people with different backgrounds, skills and interests as well as topics that are as general and varied as possible, relating to all possible aspects of an individual's life. Even if individuals cannot identify with all the decisions taken in a public sphere, they are still associated with the basic values that shape the institutions and processes through which these decisions are taken and recognition becomes meaningful. In contrast, multifunctional entities formed inside the international civil society cannot similarly cover such a need for diversity and inclusiveness in the formation of individuals. They are restrained in their actions because each of them is specialized only in a number of issues, for example, in monitoring human rights or eradicating common diseases in certain parts of the world. They are also limited in their actions by the common profile of their members. Members of international civil society's groups tend to be quite specific about which kind of issue they support as well as the kind of action they are prepared to take to back a cause.

Second, the state acts as coordinator of the various social engagements that help defining individuals along their lives. In the exercise of reciprocity that takes place through structurally defined and lasting state mechanisms, individuals can coherently construct an ensemble perspective of the components of their identity. As citizens of a state, they contribute and are subject to a system of rights that define the various social roles they perform in their private and public life, such as family member, professional, religious person and member of an ethnic group. This system ends by amalgamating a collective vision of priorities that affects these different aspects of individuals' lives. Such a phenomenon, which results from individuals' direct or indirect participation in the formulation and implementation of public policies qua free claimants able to mutually recognize themselves, is not clearly guaranteed by multifunctional agencies whose relationship is marked by diffusion of interests and power.

Third, the state can use its enforceable power to guarantee that the exercise of reciprocity takes place. State's authority is endowed with the legitimate use of force and not derived merely from negotiating skills, habits, informal agreements or shared premises as it is the case with multifunctional agencies and other forms of governance. The state has the unique ability to guarantee that agreements are in fact realizable, no matter the equilibrium of forces or the particular interests involved (Knowles, 2010, p. 17–30).

Fourth, the exercise of reciprocity implied in the relationships of citizens is historically situated (the definition of a certain system of rights in a determined space and time). A social environment, and the way it is organized over time and across space, is important because it is still the primordial locus where individuals can contextualize, and thus have a clear grasp of their basic capacity for thinking and acting towards otherness on a moral basis. A historically situated system of rights embodies a singular understanding of a collective way of life, meaning common interpretations and evaluations about what is generally accepted as individuals' leading good lives. These interpretations reflect shared experiences and a socialization process that, while helping to define the singularity of a particular public political culture, offer concrete meaning to individuals' thinking capacities and actions. Therefore, they constitute a more coherent comprehension of where individuals stand as distinct moral personalities, offering them the motivation to act on the basis of agreed principles.

Nonetheless, it is fundamental to realize that national and international environments are interrelated in a globalized world. While a historically situated environment is important to the construction of a moral individual, it cannot be considered self-sufficient. National and international environments are open to each other's influence. Such openness, when well managed by the states, can help them to reshape their roles and reinstate their importance. It could potentially allow a cross-examination and re-evaluation of states' historically contingent presuppositions on fundamental individual rights and then the derivation of common conclusions that underpin the robustness of global institutions, their legitimacy and enforceable power. It is such a robustness that paves the way to a more organized and stable international order.

The capacity of carrying up structured openness therefore becomes another distinctive characteristic of states. They are still potentially able to put in place structures and procedures, born from concerted arrangements among themselves and with civil society, to secure individuals' widespread exercise of public reasoning both at national and international levels.

Two points, however, are important to make when thinking about structured openness. First, civic groups and movements, which increasingly assume a transnational dimension, have to become meaningful and useful in politico-ethical terms. They have to become a partner of the state in the construction of new international structures and procedures. Rather than choosing to depreciate the activities and the influence of these groups and movements, the states have to institutionally acknowledge their impact in individuals' formation and formally incorporate them as inputs not only in the definition of national legislation and policies but also in the interpretations of international regulative procedures. This will enhance the ethical appeal of the state and allow it to re-affirm its importance in securing an environment where globally moral individuals can develop.

Second, the state has to understand the process of deliberation of international principles, particularly human rights principles, as a speculative and dynamic exercise of grasping and surpassing the anthropological features that define these systems of rights and limit their ethical capacities. The state should therefore develop its representatives' abilities: 1) to be mutually decentered in the deliberation process; 2) to focus on what message the other wants to pass, looking from inside the social roles the other lives by and to let their intuitions momentarily guide their actions; 3) to respect each others' inalienable dignity as an interlocutor; 4) to be aware of their limited capacities to acquire and apply knowledge. State representatives should in this sense become lucid about how historical circumstances surrounding them have influenced the construction of who they are today, and the perception they have of a distant other.

Conclusion

The arguments here defended are based on the rationality of the state, whose basic features can be seen as acceptable and realizable to a significant degree in the world today. The state is, therefore, understood as a realistic utopia. In great part, this ideal construction refers to the values of freedom and equality and institutional elements, such as democratic procedures and the rule of law, which characterize liberal societies nowadays. However, it is worth pointing out that this ideal construction is not circumscribed in terms of reference and its applicability to liberal societies

To fully realize themselves as ethical unities, the states have to comprehend themselves in a relationship of mutual recognition with other states so as to test and contest their temporally and spatially contingent interpretations of the morally foundational principles embedded in their system of rights. In the context of socio-economic interdependence, it becomes increasingly necessary for liberal states to be able to openly exchange points of view with other liberal states that differently interpret the values of freedom and equality as well as with non-liberal states that question the extent of the significance of these values in the formulation of just international principles. It is such an openness that can eventually help to construct a more stable international order, one in which the individuals emerge more conscious about their place in an increasingly interdependent world.

REFERENCES

Archibugi, Daniele, and David Held. 1995. "Principles of Cosmopolitan Democracy." In *Cosmopolitan Democracy: An Agenda for a New World Order*, edited by Daniele Archibugi, and David Held, 198-228. London: Polity Press.

Archibugi, Daniele, David Held, and Martin Kohler, eds. 1998. Re-*imagining Political Community: Studies in Cosmopolitan Democracy*. Cambridge: Polity Press.

Avineri, Salomon. 1995. *Hegel's Theory of the State.* Cambridge: Cambridge University Press.

Bache, Ian and Matthew Flinders. 2004. *Multi-Level Governance*. Oxford: Oxford University Press.

Bayart, Jean-François. 2008. *Global Subjects: A Political Critique of Globalization.* Cambridge: Polity Press.

Drache, Daniel. 2008. *Defiant Publics: The Unprecedented Reach of the Global Citizen*. Cambridge: Polity Press.

Hay, Colin, Michael Lister, and David Marsh, eds. 2006. *The State: Theories and Issues.* Hampshire: Palgrave Macmillan.

Hegel, G. W. Friedrich. 1975. *Lectures on the Philosophy of World History: Introduction*, translated by H. B. Nisbet. Cambridge: Cambridge University Press.

Hegel, Georg. W. F. 1996. *Elements of the Philosophy of Right*, translated by H. B. Nisbet. Cambridge: Cambridge University Press.

Held, David. 1991. "Democracy, the Nation-State and the Global System." In *Political Theory Today*, edited by David Held, 197-233. Cambridge: Polity Press.

Held, David. 1996. *Democracy and the Global Order: From the Modern State to Cosmopolitan Governance.* Cambridge: Polity Press.

Held, David. 2002. "Law of states, Law of peoples: Three Models of Sovereignty." *Legal Theory* 8: 1-44.

Held, David. 2010. *Cosmopolitanism: Ideals and Realities.* Cambridge: Polity Press.

Held, David, and Anthony McGrew. 1999. *Global Transformations: Politics, Economics and Culture.* Cambridge: Polity Press.

Held, David, and Anthony MacGrew. 2007. *Globalization/Anti-Globalization: Beyond the Great Divide.* Cambridge: Polity Press.

Hirst, Paul, and Grahame Thompson. 1999. *Globalization in Question.* Cambridge: Polity.

Honderich, Ted, ed. 1995. *The Oxford Companion to Philosophy*. Oxford: Oxford University Press.

Jones, Andrew. 2010. *Globalization: Key Thinkers*. Cambridge: Polity Press.

Kant, Immanuel. 1996. "Perpetual Peace: A Philosophical Sketch." In *Kant Political Writing*, edited by H.S. Reiss and translated by H.B. Nisbet, 93-130. Cambridge: Cambridge University Press.

Lake, David. 2010. Rightful Rules: Authority, Order, and the Foundations of Global Governance. *International Studies Quarterly* 54: 587–613.

McGrew, Anthony. 1992. "Conceptualizing Global Politics". In *Global Politics,* edited by Anthony McGrew, Chapter 1. Cambridge: Polity Press, 1992.

Rosenau, James. 2003. *Distance Proximities: Dynamics Beyond Globalization.* Princeton: Princeton University Press.

Rosenau, James. 2004. "Strong Demand, Huge Supply: Governance in an Emerging Epoch. " In *Multilevel Governance*, edited by Ian Bache and Matthew Flinders, 31-48. Oxford: Oxford University Press.

Scholte, Jan Aart, ed. 2011. *Building Global Democracy: Civil Society and Accountable Global Governance.* Cambridge: Cambridge Press.

Wood, Allen. 1995. *Hegel's Ethical Thought*. Cambridge: Cambridge University Press.

CHAPTER 5

The Many Faces of Globalization: Grobalization and Glocalization in MNCs

Stefan Litz

INTRODUCTION

Even though some dissenting scholars like, for example, Hirst and Thompson (1999) and Rosenberg (2000) challenge the idea that states and societies around the globe are currently confronted with an unprecedented process of social change which may best be labeled as "globalization", the overwhelming majority of scholars do hold the view that such a unique process indeed exists (Kellner 2005). Wallerstein (1979), Giddens (1990), Robertson (1992), Albrow (1996), Castells (1996; 1997), Rosenau (1990, 2000), Held (2004), Held and McGrew (2002), Ohmae (1990; 1996), Beck (2000), and Sklair (2000; 2002), to name just a few prominent scholars, all share the view that the globalization process is a matter of fact. But they may nevertheless hold different opinions when it comes to evaluating the impact of this process on the social fabric of modern societies (McGrew 2007). But what applies to nation states and other kind of societies as large scale socio-political entities also applies to Multinational Corporations (MNCs) as another important type of collective actors (Coleman 1982).

In fact, some of these MNCs may be considered, at least from an economic point of view, to be even more important and powerful than some nation states. Sklair (2002, 37), for example, has demonstrated that some of the world biggest economic entities, measured by revenues, are not nation-states but large MNCs. Particularly such large MNCs, like those listed annually as the "Fortune Global 500", are important agents and vehicles of the process of capitalist economic globalization (Sklair 2002; Dicken 2003). The number of such large MNCs as the number of MNCs in general, as Collinson/Morgan (2009, 4) have highlighted, seemed to have grown continuously in the last few decades. Collinson and Morgan (2009), drawing on UNCTAD statistics, reported that an estimated number of MNCs has jumped from 37 000 with approximately 170 000 foreign subsidiaries in the early 1990s to around 77 000 MNCs with more than 770 000 subsidiaries in 2005. In fact, the most recent UNCTAD statistics reports 82 000 MNCs with 810 000 subsidiaries employing directly about 77 million people (UNCTAD 2009).

But MNCs are not all the same and the degree to which they are involved in cross-border business operations at any point in time may vary significantly. In order to understand and measure the degree of internal globalization of MNCs two approaches, a quantitative and qualitative approach, have been utilized. For example, the UNCTAD measures the degree of corporate globalization calculating its "Transnationality Index" (TNI) for MNCs. The TNI is calculated as a composite indicator of a company's degree of globalization considering 1) the ratio of foreign assets to total assets; 2) the ratio of foreign sales to total sales and 3) the ratio of foreign employment to total employment (UNCTAD 2009). The OECD suggested other metrics for measuring the degree of the globalization of MNCs like, for example, the degree of geographic diversification of foreign control (OECD 2005). These measurements of an MNCs degree of globalization, although some are more known and complex than others, are all important indicators that allow us to track the unfolding process of globalization in MNCs. Notwithstanding the importance of measuring the degree of globalization in MNCs investigating intracorporate globalization processes also requires qualitative approaches.

Several authors have developed qualitative conceptualizations of MNCs. Heenan and Perlmutter (1979), Bartlett and Ghosal (1989; 1998), and Doz et al. (2001) have outlined qualitative criteria to distinguish between different types of MNCs that may coexist at any time in a particular "organizational population" (Hannan/Freeman 1977; Aldrich 1999). In fact, as the globalization process unfolds within MNCs, the "organizational blueprint" (Hannan and Freeman 1977) or essential characteristics of an MNC, may evolve (Westney and Zaheer 2001). Heenan and Perlmutter's (1979), Bartlett and Goshal's (1989; 1998), and Doz's et al. (2001) typologies of MNCs are certainly useful in terms of differentiating various MNCs but fall short of providing a conceptual approach allowing to distinguish and analyze various types of internally unfolding globalization processes that lie behind the evolution process. In this regard Ritzer's (2003; 2007; 2010) typology of globalization processes seems to provide a useful conceptual tool in order to analyze and highlight issues of intracorporate globalization processes that were not taken into consideration by Hennan and Perlmutter (1979), Bartlett and Ghosal (1989; 1998) and Doz et al. (2001). Drawing on Ritzer's (2003; 2007; 2010) approach, this paper applies his conceptualization of globalization processes to MNC organizational analysis. I will also elaborate on the results of an explorative study which demonstrates for two cases how applying Ritzer's (2003; 2007; 2010) conceptualization distinguishing between different types of globalization processes may help to shed new light on the internal globalization of MNCs and help to better understand subtle yet important differences between globalizing MNCs.

GROBALIZATION OF NOTHING?

Ritzer's (2003; 2007; 2010) approach to globalization invaluably makes a significant contribution to the existing body of literature on globalization. Before I discuss Ritzer's approach, I will introduce a meanwhile popular definition of "globalization". Giddens (1990) was one of the first scholars and certainly one of the most influential academics who provided a meanwhile popular definition of the term "globalization". Giddens (1990) highlighted that "globalization" refers to the process of "distanciation or separation of time from space" (Waters 1995, 48) which leads to a "disembedding of social relations from the exclusive focus on the immediate local contexts" (Waters 1995, 49). Giddens (1990, 64) emphasized that globalization is manifested in the "intensification of worldwide social relations which link distant localities in such a way that local happenings are shaped by events occurring many miles away and vice versa". In other words, the imminent impact of events occurring at one locality on events occurring at another distant locality (i.e. the intersection of the various local forces) are the defining characteristics of the globalization process. The expanding and extending interrelatedness of distant events in turn, as Giddens (1991) has maintained, influences the way in which people experience their world as some faraway events significantly affect people's experience of "everyday life"(Berger and Luckmann 1966). Instead of imagining a universal and homogenous globalization process, however, Ritzer (2003; 2007; 2010) has recently identified different types of globalization processes. According to Ritzer (2003; 2007; 2010), there are four types of globalization for which he distinguished between four fundamentally different categories which he called "glocalization" and "grobalization" as well as "nothing" and "something".

In Ritzer's (2003; 2007; 2010) conceptualization the term "grobalization" is emphasizing the phenomenon that the impact of economic, social, cultural, political and other kind of forces on various localities are quite similar or even identical on a global scale. For example, social practices like contingent pay may be universal around the globe and the variety in this practice may be rather marginal. Grobalization is the process of global standardization as people at various places adopt certain identical social practices. The tendency of globalization to standardize processes, products and behaviour has been extensively discussed by Ritzer (1995) in his earlier work such as the

"McDonaldization of Society" which at that time largely ignored the proliferation of local adjustments, hybrids, and new varieties. Barber (1996), on the other hand, has early emphasized in his contribution to globalization theory entitled "Djihad versus McDonaldization" that some localities are resisting the global standardization of products, processes and behavioural patterns. Instead, as Barber (1996) and others highlighted, various localities around the world struggle to maintain local uniqueness and socio-cultural differences. The notion of "glocalization" employed by Ritzer (2003; 2007; 2010) and others emphasizes also the omnipresent impact of one particular kind of social force on localities all around the world but highlights at the same time the fact that these globally identical factors are being locally adapted. In other words: they become differently integrated into the everyday life of people (Berger and Luckmann 1966) and the phenomenological experience of it (Schutz 1970) and therefore create new variety instead of homogeneity. While the notion of "glocalization" is quite well known to most people as it highlights those local differences created by various local adaptations of one kind of process, practice, product etc. (e.g Robertson 1992, 2010; Pieterse 2001, 2003; 2010), the notion of "grobalization" is a less well known neologism. It highlights an opposite social process, namely the uniform impact of some events at one locality at various different remote localities around the globe resulting in more homogeneity. Noting the dialectic relationship between the "grobal" and the "glocal" forces, Ritzer (2003, 193p.) stated:"Glocalization can be defined as the interpenetration of the global and the local, resulting in unique outcomes in different geographic areas. This view emphasizes global heterogeneity ... [and] economic, political, institutional, and – most importantly – cultural homogeneity. [...] grobalization focuses on the imperialistic ambitions of nations, corporations, organizations, and other entities and their desire – indeed, their need – to impose themselves on various geographic areas". Ritzer's (2003) notion of "grobalization" seems, in fact, to be a logically necessary term dialectically required in order to complement the previously existing term "glocalization". It is highlighting "homogenization" in contrast to "heterogeneization" as characterizing the impact of globalization. Ritzer (2003, 194) maintained:" Globalization as a whole is not unidirectional, because these two processes coexist under that broad heading and because they are, at least to some degree, in conflict in terms of their implications for the spread of nothingness [and something] around the world". The contrast between homogeneity and variety triggered by globalization is in fact constituting an area of disagreement or fruitful tension within globalization theory (Pieterse 2010).

Before I continue to embark on the seemingly odd terms of "something" and "nothing" used by Ritzer (2003), it is important to discuss implications of "grobalization" and "glocalization" for organizational analysis. Glocalization processes within MNCs will result in the fact that some organizational forces (e.g. practices) having an impact on all subsidiaries of a MNC will be adjusted, adopted, and therefore differently integrated into the operating patterns of the various subsidiaries. Glocalization processes within one MNC are therefore resulting in some kind of new local variety or diversity in practices while these practices are everywhere linked to the same underlying factor. For example, the principle of gender equality in a MNC may result in different practical manifestations in different subsidiaries, perhaps due to different legal systems, resulting in new variety. Grobalization processes, on the other hand, will result in the implementation of practices originated at one organizational entity of the MNC in a more or less identical manner in all other subsidiaries and will, therefore, increase or lead to some kind of similarity or homogeneity.

But, as mentioned, Ritzer (2003; 2007; 2010) linked the concepts of "grobalization" and "glocalization" to two other concepts, that is, to "nothing" and "something". Ritzer (2003, 195) explained the meaning of these two seemingly odd concepts as follows: "Nothing is defined here as a social form that is generally centrally conceived, controlled, and comperatively devoid of distinctive substantive content. This leads to a definition of something as a social form that is generally indigenously conceived, controlled, and comperatively rich in distinctive substantive content [italics removed]". In other words, the concept of "something" highlights the decentralized emergence of distinct practices, for example, and the concept of "nothing" highlights the role of a central entity in creating practices. For example, if one would highlight a MNC as characterized by processes of "nothingness", the role of one particular centre (in most instances likely but not necessarily the corporate headquarters or central R&D facilities of the organization) would be pivotal for product innovation or the development of management practices. On the other hand, in a MNC characterized largely by unfolding "something" processes various different local organizational entities or subsidiaries could be either simultaneously or interchangeably be involved in the creation of new practices and products. In the first case, there would be a clear and stable hierarchy with a clearly defined centre in the MNC resembling a "hierarchically integrated" organizational network (Bartlett and Goshal 1989;1998) and in the latter case the MNC and its various subsidiaries may be characterized by a fluctuating "heterarchical network" (Hedlund 1986; 1993).

Even though there is, according to Ritzer (2003; 2007; 2010), a natural affinity between "grobalization" and "nothing" as well as between "glocalization" and "something", other combinations are possible. Ritzer (2003; 2007; 2010) has therefore interrelated the dialectically structured concepts resulting in a typology differentiating between four types of globalization processes. Ritzer (2003; 2007; 2010) claimed that this further differentiation of the globalization process enhances our analytical capability and ability to understand the unfolding process of a large and unique kind of social transformation. But the combination of "grobalization" and "something" is, according to Ritzer (2003), a rather rare occurring event. Ritzer (2003) offered the example of handmade crafts to illustrate this type of globalization process, as, for example, various particular locally handmade or individualized crafts are sold globally at various locations by one MNC. It could also mean, if we relate this conceptual distinctive type of globalization process to organizational analysis, that various originally unique and individualized products and services developed at one of the various subsidiaries of a MNC are later on offered in an identical manner by other subsidiaries. However, there is, as Ritzer (2003, 198) has mentioned little "affinity between grobalization and something" since the production of "something" (i.e. decentral conceived individualized products or services) is much more expensive than the production of "nothing" (i.e. centrally conceived distinctive products or services). Moreover, the global demand for these rather expensive forms of individualized or tailor-made production and services seems to be rather small. It is therefore much more reasonable to assume that "grobalization" and "nothing" may characterize the globalization process unfolding within most MNCs. Ritzer (2003, 199) maintained that it is much easier to "mass-produce and mass-distribute the empty forms of nothing than the substantively rich forms of something" and, since mass-produced products and services are cheaper, there is much more demand for centrally conceived standardized products and services. Even though this may be the case for the production of commodity or tangible goods the situation may be quite different when it comes to services or intangible goods. However, the third possible type of globalization process, less important to Ritzer (2003), is "glocalization" of "nothing". This kind of globalization process unfolds according to Ritzer (2003, 201), for example, when the global tourist meets the local manufacturer of goods and services and buys locally available products or services which are, however, principally similar or identical at various localities around the world but are provided by local manufacturers. Finally, Ritzer (2003) distinguished "glocalization" of "something" from the other three previously discussed types of globalization processes. Ritzer (2003, 202) illustrated this type of globalization processes focusing on local crafts and pottery and wrote: "Such craft products are things, and they are likely to be displayed and sold in places such as craft barns. The craftperson who makes and demonstrates his or her wares is a person, and customers are apt to be offered a great deal of service. Such glocal products are likely to remain something, although there are certainly innumerable examples of glocal forms of something that have been transformed into glocal – and in some cases grobal – forms of nothing". In order to give an example which is more in tune with the analytical focus of this paper, "glocalization" of "something" could mean for an MNC that the various local subsidiaries of a global company produce their own local versions of a particular product which has been originally developed in a decentral manner by another subsidiary.

Ritzer (2003; 2007; 2010) developed his framework or typology distinguishing four types of globalization processes outlined so far by drawing on various examples primarily from the field of consumption for illustrative purposes. But Kellner (2005; 2010) and others have criticized Ritzer's (2003; 2007; 2010) "consumption bias" in outlining the theory of four globalization processes and concluded that there is, as a matter of fact, a "production deficit" to worry about (Kellner 2005, 264) when it comes to globalization studies. This paper will focus on the "production side" and will be concerned with the question of what kind of globalization processes may be observed to unfold in MNCs. It investigates questions like: Is the distinction of the four globalization processes proposed by Ritzer (2003; 2007; 2010) helpful for organizational analysis? Are there particular internal globalization patterns which may likely set some types of MNCs aside from other types of MNCs? Such questions can only be answered by applying Ritzer's (2003; 2007; 2010) four different types of globalization processes in the context of empirical organizational analysis. In the next step, I will report the results of an explorative qualitative study analyzing what kind of globalization processes are indicated to unfold within two MNCs according to the narrated experience of some interviewed managers.

Methodology

The explorative study was adopting a qualitative approach to empirical research and employed a case study design. Qualitative case studies are useful for generating data which allow a rich description of some phenomena in question, to generate new concepts, conceptual frameworks, hypotheses, and theory (Eisenhardt 1989, 535 & 545). Yin (2003) suggested that a multiple comparative case study rather than a single case analysis may provide a more sufficient "empirical ground" (Glaser and Strauss 1967) from which concepts, models, hypotheses, a theory or theoretical generalizations may be derived from (Bryman 2008, 544). Glaser and Strauss (1967, 21 pp) have emphasized that a comparative analysis of cases should highlight the particularities of each case next to commonalities for the purpose of concept generation. Eisenhardt (1989, 537) and Yin (2003) have both stressed that the selection of the cases for a comparative explorative qualitative research should be rather based on purposive instead of random sampling. In this manner, DaimlerChrysler and Accenture, two large MNCs belonging to two different economic sectors (commodity & service) have been selected for an analysis of internal globalization processes applying Ritzer's (2003; 2007; 2010) typology. Moreover, the purposive sampling allowed to analyze a company which has an "administrative heritage" (Bartlett and Ghosal 1989; 1998) or "development path" (Schreyögg et al. 2009) characterized by organic growth (Accenture) and to contrast it with a MNC which emerged from a large cross-border M&A process (DaimlerChrysler). However, given the nature of explorative research, the results of such studies may be limited to identify if a certain phenomena theoretically assumed seems to exist or not, or to see which kind of phenomena in terms of an ordinal scale evaluation seem to be more important. It is important to keep in mind that qualitative explorative studies are most suitable in areas of research in which not much knowledge exists (Schutt 2009).

In order to generate the necessary data required to answer the research questions outlined further above, several semi-structured interviews were conducted with managers in the two MNCs working in Germany. In the case of DaimlerChrysler seven and in the case of Accenture five managers could be interviewed. Hence, a phenomenological approach (Schutz 1970) focusing on the experience of internal globalization processes as a relevant phenomenon of everyday life experience (Berger and Luckmann 1966) of managers has been adopted for this explorative study. The number of interviewees was determined by the number of managers accessible for interviews as well as by the need to establish "theoretical saturation" (Eisenhardt 1989) indicating that additional interviews are unlikely to generate new information. In fact, for both companies, the data generated by the interviews tended, at one point, largely to reproduce the data generated by earlier interviews. For the purpose of an explorative study concerned with concept application and theoretical generalization, the numbers of conducted interviews seemed therefore to be sufficient.

The interviewees were asked during the interviews to describe the strategy, structure and culture of their corporations and to elaborate on the relationship between the headquarters and their subsidiary and their subsidiaries with other subsidiaries. The generated narrations were transcribed and a qualitative content analysis (Krippendorf 2004) of the transcribed data was conducted in order to identify narration revealing information about the kind of internally unfolding globalization process. The central research questions were: How is globalization experienced to unfold within the companies of the interviewees? Is there indication in the sensemaking process (Weick 1995) that only one type of globalization process as distinguished by Ritzer (2003; 2007; 2010) is existing, or do rather several types of globalization processes seem to unfold at the same time? If so, what kind of globalization processes seem to have had more momentum or to be more relevant? Are there significant differences between the two companies? If so, what kind of general conclusions or assumptions may these differences support?

DAIMLER CHRYSLER AND ACCENTURE

It seems that at Accenture, as the interview material suggest, internal management routines are standardized to a large extent. Accenture seems to be characterized, in Ritzer's (2003; 2007; 2010) terms, by extensive internal grobalization processes and forces when it comes to managerial issues. One interviewee, for example, outlined:

> Accenture is, even though there are local structures and peculiarities, nevertheless a very central and strictly managed corporation. (...) there are uniform rules and they are valid across the whole world. If you travel to China and you want to make a deal there and you have to deal with employees of Accenture, then you know: they are using the same tools, they are following the same rules, they are talking the 'same language'.

Another interviewee expressed the view that the independence of the various subsidiaries from the headquarters has decreased over time:

> Well the degree of autonomy of the various country level subsidiaries has, at least in my opinion, decreased. During the last couple of years it became more centrally managed from the USA.

In terms of Ritzer's (2003; 2007; 2010) terminology, the interviews provided overall strong evidence for the existence of "grobalization of nothing" processes when it comes to internal managerial processes and, therefore, homogeneity at Accenture.

It is important to note that at the same time, according to the interview material, product innovations may be developed or may emerge at any of the various subsidiaries of Accenture and not only at one subsidiary or the headquarters. Any local subsidiary of Accenture which has developed leading-edge knowledge in a particular area may serve as a "strategic leader" for the whole network of organizational entities of the MNC while others may be considered to serve as "implementers", "supporters" or, in the worst case, as "black holes" in terms of Bartlett and Goshal's (1989; 1998) typology of subsidiary roles. Many of the services and products offered by Accenture do emerge first at various local subsidiaries triggered by differences in local standards, business requirements and culture as well as different legal requirements. For example, while elaborate risk management reporting regulations may be implemented first of all in the U.S., they may, even though with some local differences, later on become required in other countries. Accenture may, in such a case, profit from the experiences of one subsidiary as the developed knowledge or expertise in this field, in the terminology of March (1991) an "exploration learning" achievement, becomes transferred and adjusted and applied by other subsidiaries in terms of "exploitation learning" (March 1991). It may be, however, by no means always the US subsidiary of Accenture which is at the leading edge of knowledge development due to different regulations worldwide. For example, the need for green reporting related IT systems helping to track the "carbon footprint" of a corporation may have been developed first by another subsidiary. Hence, knowledge development seems to emerge at Accenture at the level of the various local subsidiaries and is not usually centrally conceived at the headquarters or continuously at one subsidiary only. However, other subsidiaries, and subsequently Accenture at the whole profits from this knowledge transfer from various subsidiaries to the whole network as this enables the corporation to offer identical services at identical quality standards at various localities around the world. In fact, this capability to offer identical services at the same standard worldwide is perceived by some interviewers to be of key importance when it comes to the generation and maintenance of Accenture's competitive advantage. In Ritzer's (2003; 2007; 2010) terminology, Accenture seems to be characterized by "grobalization of something" processes when it comes to the globalization of its products and services.

However, it is also important to emphasize that there was at the same time some indication for the existence of "glocalization of something" processes. Since some of the large MNCs which Accenture serves require individualized services, existing standard knowledge and routines will have to be modified and adopted to the particular situation of these MNCs in different countries. Large MNCs as corporate clients may request tailor-made services for their operations by Accenture in either only one country, all countries they are operating in, or even different tailor-made services for their various operations in several countries at the same time. Moreover, different issues requiring advisory service may be relevant at the same time in different markets and subsidiaries must adjust their service or product portfolio to meet this situation. For example, one interviewee mentioned:

> But as a matter of fact, the markets are developing in a different way, and therefore, you must offer different services in the different markets. Or different topics are important and, therefore, there are different services which must be offered by Accenture in the local marketplaces. (...) For example, there may be a global offering like "Enterprise Risk Management", and this would be differently defined for the different markets. In Austria, Switzerland and Germany (ASG), this would feature different components compared with Asia since in Asia, or over there in America, this topic may be more important than here.

In such cases, Accenture's national subsidiaries will usually draw on corporation wide available standard knowledge and services and adopt them to meet particular local requirements. Hence, some services are triggering "glocalization of something" processes within Accenture.

In fact, based on the indications from the interviews, the conclusion seems to be warranted that "grobalization of something" is as important as "glocalization of something" when it comes to the services provided by Accenture. In any case, these types of globalization processes seem to fall both predominantly into the category of "something" as the tailor-made services as well as the standardized services usually will have been initially developed by some local subsidiaries rather than by a continuously dominating entity like the headquarters or one subsidiary. On the other hand, internal regulations, rules, or more generally speaking "managerial processes", seemed to be quite standardized in Accenture and originated at the organizational entity in the country of origin. According to Ritzer's (2003; 2007; 2010) terminology, the internal managerial processes in place at various subsidiaries seem to be subject of "grobalization of nothing" processes. However, there may be some minor local adjustments to these standards, that is, there are some "glocalization of nothing" processes in place resulting in some minor variety, but, they seem to be clearly subordinated to the standardization process.

It seems that the configuration of internal globalization processes was quite different at DaimlerChrysler, at least according to the narrations of the interviewed managers. DaimlerChrysler seems to have been characterized by much more internal heterogeneity when it comes to managerial processes. For a significant period in time even no overarching strategy for the various business units seemed to have existed. One interviewee, for example, mentioned:

> Well strategy, at DaimlerChrysler, if one is considering this topic in more detail, it was simply for a long time a fact that every business unit had made its own strategy and above was no strategy. (...) there are efforts, from a strategic point of view, to bring the units closer together. That this transnational DaimlerChrysler world comes closer together. In the past, there were many differences.

As the interview data suggested, there were attempts by the headquarters to homogenize managerial practices which, in Ritzer's (2003; 2007; 2010) language, would translate into "grobalization of nothing" processes within the MNC. For example, some respondents mentioned that the compensation structure at the top management level, part of the HRM practices, had to been standardized worldwide at one point after the merger. One interviewee, for example, stressed:

> ... this was one aspect which was harmonized over time, since the German managers said, why do you guys [from Chrysler] earn three times as much as we do?

But the data suggests that these unifying "grobalization of nothing" processes characterizing internal managerial practices and resulting in more homogeneity were of secondary importance compared to the simultaneously unfolding "glocalization of nothing" processes resulting in locally different adaptations of the same managerial practices. Even though there were attempts of the headquarters to create at least at the very general level some homogeneity when it comes to managerial routines and regulations, these attempts seemed according to the interviews to have rather resulted in "glocalization of nothing" processes. Due to DaimlerChrysler's continued operation of various brands, each brand characterized by its own administrative heritage and unique processes and products, internal variety of managerial processes seemed to have prevailed. In other words: managerial processes at DaimlerChrysler corporation may be characterized in Ritzer's (2003; 2007; 2010) terminology as featuring a great deal of internal variety and "glocalization of nothing" processes, most likely due to different administrative heritages of the various formerly independent firms which became later on business units of DaimlerChrysler.

The processes and practices of product development, including the design and construction of new vehicles, as well as the production and sales process were quite different between Mercedes-Benz, Dodge, Chrysler and others in the CarGroup and knowledge sharing seemed to have remained quite limited. The interview data suggested that the perception of only limited cooperation between the automotive brands was dominating the interviewed manager's mindset. Knowledge sharing and even joint development projects, like a new truck engine dubbed "World Engine", seemed on the other hand to have worked quite well for the Truck Group. For example, one interviewee mentioned:

> There are efforts to share [knowledge]. This is more so the case in the Truck Group than in the Car Group. If one is really precise, one must distinguish between the Truck Group and the Car Group since there are many differences in the design [of knowledge generation and sharing].

Insofar as there were globalization processes unfolding in terms of knowledge development and sharing it seems that these were characterized by "grobalization of something" in the TruckGroup. If knowledge sharing occurred at the various brands of the CarGroup it may have rather triggered "glocalization of something" processes as innovations generated at one brand needed to be adjusted to the various other "brand identities". But the automotive products produced by one brand, even though there are various models, are greatly standardized. For example, an A-class Mercedes car offered in Germany and in Korea is expected to be principally identical regardless of where this car actually has been produced. In Ritzer's (2003; 2007; 2010) terminology this is some evidence for "grobalization of nothing" as the car design was centrally received at the R&D centre of Mercedes-Benz headquarters. But if one takes some minor local product adjustments into consideration, for example the windshield of the cars may be offered in tinted version in Korea while no such thing would be offered in Germany due to legal restrictions there is also some indication for "glocalization of nothing" processes. However, these processes are secondary as the basic design of the product remains the same and changes may be only of minor scope.

Conclusion

The results of the explorative study indicate that it seems too simplistic to speak of globalization in MNCs in general but one must instead identify what kind of globalization processes are unfolding in order to understand the quality of intracorporate globalization. Ritzer's (2003; 2007; 2010) framework helps to advance organizational studies as it enables to identify unfolding globalization processes within MNCs in a more elaborate and differentiated manner. The analysis has demonstrated that, when it comes to the task to capture the globalization processes existing in MNCs, it is important to distinguish between managerial processes, product development processes, and finally the products offered by the companies. This distinction may easily be overlooked as much literature focusing on the issue of homogenization (grobalization) vs. variation (glocalization) focuses on the types of generated products and services only and not on the underlying organizational processes. The results of the explorative study presented in this paper also help to become aware of the fact that, in addition to analyzing the unfolding types of globalization processes at a particular point in time, the concurrently existing configuration of managerial processes, product development processes, and the nature of the products (i.e. homogeneity vs. diversity) has to be taken into account. Depending on which kind of globalization processes may be identified (e.g. grobalization or glocalization) given either a large degree of homogeneity or heterogeneity of the internal managerial processes, product development processes, and the nature of the products, the pinpointed particular combination may suggest the existence of either organizational change or organizational inertia.

It may also be argued as a result of this study that it is more likely that organizations in the service sector will be prone to be characterized by "grobalization of something" and "glocalization of something" processes and consumer commodities producing companies by "grobalization of nothing" and "glocalization of nothing" processes when it comes to their products. Even though Ritzer (2003: 198) has argued that there is little "affinity between grobalization and something" the case of Accenture may demonstrate that this kind of globalization process may be in fact one of the most important sources for competitive advantage of MNCs in the service sector. The standardization of knowledge and expertise developed at one of the MNC's subsidiaries in terms of initial "exploration" (March 1991) of a new product or service and the subsequent "exploitation" (March 1991) of this knowledge by other subsidiaries is a key competitive advantage for consultancy firms operating in various countries. The various subsidiaries must be able, as the case of Accenture has demonstrated, to adopt and modify such knowledge, if necessary, leading to "glocalization of something" processes while at the same time "grobalization of something" processes are also possible. It seems much more likely that MNCs in the consumer commodities sector will feature "grobalization of nothing" and "glocalization of nothing" processes when it comes to the products they offer. Due to the tangible nature of their products and the large initial capital investment for their production the individual adaptability of the product is limited and economics of scale are an important factor.

The evidence also indicates that the "development path" (Schreyögg et al. 2009) or, in other words, the "administrative heritage" (Bartlett/Goshal 1989; 1998) of a MNC may have a significant impact on the likelihood which kind of globalization processes may be dominating and which may be secondary. It may be inferred from the case studies that it is more likely to expect for organically grown MNCs a large degree of homogeneity and "grobalization of nothing" processes when it comes to their internal managerial regulations and processes. For companies emerging from a cross-border M&A process it seems to be more likely to encounter "glocalization of nothing" next to some "grobalization of nothing" processes at least on the very top level. This may particularly be expected in situations in which it is important to maintain the distinct identities of the previously independent firms.

The results of the study also highlight the fact that it is important to pay attention to the hierarchical level while analyzing the globalization processes within MNCs. While the interviews at Accenture contained no qualifying comment indicating that "grobalization of nothing" processes are only limited to the top level, the interviews with DaimlerChrysler managers emphasized the limitation of "grobalization of nothing" processes to homogenize managerial processes at the top corporate hierarchical level only.

In sum, the results of the explorative study suggest that for any MNC various types of globalization processes may be simultaneously unfolding within. Any organizational analysis concerned with applying Ritzer's (2003; 2007; 2010) framework should therefore adopt an "as-well-as" rather than an "either-or" perspective. An inclusive pluralistic perspective is pivotal for all postmodern organizational analysis (Alvesson/Deetz 1996; Cummings 2001) and, as a matter of fact, also characterizes the very nature of the postmodern organization. However, some of these globalization processes may be dominating while the other types may be of relatively minor importance and of lower intensity. In other words, the different configuration of the various types of ongoing internal globalization processes needs to be investigated in order to be able to understand the quality or characteristic nature of internally unfolding globalization processes in MNCs and to highlight similarities and differences. The case study evidence suggests that when it comes to managerial processes, the influence of a center, usually the headquarters, on the various subsidiaries of the MNC is likely. But, when it comes to the development of products and services, MNCs may be more likely to take advantage of developments occurring decentrally at the same time at various subsidiaries. MNCs in the service sector may therefore most likely feature a network of organizational units governed by the principle of "heterarchy" (Hedlund 1986; 1993) for product development while, at the same time, the organizational network may be governed by the principle of "hierarchy" when it comes to internal managerial or administrative processes. In other words: the role of any specific subsidiary in terms of Bartlett/Goshal's (1989; 1998) distinction between "strategic leader", "implementer", "supporter", or "blackhole" may change over time in the context of product development. Moreover, one specific subsidiary may be a "strategic leader" and therefore crucial in knowledge development for one service or product, while the same subsidiary may be at the same time only one of several "implementers" of another kind of service. But when it comes to managerial processes, as both cases indicated, a centre in the "hierarchically integrated" network (Bartlett/Ghoshal 1989; 1998) seems to be likely to impose standards concerning the design of the managerial processes. These results indicate that the governance principles linking the various subsidiaries of the organizational network of an MNC may operate at the same time according to different logics.

REFERENCES

Albrow, Martin. 1996. *The Global Age. State and Society beyond Modernity.* Cambridge: Polity Press.

Aldrich, Howard. E. 1999. *Organizations Evolving.* London: Sage.

Alvesson, Mats, and Stanley Deetz 1996. "Critical Theory and Postmodernism Approaches to Organizational Studies" In *Handbook of Organizational Studies*, edited by Steward Clegg, Cynthia Hardy, and Walter Nord, 191-217: Sage: London.

Barber, Benjamin. 1996. *Jihad versus McWorld.* New York: Ballantine Books.

Bartlett, Chris, and Sumantra Ghoshal. 1989. *Managing Across Borders. The Transnational Solution.* Boston: Harvard Business School Press.

Bartlett, Chris and Sumantra Ghoshal 1998. *Managing Across Borders*. Boston: Harvard Business School Press. 2nd edition.

Beck, Ulrich. 2000. *What is Globalization*?. Cambridge: Polity Press.

Berger, Peter .L., and Thomas Luckmann. 1966. *The Social Construction of Reality. A Treatise in the Sociology of Knowledge*. Garden City: Doubleday.

Bryman, Alan. 1998. *Social Research Methods*. Oxford: Oxford University Press.

Castells, Manuel. 1996. *The Rise of the Network Society. Vol 1: The Information Age. Economy, Society and Culture.* Oxford: Blackwell.

Castells, Manuel. 1997. *The Power of Identity. Vol. 2: The Information Age: Economy, Society and Culture*. Oxford: Blackwell.

Coleman, James. 1982. *The Asymmetrical Society*. Syracuse: Syracuse University Press.

Collinson, Simon, and Glenn Morgan. 2009." Images of the Multinational Firm" In *Images of the Multinational Firm.*, edited by Collinson, Simon and Glenn Morgan, 1-22. Chicester: Wiley & Sons.

Cummings, Stephen. 2002. *ReCreating Strategy*. London: Sage.

Dicken, Peter. 2003. *Global Shift: Reshaping the Global Economic Map in the 21st Century*. New York. Guilford Publications.

Doz, Yves L., Jose Santos, and Peter J. Williamson. 2001. *From Global to Metanational. How Companies win in the Knowledge Economy*. Boston: Harvard Business School Press.

Eisenhardt, Kathleen M. 1989. "Building Theory from Case Study Research" *Academy of Management Review* 14: 532-550.

Giddens, Anthony. 1990. *The Consequences of Modernity*. Cambridge: Polity Press.

Glaser, Barney .G., and Anselm L. Strauss. 1967. *The Discovery of Grounded Theory. Strategies for Qualitative Research*. Chicago: Aldine.

Hannan, Michael .T., and John Freeman. 1977. "The Population Ecology of Organizations" *American Journal of Sociology* 82: 929-964.

Hedlund, Gunnar.1986. "The Hypermodern MNC – A Heterarchy" *Human Resource Management* 25: 9-35.

Hedlund, Gunnar. 1993. "Assumptions of Hierarchy and Heterarchy, with Applications to the Management of the Multinational Corporation" In *Organization Theory and the Multinational Corporation*, edited by Sumatra Ghoshal, and Eleanor Westney, 211-236: London: Macmillan.

Heenan, David .A., and Howard V. Perlmutter. 1979. *Multinational Organization Development*. Reading: Addison-Wesley.

Held, David. 2004. *Global Covenant*. Cambridge: Polity Press.

Held, David, and Anthony McGrew. 2002. *Globalization/Antiglobalization*. Cambridge: Polity Press.

Hirst, Paul, and Grahame Thompson. 1999. *Globalization in Question*. Cambridge: Polity Press.

Kellner, Douglas 2002. "Theorizing Globalization" *Sociological Theory* 20: 285-305.

Kellner, Douglas 2005. "Dialectics of Something and Nothing" *Critical Perspectives on International Business* 1: 263-272

Kellner, Douglas 2010. "Dialectics of Something and Nothing: Critical Reflections on Ritzer's Globalization Analysis" In *Readings in*

Globalization: Key Concepts and Major Debates, edited by George Ritzer, and Zeynep Atalay, 372-379: Wiley-Blackwell: Chichester.

Krippendorf, Klaus. 2004. *Content Analysis: An Introduction to its Methodology*. Thousand Oaks: Sage.

March, James G. 1991. "Exploration and Exploitation in Organizational Learning" *Organizational Sience* 2: 71-87.

McGrew, Anthony. 2007. "Globalization in Hard Times: Contention in the Academy and Beyond" In *The Blackwell Compagnion to Globalization*, edited by George Ritzer, 29-53. Oxford: Blackwell.

OECD (2005): *Handbook on Economic Globalisation Indicators*. Paris: OECD Publishing.

Ohmae, Kenichi. 1990. *The Borderless World*. London: HarperCollins.

Ohmae, Kenichi.1996. *The End of the Nation-State*. London: Harper Collins.

Pieterse, Jan N. 2001. "Hybridity, so What? The Anti-Hybridity Backlash and the Riddles of Recognition" *Theory, Culture and Society* 18: 219- 245.

Pieterse, Jan N. 2003. *Globalization and Culture: Global Mélange*. Lanham: Rowman and Littlefield.

Pieterse, Jan N. 2010. "Globalization as Hybridization" In Readings in Globalization: Key Concepts and Major Debates, edited by George Ritzer, and Zeynep Atalay, 326-333. Chichester: Wiley-Blackwell.

Ritzer, George. 1995. *The McDonaldization of Society*. Thousand Oaks: Pine Forge Press.

Ritzer, George. 2003. "Rethinking Globalization: Glocalization/Grobalization and Something/Nothing" *Sociological Theory* 21: 193-209.

Ritzer, George. 2007. *The Globalization of Nothing*. Thousand Oaks: Pine Forge Press.2nd Edition.

Ritzer, George. 2010. "Rethinking Globalization: Glocalization/Grobalization and Something/Nothing" In *Readings in Globalization: Key Concepts and Major Debates*, edited by George Ritzer, and Zeynep Atalay, 361-371. Wiley-Blackwell: Chichester.

Robertson, Ronald.1992. *Globalization: Social Theory and Global Culture*. London: Sage.

Robertson, Ronald. 2010. "Glocalization: Time-Space and Homogeneity-Heterogeneity" In Readings in Globalization: Key Concepts and Major Debates, edited by George Ritzer, and Zeynep Atalay, 334-343. Wiley-Blackwell: Chichester.

Rosenau, James N. 1990. *Turbulence in World Politics*. Princeton: Princeton University Press.

Rosenau, James N. 2000. *Distant Proximities*. Princeton: Princeton University Press.

Rosenberg, James N. 2000. *The Follies of Globalization Theory*. London: Verso.

Schreyögg, Georg, Jochen Koch, and Jörg Sydow. 2009. "Organizational Path Dependence: Opening the Black Box" *Academy of Management Review* 34: 689-709.

Schutt, Russell. 2009. *Investigating the Social World.* Newbury Park: Pine Forge Press.

Schutz, Alfred. 1970. *On Phenomenology and Social Relations*. Chicago: Chicago University Press.

Sklair, Leslie. 2000. *The Transnational Capitalist Class*. Oxford: Blackwell Publishers.

Sklair, Leslie. 2002. *Globalization. Capitalism and its Alternatives*. Oxford: Oxford University Press.

UNCTD. 2009. *World Investment Report*. Geneva: United Nations.

Wallerstein, Immanuel. 1979. *The Capitalist World Economy*. Cambridge: Cambridge University Press.

Waters, Malcom. 1995. *Globalization*. London: Routledge.

Westney, Eleanor, and Srilata Zaheer. 2001. "The Multinational Corporation as an Organization" In *Handbook of International Business*, edited by Alan Rugman, and Thomas Brewer, 349-379. Oxford: Oxford University Press.

Weick, Karl.1995. *Sensemaking in Organizations*. London: Sage

Yin, Robert K. 2003. *Case Study Research. Design and Methods*. Thousand Oaks: Sage

CHAPTER 6

A Transversalist Justice: Responses to the Corporate Globalization

S. A. Hamed Hossein

INTRODUCTION

Concerned with global inequalities and crises, a new wave of grassroots activism has opened up prospects for reformulating social and environmental justice in the 21st century. This new global resistance is shaped around a set of shared goals for advancing social, political, economic and ecological justice across the world although definitions of global issues may vary among the participant groups (Hosseini 2010; della Porta 2007). The main concerns are related to the international financial institutions and trade agreements, related domestic and foreign policy changes, neoliberal financial policies, privatization, structural adjustment programs in the South, transnational corporations, and the recent war and peace issues (Broad 2002). Although a great number of massive protests across the world (especially in the West since the late 1990s) have given popularity to the resistance, the movement in fact is not limited to these events. The incidence of massive uprisings and protests has experienced ups and downs during the last decade. While the September 11, 2001 terrorist attacks and the following sharp shifts in public discourses diverted the public attentions from the movement, it has been able to regain its potency once again, thanks to the rising disappointment with the exhaustive costly war in Iraq and Afghanistan, and the recent collapse of giant capitalist institutions.

This growing resistance has created new visions and new spaces for exchanging experiences in confronting the global agents of disempowerment and inequality. As Callinicos (2003, 15), a political theorist and socialist activist, mentions, the recent transnational movements are now motivated by a sense of the interconnection between an immense variety of different injustices and dangers. The scholarly literature on the global resistance has been rapidly growing. A growing number of authors have identified the issue of justice as the core concern of many participants in the movement (Opel and Pompper 2003;

Amoore 2005; della Porta 2007; Moghadam 2009; Hosseini 2009). However, little attention has paid to the definitions of justice adopted or developed by the main actors in the movement.

Is the movement in fact a plural space comprised of myriad local campaigns demanding for putting particular-localized modes of justice into practice or a cohesive global movement with a universal notion of justice? What concept(s) of justice can be attributed to these movements? How is justice understood in the movement when compared to the notions of justice which used to be embraced by the so-called new (or identity-based) movements (NSMs) like feminism or the so-called old social movements (OSMs) like many labor, socialist and anarchist movements? Is this a movement for redistributive fairness or recognitive justice? To what extent are the complexities of global inequalities translated into the new conceptions of justice? Who are the most liable actors in the movement to adopt and call for the application of such notions of justice? In this article, I hope I will contribute to answering the above questions by drawing on: (1) a short critical review of mainstream justice theories; (2) a conceptual analysis of the notions of justice underlying some prototypical activist discourses and practices; (3) an argument about the complexity of global social changes and inequalities; and (4) an examination of a grassroots HIV/AIDS advocacy network (ACT UP) as an illustrative case study.

Global Oppositions to Global Injustices

The global resistance to corporate globalization has not been created ex nihilo. Rather, it has ideological-experiential roots in both the so-called new Left middle class (such as green, identity-based, welfare, and cultural movements), old Left movements (socialism, unionism, and anarchism), and the most recent transnational protests and resistances. It consists of: single-issue protests (anti-sweatshops, debt relief, fair trade, AIDS, farmers, youth groups, etc.); larger activist networks (such as anti-war and human rights, advocacy networks, organized labor, international hunger and slum dwellers, Zapatista solidarity networks); inter-national uprisings (such as the Occupy movements, Arab Spring, and the European anti-austerity protests); infrapolitical everyday life resistances (as experienced by myriads of ordinary citizens, migrants, peasants and villagers in opposing adjustment programs in the Third World); INGOs (such as the Global Exchange, Focus on Global South, the Peoples' Global Action against Free Trade and WTO, and many corporate watchdogs); and annual international and regional forums (like the International Forum on Globalization, the World Social Forum, and its local chapters).

Many in the movement have aimed to identify and oppose the major sources of inequality. Ayres (2004), in a brief review, shows how diagnostic and prognostic frames have come out of scattered resistances, and shaped inclusive master frames, critical of the whole process of neoliberal globalization. According to these frames, the free trade ideology undermines democratic politics and democratic identities. Insofar as an ideology legitimizes social inequalities and revokes the principles of fundamental social justice and security, it threatens the culture of democratic freedom. Many in the movement stand up against injustice and hegemony by questioning the legitimacy of such ideologies. However, it remains arguable if the movement has been able to develop a unique mode of conceptualizing and practicing justice as an alternative to mainstream discourses. Social movements can provide a breeding ground for new theories (of justice) even though they may not be explicitly articulated. Analyzing activists' discourses, practices, ideas, and solidarities in terms of their underlying definitions and assumptions can help us extract such "direct theories" (Sturgeon 1995). For instance, the second paragraph of the Call of Social Movements, issued at the end of the 2002 World Social Forum in Porto Alegre, outlines an idealized perception of a specific mode of solidarity among actors within the global field of resistance who have been experiencing different but interdependent systems of disempowerment:

> We are a global solidarity movement, united in our determination to fight against the concentration of wealth, the proliferation of poverty and inequalities, and the destruction of our earth. We are living and constructing alternative systems, and using creative ways to promote them. We are building a large alliance from our struggles and resistance against a system based on sexism, racism and violence, which privileges the interests of capital and patriarchy over the needs and aspirations of people. (WSF 2002)

This can be interpreted as a new stage for global resistance in which people's experiences of injustice in different contexts can be heard, exchanged and compared; a new phase that represents a shift from self-interested and particularist movements, to flexible and adaptive cooperation with 'others', from fugitive events to flexible networks of solidarity, and from a negative to a positive position. All these mentioned happenings, their continuity, intensity, and cosmic spread, reflect a common concern about the growing global complexities and have implications for justice at the global level.

TOWARDS AN INTEGRATIVE THEORY OF JUSTICE?

A short review of major theoretical controversies over the definition of social justice can provide us with a basic framework for mapping the definitions of justice among the movement actors. Theoretical controversies can be roughly discussed in terms of: (1) the units of justice; (2) content of justice; and (3) the institutional bases of justice. In terms of the units, controversies have been shaped around the dualism of individual vs. collective (or liberty vs. equality). In terms of the content, redistributive (material-economic) justice has been considered as an opposite view to recognitive (social-cultural) justice while in terms of the institutional bases, those who argue for the adequacy of national and local institutions are disputed by those who argue for the necessity of establishing new global rules.

One of the most important dilemmas for both liberalism and neoliberalism is the issue of balancing individual and community (society) in their definition of justice. Classical liberalism and libertarians equate justice with the sovereignty and autonomy of the individual rather than community and therefore fail to acknowledge preexisting sources of difference and inequality. The most basic ideal of liberal society is individual liberty. Individual liberty and social equality are held as conflicting ideals and therefore social inequalities are inevitable consequences of liberty as people are naturally different in terms of their abilities and merits. The only credible equality is the equality before law and rules of conduct. By affirming abstract and universal concepts of justice around the negative rights to property and entitlements, (neo-)liberalism misrecognizes cultural and identity differences. Therefore, in terms of distributive justice, it endorses class differentiation as natural outcome of difference in individuals' merits, and overlooks the recognitive dimension of justice.

Egalitarian liberalists like Rawls (1971), however, attempt to combine both individual liberty and social equality into one ideal by expanding the notion of justice beyond economy into political realm where individuals' original position of equality is assumed. Although social and economic inequalities are inevitable, from a Rawlsian perspective, they can be arranged in a way that they benefit the least well-off (Rawls 1971, 302). Egalitarian liberalism, however, remains blind to cultural and social differences by keeping its notion of fair distribution away from what communities and people may believe as good. Egalitarian justice like the other forms of liberal justice transcends social, cultural and symbolic roots of inequality by stressing on a universal conception of human needs and rationality.

Quite contrary to the liberalist ideas of justice, a communitarian response to the dilemma of redistribution vs. recognition is to stress on cultural context and the values associated with common good. They believe that social justice is inextricably linked with shared identities like nationality, shared beliefs and ideologies, and public cultures (Kymlicka 1995; 2001). The endorsement of moral relativism by communitarianism requires a rejection of transcendental cosmopolitanism in favor a particularism (Okereke 2007, 45-47).

A new generation of justice theorists, such as Fraser (1995; 1997; 2005), Honneth (1995; 2001), and Young (1990; 2000), have argued for the reconciliation of recognitive and redistributive justice. For them, recognitions and misrecognitions, like racism, happen through social and cultural relations and therefore they are not simply limited to political and economic institutions. Therefore, recognition of differences is not only a primary good but also a precondition of entitlement. Realization of social justice requires examination of existing differences, privilege and oppression. Compared to reductionist accounts raised by liberalist and communitarianist views, such a theoretical endeavor for balancing between both allegedly conflicting aspects of justice must be celebrated as a significant advancement. However, a great body of these arguments remains highly sophisticated and abstract.

These integrative views, in order to defend the necessity, possibility and plausibility of establishing balance between redistribution and recognition, assume an analytical separation between economic, political and cultural realms. This assumption can be questioned regarding the nature of many current globalization processes. They argue that neither recognition nor redistribution can be reduced to one another as each belongs to a different realm with different mechanisms of regenerating inequality and injustice (Schlosberg 2004). Therefore, the inter-sectional nature of inequalities and intertwined causes of injustice have remained undertheorized in these integrative theories of justice. These theories rightly argue that an essential element of developing normative theories of justice is to analyze the actual roots of injustice in different contexts. But what I will define as the complexities of global structural changes have not been investigated adequately. Moreover, there is not consent about the applicability of these integrative theories of justice in a more global perspective. In the context of global justice solidarities, as Gould (2008) argues, "a multitude of difference comes to play" and this questions the reduction of cultural and identity differences. The following section will explore a new notion of justice in the movement which has constructive lessons for both academic theories of justice and theories of global change.

A Transversalist Notion of Justice

The first glimpses of global resistance against neoliberalism emerged with many scattered local and national conflicts over welfare issues and in opposition to new policy shifts towards structural adjustments in developing countries alongside economic deregulations in the North. Numerous studies of such dispersed pockets of resistance show that many contemporary social movements in varying degrees have raised issues about both redistribution and recognition (for instance, see Martin 2001, 361, on new welfare movements). Contemporary movements usually combine identity politics with social policy goals. Since the rise of neoliberal regimes and economic rationalization at the national level, the resistance against social policy changes happened to grow up in many local communities. Hence, strong links between the politics of recognition and their appeals for changes in distributional policies have surfaced and been identified by some scholars such as Taylor (1998) and Fraser (1995).

Unlike identity-based movements that usually aim to address and solve problems related to their own lifestyles, many in the recent uprisings deal with problems which cross identity boundaries, while affecting their own lifestyles as well. This can be interpreted as the unique ideational feature of recent movements. An increasing number of counter-hegemonic discourses usually deal with issues beyond both recognition and redistribution. In contrast to the new welfare and policy movements, current global concerns cannot even be reduced to a combination of the two. Rather, they carry a social and moral responsibility for the interests and recognition of the Other. This can be easily identified in, for instance, the civil rights of women and children from the South in the case of defending refugees, the rights of workers exploited in sweatshops in the case of anti-sweatshop movements, and the issues of unemployed people and global poverty in the case of the anti-debt movement.

Although the acknowledgement of social differentiations is important in the practical formation of ideas about justice in the movement, identity-affirmation is not an end in itself. The idea of justice has been redefined by many in the movement in accordance with both collective identities and the totality of a globalizing capitalist system at the same time. According to Burgmann (2003), the recent counter-capitalist movements, by targeting the 'whole' of globalization, question any postmodernist inspired skepticism about radical intellectual appeals for challenging the whole world system. How can the movement actors hold the significant position of identity-affirmation within their understanding of justice, while avoiding its implication for a paralyzing fragmented subjectivity? One solution is to attribute a broader, more inclusive, and 'transversalist' meaning of justice in these movements.

Although there is sufficient evidence to signify the emergence of new structural changes (della Porta and Diani 1999, 55) there is no evidence that materialist values have lost their relevance in resistance led by non-working class movements (Brooks and Manza 1994). The contemporary history of mobilizations in advanced societies, even during the 1980s, has witnessed the emergence of alliances between working class and community groups (see Burgmann 2003, 270-276, for some examples of the new patterns of alignment between unions and communities). Drawing upon two cases from the present context of struggles, i.e. the Community Unionism and British Firefighters' Dispute, Edwards (2004, 114) contends that labor movements retain "a key role in generating a relatively autonomous space for public debate in advanced capitalist societies." Besides, such cases bear witness to the uprising of many movements concerned with the quality of life and with the allocation of material rewards to different social groups (Brecher and Costello 1990). As Edwards (2004, 126) concludes, rather "than old class conflict being divorced from the new postmaterialist concerns to reassert communicative rational action, they are fundamentally implicated in it".

One way of understanding the movement's conception of justice is to investigate the modes of solidarity in the movement in terms of their underlying assumptions. The growth of horizontal alliances, affinity groups, and collaborative networks across communities with different interests and identities point to a new tendency to go beyond the incompatible conceptions of social differentials – around issues like gender, race, cultural identity, individuality, and community – in establishing a flexible solidarity based on a collaborative inclusion of the Other into the definition of Self. In its mission statement, the Queers for Economic Justice, a non-profit organization promoting social justice in sexual and gender contexts, states:

> We are a multi-racial, multi-classed, multi-cultural group of people of diverse marginalized sexual and gender identities, as well as diverse ages, skills, educational levels, backgrounds and abilities ... We understand the interconnections between different oppressions that perpetuate economic injustice, and we work on multiple levels to eradicate them. (Queers for Economic Justice, 2004)

Contextualizing and operationalizing the universal values such as tolerance, justice, equality and those that are implied by human rights discourses, through particular debates is the major aptitude of the World Social Forum for synthesizing universality and particularity. As reflected on the Forum's website, the WSF 2005 started as the expression of world diversity, polyphony of voices that meet the universal wishes for tolerance, justice, peace, and equality (see WSF 2005).

'Transversalism' here is within the domain of groups critical of different forms of injustice caused by corporate globalisation, reflecting a foundational consensus with a creative approach to their contentions. It suggests that understanding problems like inequality must follow the lines of anti-dualist, anti-reductionist, and anti-hierarchical principles. This emerging notion of social justice (and democracy) requires affirming a few general principles:

- Inequalities at any level from local to global should be systemically addressed in relation to each other;
- The intersectionality of global inequalities must be recognized both in the analyses of reality and the articulation of normative alternatives;
- Integrative visions of justice and equality ought to be articulated through freely exchanging ideas and experiences in autonomous and horizontally structured open spaces of action and deliberation;
- Material and post-material, economic and cultural bases of inequality, and recognition and redistribution issues are deeply interdependent, and none should be weighted over the other (both the life-word and system must be democratically restructured);
- The asymmetrical nature of globalization processes can only be effectively dealt with if subjects think and act as effectual globally as locally;
- All personal grievances and experiences of surrounding conditions must gain equal opportunity to be expressed publicly and all public issues must be taken personally; and,
- Neither revolution nor reform makes sense without developing relative autonomous spaces where actors can practice and examine their alternative ways of organizing social life.

Such a consciousness is best embodied perhaps in the principles of the World Social Forum – that any alternative must be democratic and have well-built commitment to shared dignity or rights; that it must take us away from the neoliberal, hegemonic world order, homogenizing consumerist culture, and corporate commodification. Although transnational solidarities, forums, and interactions carry many paradoxes, caused by persisting undigested experiences of the past practices, experiencing this uncertainty or confusion itself has resulted in the emergence of creative intellectual demands which convey a transversalist mode of conceptualizing justice.

Global Complexities as Structural Factors

The question I will be attempting to answer in this section is how we can explain the rise of such a transversalist notion of justice in terms of the major social changes in the current global context especially since the end of Cold War. Many European studies of the post-1960s Western social movements argued that due to main transformations in the nature of capitalism, i.e. a shift from an industrial to post-industrial society, a historical rupture could be identified in the politics of opposition. A significant decline of interest in ideology, politics and redistributive justice and a growing concern about identity, cultural representations and recognitive justice among the new social movements (NSMs) is what supposedly marks the post-1960s politics of protest.

The post-1960s (or the so-called new social) movements were considered the result of, and the response to, their historical conditions including: the bureaucratization of trade unions and labor movements; the internal immobility of political parties; the neglect of discriminating issues other than class by earlier social movements; an emerging new middle class; increasing levels of intellectual capital; the emerging importance of cultural reproduction instead of material production; and marketization of knowledge (Burgmann 2003). In addition, these conditions had a strong correlation with the post-WWII political economy: the rising welfare state, the Keynesian economic system, the corporatist state, the embourgeoisement of the working class, state protectionism, and higher levels of employment and accountability of social democratic states, higher real income levels, and post-materialist needs and values (Inglehart 2000, 228). Accordingly, all these conditions (generally referred to under titles such as 'post-industrial society', 'welfare capitalism', or 'late modernity') has made social and political activists launch themselves into a new process of social learning.

According to these accounts, the rise of welfare state in the West has caused social cleavages to be no longer derived from the control of the means of production, but rather from the means of survival. Therefore, the emergence of single-issue movements for the re-allocation of public resources such as housing and health would be more likely. However, many of these structural speculations, especially those related to the growing role of the state, are now deeply questioned regarding the changing conditions caused by the relative retreat of the welfare state in the West, and the definite decline of protectionist policies in most of the post-colonization South. Since the early 1980s, state interventions, such as protectionist policies for education, health and civil activities, have been under pressure by neoliberalist ambitions, such as 'austerity measures' in the North and 'structural adjustment programs' in the South (Laurell 2000).

Welfare states in all developed countries have been experiencing enormous financial pressures. Many scholars argue that in responding to such pressures, governments have begun to adopt the marketization and privatization approaches, which eventually lead to the destruction of social democracy and to the polarization of society. Although the growing resistance and the "strength of support for public social provision in most countries makes the dismantling of the welfare state highly unlikely" (Pierson 1998, 539) the real challenges and pressures to welfare states due to the neoliberalist reforms are undeniable.

As Bartholomew and Mayer (1992) argue, issues of inequality and hierarchy must no longer be discarded in favor of the politics of identity and in a cultural reductionist type of analysis. Fostering the de-politicization of public spheres and neoliberal public policies on the deregulation of labor markets have weakened institutionalized opportunities for tripartite negotiations among the state, capital and labor (the so-called capital-labor compromise), or the social corporatist patterns of interest representations (Navarro 1998). Besides, the protecting measures for disempowered groups and long-term peace and justice perspectives secured by the state in post-industrial societies have become less persuasive.

However, the retreat of the welfare state, since the 1980s, does not necessarily mean the resurrection of cruel types of industrial capitalism that sparked in the 19th Century. Hence, such an event per se does not discredit the cultural and cognitive approaches in favor of a class-based and economic deterministic model. New structural inequalities fit neither into materialist nor into post-materialist models of explanations.

The retreat of a welfare oriented and centralized planning paradigm from the private sphere of life in favor of economic rationality has pushed forward the radical Left to rearticulate what they mean by 'justice' and to radicalize their basic ideas of democracy to remove ambiguities which might overlap with the ideas of new liberal democracy. The new situation caused by the emergence of neo-liberal governments and the withdrawal of state interventions for social protection, has required some scholars to extend the European approach beyond the analyses of the welfare state (Maheu 1995; Melucci 1995c; Castells 1997).

The recent extensions of European and late modernity approaches have embraced growing discourses around notions such as network society, information age, communication revolution, and the agential role of movement actors in these new historical situations. Among scholars who have given significant attention to the changing conditions and situation of the current global social movements (GSMs) are Melucci (1995b; 1995a; 2000), Castells (2000; 2004), and to some extent Giddens (1991; 1994). It is argued that the idea of the State as the fundamental element of change has been weakened because of certain factors such as: the growing rates of employment in informal sectors; stronger economic interdependence among states; the diffusion of mass communication across borders; the emergence of public awareness of supranational dimensions of social life; as well as a growth of organisms of supranational sovereignty and various decentralizations (della Porta and Diani 1999, 34). These factors have limited the power of the State in controlling civil society. At the same time, the resulting proliferation of diverse global public spheres and subnational autonomies brings about significant changes in the nature of collective action-ideation.

Besides, the growing influence of the media and the importance of symbolic production have provided new spaces for conflict. For instance, some new spaces for conflict about the different uses of scientific and technological knowledge have opened up by way of the new scientific developments in biotechnology. Growing consumerism and commercialization of cultural products have always been associated with the intervention of the market into private aspects of life, such as eating habits, styles of clothes, leisure, entertainment, and emotional expressions. This intervention has resulted in new forms of political-cultural reactions, perhaps best crystallized in the rise and demise of new antagonistic lifestyles such as popular music, youth movements and countercultures plus the increasing diversification among social groups (Eyerman and Jamison 1998). All the above-listed factors are mainly referred to in order to explain the growing cultural-ideological diversity and even individualization of current global movements, rather than to explain their growing convergence, interdependence, and new integrative features. Therefore, from this point of view, justice as the recognition of difference remains as the prime demand in the global age. The weakness of national political and welfare institutions in securing distributive and recognitive justice cannot be compensated by fortifying unified global governance, as this would exacerbate local injustices by downplaying local differences.

These sorts of theoretical extensions insist that in the present era of economic austerity, class struggles have remained superseded by powerful new interest groups of welfare-state clients capable of largely resisting pressures from neoliberal states. However, in fact, regarding cases of 'new welfare movements' (Fagan and Lee 1997), the demands for challenging interventionist states in the 1960s-1970s have been largely replaced with recent mobilizations heading for extending State responsibilities for providing distributive justice for the disadvantaged groups in the process of economic reform. How could these movements requesting welfare for disadvantaged communities challenge the totality of injustices caused by systemic application of post-welfare policies across societies and localities?

Just recently the rise of anti-corporate and anti-capitalist (anti-globalization) movements has revealed, for many social researchers and theorists, the importance of integration between infrastructural-material and postmaterial-cultural issues. This has just recently encouraged the revision of both culturalist and structuralist accounts of current global movements. Though the multiplication of identities and interests in the era of globalization has remained high in comparison to the industrialization era, different segments of society have manifested many common grounds of concern about both the so-called infrastructural and super-structural bases of social inequalities and exclusion.

Since the crisis of the welfare-state capitalist system in the 1960s and the reemergence of liberalist capitalism, the social and political-economic conditions have transformed significantly due to the globalization of neo-liberalism, the partial withdrawal of welfare-state protectionism, de-politicizing and de-radicalizing policies, and growing levels of unemployment and inequality. However, these structural transformations have not followed any linear or convergent path towards the entire dominance of any specific epoch. Therefore, the movements for recognitive justice, now after thirty years of structural changes, have been transformed (whether through being politically institutionalized or through losing their relevance) in responding to these changing conditions. Such a transformation can be explained in terms of the complexities of global change.

A general explanatory model that assists in understanding how the recent structural complexities and inequalities have factually translated into new elements of conceptualizing justice is needed. Investigation of the 'complexities of global change' allows for questioning of the reductionist frames of reference within which most conventional explanations of solidarity among diverse identities and concerns operate. Global complexities can be defined in terms of following components: (1) the multiscalar nature of social inequality (inequalities and injustice at all levels from local to global have become more interdependent); (2) the multi-dimensional nature of global inequalities (both the material and post-material aspects of inequalities are highly intertwined); and (3) the cross-sectionality or multi-polarity of global inequalities (though social inequalities shaped around race, class, gender, and ethnicity have different dynamics and trajectories, they are practically enmeshed, more so than before). While the first component accounts for changes in the necessary institutional bases of justice, the second and third components influence the content and units of justice, respectively.

The following section will mostly focus on the second component of global complexity which can be considered as determining factors for the rise of transversalist justice especially the integration between recognitive and redistributive ideas of justice (for an extensive discussion of other components, see Hosseini, 2009). Unlike new integrative justice theorists, this section will show that in fact due to the interminglement and interdependence between the economic and social-cultural aspects of global change, demands for transversalist justice have been appealing for many activists. Giving attention to the 'complexity' of global change helps us to go beyond the limits of dualisms, like those of lifeworld-system, global-local, and material-postmaterial that are associated with theoretical controversies around the definition of justice (Hosseini 2013; 2006). It is the 'complexity' of current global transformations that has provided a structural backdrop for both the movements for recognitive justice (i.e. the so-called NSMs) and the movements for redistributive justice (i.e. the so-called OSMs like the labor movement) to reconstruct their original concerns and ideas about social changes in a more accommodative manner.

The Complexity of Global Inequality

I will now discuss the complexity of global inequality and discuss the questions of recognition vs. redistribution, identity vs. ideology, social vs. economic, material vs. postmaterial.

The dualisms of socio-cultural vs. political-economic and recognition vs. redistribution, in association with the dualism of the 'lifeworld' vs. 'system', can be challenged with respect to the globalization processes through which social inequalities are reproduced. Articulation between culture and economy has become much more intense and complex than before (Gregson, Simonsen, and Vaiou 2001). As Lash and Urry (1994, 64) argue, economies are increasingly "interarticulated" with culture, in view of the fact that culture has become a tool in economic development, and knowledge and information have gained more importance within current economies. For instance, examining the movement of a Mexican traditional food artifact (tortilla) between the local and global contexts, Lind and Barham (2004) show how powerful, homogenizing forces of the capitalist market have commodified an authentic cultural food. However, as they conclude, the commodification processes illustrate "the interconnectedness between material and symbolic exchanges" and represent a "continuous convergence of economic, social, cultural, political, and moral concerns" (Barham 2004, 47). Goods and markets have become more entwined with cultural signs and issues thereby influencing the processes of identity formation (Salcedo, 2003, 1099).

Along with such a growing interarticulation and co-evolution between culture and economy, associated recognitive and redistributive aspects mediated by the role of the welfare state have changed. In the 19th Century, many recognition claims were bound with the material concerns of women, anti-slavery and nationalist movements. This situation finally ended up with the development of the post-WWII welfare state due to the pressures from labour to ensure a less unequal redistribution of opportunities, resources, and income between classes.

The corporatist compromise between government, business, and labour (known as tripartism) softened class differences and created a new opportunity for acknowledging the recognition aspects of social justice issues; in fact, the state was under more pressure to recognize the rights and entitlements of many other excluded groups (such as indigenous and homosexual groups). The result was a growing political potential, mediated by the redistributive welfare state, for the inclusion of the Other into a civic covenant (O'Neill 2001). At the same time, the model was also commonly adopted by anti- and post-colonization nationalist states in the South.

However, the post-Cold War globalization of the neoliberal state has been associated with the rejection of any serious possibility of political treatment to the market that might redistribute income and resources between and within groups including classes. In evading these institutionalized social recognitions in their post-Cold War austerity policies, neoliberalist regimes have shown feeble tendency to accept responsibilities for mediating between the rights different groups may claim for themselves and the requirements of their rationalized economic systems. Consequently, through the global expansion of neoliberalist economic regimes, tensions between different recognition claims based on different conceptions of Self are expected to rise.

In the post War welfare state era, with its higher level of centralized planning, recognition claims did target the national government as the primary responsible body for social exclusions. However, in a less centralized planning system, the clash between recognition claims can surpass the nation state and mutate into a war between chauvinist claims, as happened with ethnic conflicts in Eastern Europe due to the sudden fall of communist governments. This promotes a situation where the "wars of recognition are here to stay," as Bauman (2001, 148) claims, or "a return to the 'state of nature'" where we shall lose our "will-to-civic covenant" (O'Neill 2001, 78-9).

As Featherstone (2001, 496) argues, the capitalist economic system is not merely globalizing under its own dynamics, such as "the activities of powerful alliances of businessmen, industrialists, politicians, academics, and cultural intermediaries". Rather, underneath the global economic integration there are developing "patterns of sociality, cultural expectations, and means of orientation which recursively form and are formed by the enlarged networks of interdependence" (Featherstone 2001, 496). Like in the 18th century, today we can speak of a global market culture or a commonsense authenticity that gives people an affirmative image of social relationships based on the market. The most evident exemplar of such cultural (re)formation of the capitalist economy can be found in today's logos, i.e. the current wave of the branded corporate economy. As Klein (2000, 23) clearly articulates, "With this wave of brand mania has come a new breed of businessman, one who will proudly inform you that Brand X is not a product but a way of life, an attitude, a set of values, a look, an idea".

Alongside such transformations in the mechanisms of forming people's identities as consumers, the mechanisms of identity formation through relations of production have also partially, but meaningfully, changed. In explaining the current identity changes in terms of the changes in the capitalist modes of employment, some theorists of 'post-industrial' society have grounded their arguments on the crisis of Fordism, which has led to the globalizing post-Fordist resolution through adopting the neo-liberal stance (see Turner 1986, 104-107; Piore, and Sabel 1984; Lash, and Urry 1987). The shift is often described in terms of a series of interrelated social, economic, technological, political, and spatial transformations. These changes can be generally summed up as a shift from "the concentration and centralization" of mass production based enterprises "within the framework of the nation-state," regulated by the state, to "the deconcentration and geographic dispersal" of small-scale, networked enterprises all over the world (Lem 2002, 287). Such a structural change in the organization of production is seen to be associated with a growth in human mobility, the creation of new forms of social polarizations and disparity, employment relationships and thereby the proliferation of new forms of identity (Walks 2001; Schiller, Basch, and Szanton 1992).

The current changes under the title of post-Fordism, while linking the new questions of identity and lifestyle to quality of life, economic security and material concerns, revitalize the traditional class and labor problems into new formats (see Tomlinson 1999, for his quantitative analysis of such links). Although the negative economic and environmental impacts of neoliberal policies, such as globalizing ecological hazards and job instabilities, have transcended class divisions and national boundaries, they have not reduced the importance of class, race, and gender in political motivations. The reason, as Marshall (1999, 269) points out, is simply that people "of low socioeconomic status are systematically and disproportionately exposed to the hazardous byproducts of modernization while receiving only a fraction of the benefits". In terms of evolving gender and ethnic relations, the increase of immigrant women's participation in the growing contingent types of working has resulted in new configurations but still linked with the older forms of divisions (Walby 2000).

As women and migrants with diverse ethnic backgrounds have increasingly been involved with post-Fordist contingent modes of employment – whether in developed countries or developing societies – they have become increasingly aware of economic redistribution issues, which may have direct links to the identities on which they are discriminated against (Acker 1989; ILO 1999). This has constructive implications for integrative justice theories. Accordingly, as Walby (2001, 120) in criticizing Fraser argues, "the relationships between the role of recognition and redistribution politics is not that of alternates, in which recognition is replacing redistribution". The evidence Walby draws on is the changes in deep structures of gender relations in the US and the UK due to the greater involvement of women in labor markets and therefore in union activities (Walby 2001, 118). In sum, both the material and postmaterial bases of identity and, their associated politics of redistribution and recognition, have co-evolved into a new phase of capitalist globalization.

Besides, the co-evolution or co-development of social relations has not been consistently occurring but rather dissonantly bifurcating alongside the axes of discrimination, inequality, and exclusion. For instance, both the benefits and risks of post-Fordism have spread unequally among different social groups and statuses. The decentralization of corporate jobs has been associated with a greater use of contingent and part-time workers, who have low job security (Gardner 1995; Fallick 1996), as well as higher rates of job displacements among lower educated workers (Morris and Western 1999). The percentage of part-time, subcontracted, and self-employed jobs has increased, while the proportion of women and migrants in this increase has also been amplified (see Tilly 1996, for the case of the US; and OECD 2004, for the OECD members since 1993).

Due to the migration of labor intensive jobs to the global South, work in these regions has become "increasingly fragmented, deskilled and feminized in the race by multinational capital to increase its profits" (Freeman 1998, 246). At the same time, in the North, the cores of those who face job losses are people of color and women. Moss and Tilly (1996) investigate how the Black men's growing disadvantage in the US labor market can be explained in terms of the changes in skill requirements, particularly the increase in demands for 'soft skills'. The global expansion of a knowledge-based economy privileges those with high levels of education mainly developed in Western countries. In association with new transnational flexible relations of production, workers can develop a new collective identity that is more transversal, both in terms of their identity and class statues.

Local impacts of global warming and climate change, which seem to affect all people equally (regardless of their class and identity), have been unequally dispersed among and within different societies. While the involvement of poor societies in causing this problem is much less than that of developed societies: "Poor resource bases, inequalities in income, weak institutions, and limited technology limit the capacity of the most vulnerable to deal with the impact of climate change, and means that they will suffer most from its effects" (People and Planet Network 2004). Even inside a highly developed country, as Newman (2000, 530) mentions, "environmental degradation disproportionately affects minority communities". Even the minority and disadvantaged communities have been underrepresented in the mainstream environmentalist movements for the most part of their history. Nonetheless, the more such dissonance in the globalization of environmental risks has been recognized due to the growth of resistance among poor communities, the more cognitive shifts towards adopting more transversal discourses have occurred; for instance, reframing environmental degradation within social justice discourses rather than an utterly ecological one (Bullard, and Wright 1992; Bullard 1993), and intersectional feminist movements (Yuval-Davis 2012).

Therefore, the growing traversal cooperation between working class activists (like unions), the newly raised participation of young 'contingent workers', and the environmentally disadvantaged communities in the field, has not happened fortuitously. Rather, they have resulted from contemporary changes in which the organization of production, the distribution of risks, and culturally homogenizing forces have been amalgamated disproportionately more than ever to stabilize power relations. There has also been a transformation of social movements into more transversalist discourses with respect to cultural identities and material interests. Langmore (2001, 11) contends that "economic and social issues are closely interdependent and that the appropriate stance is to work on both together". Zinn (2003), a post-anarchist and the author of A People's History of the United States, described the anti-WTO protest in Seattle 1999 as a turning point in the history of movements since it was a departure from single-issue movements (cited in Brecher, Costello, and Smith 2000, 16).

Therefore, recognition claims for many underprivileged groups in such a complex integration between culture and the economy have not been 'merely' oriented to the affirmation of their particularities against the system (as some like Fraser suggest), or even in contrast to each other in a clash of identities. Hence, the growing global complexities have caused the global field of resistance to become bifurcated between those who still follow the reductionist traditions and those who adopt a more accommodative point of view. For instance, in spite of the growth of inequalities between and within countries since the 1980s due to the adoption of neoliberal policies (Parayil 2005; Held, and Kaya 2007), the right-shift in centre-left parties towards economic liberalism was associated with the decline of unionization and working-class representation in the public sector. Therefore, the working class identity politics, which achieved a satisfactory level of institutionalization during the post-WWII welfare states, has faced a trend of de-institutionalization. This decline happened in a period during which social inequalities have become greater, more complex and more multifaceted due to accelerated economic globalization (see Burgmann 2003, 251-253). The failure of left-wing parties in representing the concerns and interests of the working class has encouraged not only the resumption of traditional international protectionism but also new internationalist anti-capitalism within the current field of resistance.

Oscillating between traditional protectionism and internationalist anti-capitalist orientations, unions have played an ambivalent but important role in the movement (see Burgmann 2003, 205). However, what may cause the resumption of 'class' is the rise in awareness regarding interwoven webs of exploitation inside and between globalizing societies, rather than the physical juxtaposition of unionism and other different groups. Global justice ideologues have revealed their concerns about the ambivalent contribution of unionism inside the movement (see for instance, Waterman 2003). Hence, there has been a bifurcation between the old, institutionalized labor movements and "the possibility of a new social movement labor internationalism" (Waterman 2005, 152), where "a practical, non-ideological, emphatically non-partisan" labor can be an equal partner with other actors in confronting the neoliberal order (Blackwell 1998, 321).

In addressing the increasing number of part-time workers, unemployed, and low-waged labor in Japan, due to the transformation of the mode of production from Fordism to post-Fordism, Yoshitaka (2005) identifies the growth of a young cultural resistance with a strong political potential in challenging neoliberalism in the country. In contrast to the so-called NSMs, which were theorized as more cultural than political, the current generation of Japanese activists has been more able to intervene in everyday practices, practically linking the public and the private, blurring the distinction between the cultural and the political, and avoiding Leftist rhetoric and elitism. The cognitive-ideological autonomy of this young trend of resistance is rooted in the transforming nature of social inequality and the relative political-economic autonomy of the social status, from which the participants originated.

In conclusion, the ever increasingly interweaving of cultural and economic aspects of life in an unequal and disproportionate manner has required the politics of resistance to expand the meaning of social justice to bridge material and post-material rights. "The politics of identity and culture needed to be related to, rather than opposed to, the politics of class," Mayo (2005, 76) argues. As Bauman (2001, 147) concludes, "melting together the task of distributive justice and the policy of recognition is the meaning of social justice in the present … era, while campaign politics compounding the two is its prime, and perhaps its sole, available strategy".

EXPERIENCING THE STRUCTURAL COMPLEXITIES OF GLOBAL CHANGE

The influence of the structural complexities of globalization on the ideational structure of global movements and the emergence of transversalist justice are mediated by experiential and constructive mechanisms. Acknowledging this reality would help us avoid any structural determinism. In their case study of union revitalization in the late 1990s California, Voss and Sherman (2000) show that structural factors, however important, cannot explain, by themselves, the differences between union organizations in breaking out of their predominant bureaucratic conservatism. The role of leadership in convincing staff of the value of working in different ways is important. Besides, as they show, union "activists with experience outside the labor movement brought broader visions, knowledge of alternative organizational models, and practice in disruptive tactics …" (Voss, and Sherman 2000, 333)

Two major experiential mechanisms mediate the structural changes and influence the cognitive formation of the movement. The first one is the recognition of the multidimensionality and systemic reciprocality of social inequalities as well as the necessity of expanding the scope of resistance to deal with these complexities. As Starr and Adams (2003, 28) acknowledge, the first world environmentalist community-based resistance, had begun to recognize that in order to achieve goals at the local-community level, it was necessary to deal with the broader issue of international equality and to focus on taking responsibility for having underdeveloped the third world. For instance, Randy Hay, an environmentalist, at the Tropical Rainforest conference, 18 October 1987, claimed that, "to be more effective at saving tropical Rain Forests … what we need is to get our foot off the throat of the Rain Forests" (cited in Starr, and Adams 2003, 28). This process requires not only building sustainable networks of knowledge-experience exchange among like-minded organizations and agents concerned with common particular issues, but also providing forums and conferences with diverse forces of resistance such as workers, environmentalists, farmers, and women.

The second experiential mechanism, which is the most important factor in transforming identities beyond the borders of conventional social differences, is related to the movement actors' experience of changes in their own social background due to the current changes in the broader structural bases of social problems. The more participants with different social backgrounds experience common predicaments, the more likely the cross-boundary nature of social problems will be translated into identity (re)formation and the transversalist notions of justice (Yuval-Davis 2010; Hosseini 2013). The following exemplary case help clarify the above-mentioned experiential mechanism.

The Case of ACT UP and Multilateral Oppression

ACT UP, a grassroots organization of diverse individuals and groups, was formed in March 1987 at the Lesbian and Gay Community Centre in New York. They started with regular meetings and after three weeks, held their first demonstration, a direct action tactic on Wall Street, to protest profiteering by pharmaceutical companies and the Reagan administration's lax reaction to the AIDS crisis. They shut down the New York Stock Exchange and picketed St. Patrick's Cathedral.

The case of ACT UP is a good example of how a grassroots organization evolves from a single-issue movement, concerned about the issue of AIDS and health and directed by white middle-class homosexuals, to a transnational network with overlapping concerns about both recognitive and redistributive justice. This evolution simply shows the emergence of a transversalist mode of dissident knowledge and solidarity out of agential experience of structural changes at both national and international levels. Due to the recent socio-demographic changes in the patterns of Sexually Transmitted Diseases (STDs), including the AIDS epidemic, and the changing structures of inequality in terms of education and public health infrastructure, the composition of movement participants has changed.

During the last three decades, the demographical pattern of HIV infection in the United States has been changing in terms of race, ethnicity, and gender (Wasserheit 1995). At first, it was dominant among white homosexual and bisexual men. In the early 1990s, the spread among this population started to plateau while the number of heterosexually transmitted cases in women, especially women of color, rapidly increased (Wasserheit 1995). Social inequalities, exacerbated by recent economic globalization processes, lay at the heart of such an epidemiological transition (Coburn 2004).

At a global level, although the HIV virus has not shown any respect for humanity's national borders, we have been witnessing a growing gap between the South and the North in terms of the progression and understanding of the natural history of the virus, and therefore the capacity to develop its treatment. As Parker (2002) shows, the global distribution of AIDS has been highly unequal between the poor and the rich. Inside both developed and developing societies, "a range of structural inequalities intersect and combine to shape the character of HIV/AIDS epidemic" (Parker 2002, 344). Economic globalization has been associated with attempts to generalize Western research and health care models: "The latter scenario is one of the recommendations of the World Bank" (Zimmet 2001, 304). The history of AIDS started with an "utter nonchalance" about the victims by the leading national and international institutions, political and religious leaders, then with "disdain for those infected," and finally followed by a grave inequality in terms of treatment and prevention due to the rationalization of the economy (Garrett 1994, 10).

The strong correlation between the changing patterns of disease and the changing socio-economic structures of inequality on both national and international scales, accounts for recent developments in the composition and consciousness of participants in the ACT UP and similar networks. Such developments are well self-documented by the ACT UP activists like Kim (2001) of Queers for Economic Justice, Stockdill (2003), an activist-scholar and a member of ACT UP, and in the book From ACT UP to the WTO edited by Shepard and Hayduk (2002).

As Kim (2001) reveals, the early structure of ACT UP was largely dominated by white middle class homosexuals. During the 1990s, while expanding to as many as 70 chapters all around the world, the organization experienced decline and split. Due to the introduction of antiretroviral drugs in the mid-1990s, which were unequally accessible to patients from different social statuses, the AIDS activism among middle class homosexual communities declined. However, changes in the national and global distribution of AIDS influenced both the structure and praxis of ACT UP. A shift in priorities occurred from a particular self-interested group to an inclusive network of different initiatives, once the number of participants from low-income communities and the people of color increased; "ACT UP has come to focus on the global AIDS epidemic, applying constant pressure on the US government and pharmaceutical companies to facilitate generic drug manufacturing, and on international policy-makers to enact immediate debt relief for developing nations" (Kim 2001).

Analyzing empirical evidence out of his ethnographical case studies of AIDS activists in the US, Stockdill (2003) shows how multifaceted systems of oppression have shaped current AIDS solidarities. As he explains, the multiple inequalities constructed in society can easily translate into the movement resulting in movement contentions and biases; the "price of activism weighs more heavily on economically, politically, and socially marginalized groups" (Stockdill 2003, 128). For instance, middle class white men were slow in becoming concerned about people of color, and homosexuals of color have always been alienated from the hubs of solidarity networks. However, according to him, despite such dissonant influences of multiple oppressions on solidarities, interlocking inequalities at different levels (personal, institutional and cultural) necessitate developing an integrative dissident knowledge to create positive cross-movement alliances; "inclusion is key in all areas of progressive and radical organizing" (Stockdill 2003, 167). In November 1999, the organization participated in the anti-WTO protest in Seattle and committed itself to building a coalition within the global resistance against global systems of capitalism (see Shepard, and Hayduk 2002, 1-9).

Conclusion

Justice has been conceptualized by many in the global field of resistance as a multi-dimensional, multi-scalar and multi-polar issue. As argued in this article, studying the conception of justice among these movement actors and their conceptualizations of injustice on their own ground can have significant lessons for both normative theories of justice and analytical explanations of global inequalities and global movements. At least,

1. Given the movement's demands for justice, theories of justice can be proved reductionist and not adequately tied to the complexities of social inequalities in the global age.
2. On the other hand, when trying to explain the structural roots of global uprisings and its practical conceptions of justice, the available social movement and globalization theories can be shown inadequate, as they have failed to address the complexities of social change.

New theories which has rightfully insisted on the necessity of developing more inclusive notions of justice, need to take a closer look at the justice demanded by those in the global field of resistance and must consider the complexities of global change.

The growing multiplications of social roles, and increasing fragmentation lines due to the complexity of globalization processes and their bifurcating impacts, keep affecting social compositions among agents of resistance and emancipation. However, this fact does not suggest that today's history is without a positive Subject, and does not mean that effectual, sustainable solidarities for the realization of (a) just world(s) are impracticable. Complexity in any social system is not only associated with the growth of fragmentations and tensions, but also with the growth of interdependence, interconnection, and the promoted cross-fertilizing exchanges of ideas and information. As show in the case of ACT UP, in such a situation, those actors who have been experiencing interdependent and interwoven systems of exploitation and exclusion, aggravated by multi-scalar and asymmetrical processes of globalization, are more apt to develop transversalist notions of justice

REFERENCES

Acker, Joan. 1989. *Doing Comparable Worth: Gender, Class, and Pay Equity*. Philadelphia: Temple University Press.

Amoore, Louise. 2005. *The Global Resistance Reader*. London; New York: Routledge.

Ayres, Jeffrey M. 2004. "Framing Collective Action against Neoliberalism: The Case of the 'Anti-Globalization' Movement" *Journal of World-Systems Research* 10: 11-34.

Bartholomew, Amy, and Margit Mayer. 1992. "Nomads of the Present: Melucci's Contribution to 'New Social Movement' Theory" *Theory, Culture and Society* 9: 141-159.

Bauman, Zygmund. 2001. "The Great War of Recognition" *Theory, Culture and Society* 18: 137-150.

Blackwell, Ron. 1998. "Building a Member-Based International Program" In *A New Labor Movement for the New Century*, edited by Gregory Mantsios, 320-328. New York: Garland Publications.

Brecher, Jeremy, and Tim Costello, (eds.). 1990. *Building Bridges: The Emerging Grassroots Coalition of Labor and Community*. New York: Monthly Review Press.

Brecher, Jeremy, Tim Costello, and Brendan Smith. 2000. *Globalization from Below: the Power of Solidarity*. Cambridge: South End Press.

Broad, Robin. 2002. *Global Backlash: Citizen Initiatives for a just World Economy*. Lanham: Rowman & Littlefield Publishers.

Brooks, Clem, and Jeff Manza. 1994. "Do Changing Values Explain the New Politics: A Critical Assessment of the Postmaterialist Thesis" *Sociological Quarterly* 35: 541-70.

Bullard, Robert. D., and Beverly H. Wright. 1992. "The Quest for Environmental Equity: Mobilizing African-American Community for Social Change" In *American Environmentalism: The US Environmental Movement*, 1970-1990. edited by Riley E. Dunlap and Angela G. Mertig, 39-50, Philadelphia: Taylor & Francis.

Bullard, Robert D. 1993. "Anatomy of Environmental Racism and the Environmental Justice Movement." In *Confronting Environmental Racism*, edited by Robert. D. Bullard, 15-39. Boston: South End Press.

Burgmann, Verity. 2003. Po*wer, Profit and Protest: Australian Social Movements and Globalisation*. Crows Nest: Allen & Unwin.

Callinicos, Alex. 2003. *An Anti-Capitalist Manifesto*. Cambridge: Polity Press.

Castells, Manuel.1997. *The Power of Identity*. Malden: Blackwell.

Castells, Manuel. 2000. "Materials for an Exploratory Theory of the Network Society" *British Journal of Sociology* 51: 5-24.

Castells, Manuel. 2004. *The Power of Identity*. Malden: Blackwell Publishing.

Coburn, David. 2004. "Beyond the Income Inequality Hypothesis: Class, Neo-liberalism, and Health Inequalities" *Social Science & Medicine* 58: 41-56.

della Porta, Donatella, and Mario Diani. 1999. *Social Movements: An Introduction*. Oxford: Blackwell.

della Porta, Donatella. 2007. T*he Global Justice Movement: Cross-National and Transnational Perspectives*. Boulder: Paradigm Publishers.

Edwards, Gemma. 2004. "Habermas and Social Movements: What's 'New'?" *Sociological Review* 52: 113-130.

Eyerman, Ron, and Andrew Jamison. 1998. *Music and Social Movements: Mobilizing Traditions in the Twentieth Century*. Cambridge: Cambridge University Press.

Fagan, Tony, and Phil Lee. 1997. "'New' Social Movements and Social Policy: A Case Study of Disability Movements" In *Social Policy: A Conceptual and Theoretical Introduction*, edited by Michael Lavalette and Alan Pratt, 140-60. London: Sage.

Fallick, Bruce C. 1996. "A Review of the Recent Empirical Literature on Displaced Workers" *Industrial & Labor Relations Review* 50: 5-16.

Featherstone, Mike. 2001. "Postnational Flows, Identity Formation, and Cultural Space." In *Identity, Culture and Globalization: The Annals of the International Institute of Sociology*, Volume 8, edited by Eliezer Ben-Rafael and Yitzhak Sternberg, 483-526. Leiden: Brill.

Fraser, Nancy. 1995. "From Redistribution to Recognition: Dilemmas of Justice in a Post-Socialist Age" *New Left Review* 212: 68-93.

Fraser, Nancy. 1997. *Justice Interruptus: Critical Reflections on the 'Postsocialist' Condition*. New York: Routledge.

Fraser, Nancy. 2005. "Reframing Justice in a Globalizing World" *New Left Review* 36: 1-19.

Freeman, Carla. 1998. "Femininity and Flexible Labor: Fashioning Class through Gender on the Global Assembly Line" *Critique of Anthropology* 18: 245-262.

Gardner, Jennifer. M. 1995. "Worker Displacement: a Decade of Change" *Monthly Labor Review* 118: 45-57.

Garrett, Laurie. 1994. *The Coming Plague: Newly Emerging Diseases in a World Out of Balance*. New York: Farrar Straus and Giroux.

Giddens, Anthony. 1991. *Modernity and Self-Identity: Self and Society in the Late Modern Age*. Stanford: Stanford University Press.

Giddens, Anthony. 1994. *Beyond Left and Right: The Future of Radical Politics*. Stanford: Stanford University Press.

Gould, Carol. C. 2008. "Recognition in Redistribution: Care and Diversity in Global Justice." *Southern Journal of Philosophy* 46: 91-103.

Gregson, Nicky, Kirsten Simonsen, and Dina Vaiou. 2001. "Whose Economy for Whose Culture? Moving Beyond Oppositional Talk in European Debate about Economy and Culture." *Antipode* 33: 616-646.

Held, David, and Ayse Kaya, eds. 2007. *Global Inequality: Patterns and Explanations*. Malden; Cambridge: Polity Press.

Honneth, Axel. 1995. *The Struggle for Recognition: The Moral Grammar of Social Conflicts*. Cambridge, MA: MIT Press.

Honneth, Axel. 2001. "Recognition or Redistribution? Changing Perspectives on the Moral Order of Society" *Theory, Culture and Society* 18: 43-55.

Hosseini, S .A. Hamed. 2006. "Beyond Practical Dilemmas and Conceptual Reductionism: The Emergence of an Accommodative Consciousness in the Alternative Globalization Movement." *Journal of Multidisciplinary International Studies* 3: 1-27.

Hosseini, S. A. Hamed. 2010. *Alternative Globalizations: An Integrative Approach to Studying Dissident Knowledge in the Global Justice Movement*. Milton Park: Routledge

Hosseini, S. A. Hamed. 2013. "Occupy Cosmopolitanism: Ideological Transversalization in the Age of Global Economic Uncertainties" *Globalizations* 10: 425-38.

ILO. 1999. *Yearbook of Labour Statistics*: 1999, Geneva: International Labour Office.

Inglehart, Ronald. 2000. "Globalization and Post-modern Values" *The Washington Quarterly* 21: 215-228.

Kim, Richard. 2001. "ACT UP Goes Global", *The Nation*, (July 9). <http://www.thenation.com/article-act-goes-global> (accessed on 20 July 2005).

Klein, Naomi. 2000. No Logo: *Taking Aim at the Brand Bullies*. London: Flamingo.

Kymlicka, Will, (ed.). 1995. *The Rights of Minority Cultures*. Oxford: Oxford University Press.

Kymlicka, Will. 2001. *Politics in the Vernacular: Nationalism, Multiculturalism, and Citizenship*. Oxford: Oxford University Press.

Langmore, John. 2001. "Globalisation and Social Policy" *Social Work in Health Care* 34: 11-29.

Lash, Scott, and John Urry. 1987. *The End of Organized Capitalism*. Cambridge: Polity.

Lash, Scott, and John. Urry. 1994. *Economies of Signs and Space*. London: Sage.

Laurell, Asa. C. 2000. "Structural Adjustment and the Globalization of Social Policy in Latin America" *International Sociology* 15: 306-325.

Lem, Winnie. 2002. "Articulating Class in Post-Fordist France" *American Ethnologist* 29: 287-306.

Lind, David, and Elizabeth Barham 2004. "The Social Life of the Tortilla: Food, Cultural Politics, and Contested Commodification" *Agriculture and Human Values* 21: 47-60.

Maheu, Louis. 1995. *Social Movements and Social Classes: the Future of Collective Action*. London: Sage Publications.

Marshall, Brent K. 1999. "Globalisation, Environmental Degradation and Ulrich Beck's Risk Society" *Environmental Values* 8: 253-275.

Martin, Greg. 2001. "Social Movements, Welfare and Social Policy: A Critical Analysis" *Critical Social Policy* 21: 361-383.

Mayo, Marjorie. 2005. *Global Citizens: Social Movements and the Challenge of Globalization*. London: Zed Books.

Melucci, Alberto. 1995a. "The New Social Movements Revisited: Reflections on a Sociological Misunderstanding" In *Social Movements and Social Classes: The Future of Collective Action*, edited by Louis Maheu, 107-119. London, England: Sage.

Melucci, Alberto. 1995b. "Individualization and Globalization: Individualisation et globalization" *Cahiers de Recherche Sociologique* 24: 185-206.

Melucci, Alberto. 1995c. "The Global Planet and the Internal Planet: New Frontiers for Collective Action and Individual Transformation" In *Cultural Politics and Social Movements*, edited by Marcy Darnovsky, Barbara Epstein, and Richard Flacks, 287-298. Philadelphia: Temple University Press.

Melucci, Alberto. 2000. "Social Movements in Complex Societies: A European Perspective" *Arena Journal* 15: 81-99.

Moghadam, Valentine M. 2009. *Globalization and Social Movements: Islamism, Feminism, and the Global Justice Movement*. Lanham: Rowman & Littlefield.

Morris, Martina, and Bruce Western. 1999. "Inequality in Earnings at the Close of the Twentieth Century" *Annual Review of Sociology* 25: 623-657.

Moss, Philip. and Chris Tilly, C. .1996. ""Soft" Skills and Race: An Investigation of Black Men's Employment Problem" *Work and Occupations* 23 (3): 252-276.

Navarro, Vicente. 1998. "Neoliberalism, 'Globalization,' Unemployment, Inequalities, and the Welfare State" *International Journal of Health Services* 28: 607-682.

Newman, David. M. 2000. *Sociology: Exploring the Architecture of Everyday Life*. California: Pine Forge Pres.

O'Neill, John. 2001. "Oh My Others, There is No Other! Civic Recognition and Hegelian Other-wiseness" *Theory Culture & Society* 18: 77-90.

OECD. 2004. *Organisation for Economic Co-operation and Development*, Paris, v.

Okereke, Chukwumerije. 2007. *Global Justice and Neoliberal Environmental Governance: Ethics, Sustainable Development and International Co-operation*. New York: Routledge.

Opel, Andy, and Donnalyn Pompper, eds. 2003. *Representing Resistance: Media, Civil Disobedience, and the Global Justice Movement*. London: Praeger.

Parayil, Govindan. 2005. “The Digital Divide and Increasing Returns: Contradictions of Informational Capitalism” *Information Society* 21: 41-51.

Parker, Richard. 2002. “The Global HIV/AIDS Pandemic, Structural Inequalities, and the Politics of International Health” *American Journal of Public Health* 92: 343-346.

People and Planet Network .2004. *The Equity of Climate Change, People and Planet Network.* <http://www.peopleandplanet.org/aboutus/> (accessed 21 July 2005)

Pierson, Paul. 1998. “Irresistible Forces, Immovable Objects: Post-Industrial Welfare States Confront Permanent Austerity” *Journal of European Public Policy* 5 (4): 539-560.

Piore, Michael. J. and Charles F. Sabel. 1984. *The Second Industrial Divide: Possibilities for Prosperity*. New York: Basic Books.

Queers for Economic Justice. 2004. *Mission Statement, Queers for Economic Justice.*

Rawls, John. 1971. *A Theory of Justice*. Oxford: Oxford University Press.

Salcedo, Rodrigo. 2003. “When the Global Meets the Local at the Mall” *American Behavioral Scientist* 46: 1084-1103.

Schiller, Nina. G., Linda Basch, and Christina Blanc-Szanton. 1992. *Towards a Transnational Perspective on Migration: Race, Class, Ethnicity, and Nationalism Reconsidered.* New York: New York Academy of Sciences.

Schlosberg, David. 2004. “Reconceiving Environmental Justice: Global Movements and Political Theories” *Environmental Politics* 13: 517-540.

Shepard, Benjamin, and Ronald Hayduk. 2002. *From ACT UP to the WTO: Urban Protest and Community Building in the Era of Globalization.* London: Verso.

Starr, Amory, and Jason Adams. 2003. “Anti-globalization: the Global Fight for Local Autonomy” *New Political Science* 25: 19-42.

Stockdill, Brett. C. 2003. *Activism against AIDS: At the Intersection of Sexuality, Race, Gender, and Class.* Boulder: Lynne Rienner.

Sturgeon, Noel. 1995. “Theorizing Movements: Direct Action and Direct Theory” In *Cultural Politics and Social Movements*, edited by Marcy Darnovsky, Barbara Epstein, and Richard Flacks, 35-51. Philadelphia: Temple University Press.

Taylor, David. 1998. “Social Identity and Social Policy: Engagements with Postmodern Theory” *Journal of Social Policy* 27: 329-350.

Tilly, Chris. 1996. *Half a Job: Bad and Good Part-Time Jobs in a Changing Labor Market*. Philadelphia: Temple University Press.

Tomlinson, John. 1999. *Globalization and Culture*. Chicago: University of Chicago Press.

Turner, Bryan S. 1986. *Citizenship and Capitalism: The Debate over Reformism*. London: Allen & Unwin.

Voss, Kim, and Rachel Sherman. 2000. "Breaking the Iron Law of Oligarchy: Union Revitalization in the American Labor Movement" *American Journal of Sociology* 106: 303-349.

Walby, Sylvia. 2000. "Analyzing Social Inequality in the Twenty-First Century: Globalization and Modernity Restructure Inequality [Book Review]" *Contemporary Sociology* 29: 813-818.

Walby, Sylvia. 2001. "From Community to Coalition: The Politics of Recognition as the Handmaiden of the Politics of Equality in an Era of Globalization" *Theory Culture & Society* 18: 113-135.

Walks, R. Alan. 2001. "The Social Ecology of the Post-Fordist/Global City? Economic Restructuring and Socio-Spatial Polarisation in the Toronto Urban Region" *Urban Studies* 38: 407-447.

Wasserheit, Judith N. 1995. "Effect of Human Ecology and Behavior on Sexually Transmitted Diseases, Including HIV Infection" In *Infectious Diseases in an Age of Change: The Impact of Human Ecology and Behavior on Disease Transmission*, edited by Bernhard. Roizman, 141-156. Washington D. C.: National Academy Press.

Waterman, Peter. 2003. *2nd Thoughts on the WSF: Place, Space and the Reinvention of Social Emancipation on a Global Scale, Forum Social Mundial*, <http://memoriafsm.org/bitstream/handle/11398/1547/2003_07.01_Balan%C3%A70_34.pdf?sequence=1&isAllowed=y> (accessed, 26 October 2004)

Waterman, Peter. 2005. "Talking across Difference in an Interconnected World of Labour" In *Coalitions Across Borders: Transnational Protest and the Neoliberal Order*, edited by Joe Bandy, and Jacky Smith, 141-162. Lanham: Rowman & Littlefield.

WSF. 2002. *Call of Social Movements, Forum Social Mundial*, >http://viacampesina.org/en/index.php/actions-and-events-mainmenue-26/world-social-forum-mainmenu-34/377-porto-alegre-ii-call-of-social-movements< (Accessed 12 May, 2004).

WSF . 2005. *World Social Forum 2006 will be spread out*, Forum Social Mundial, <http://www.wunm.com/news/2006/02_19_06/021906_world_social.htm> (Accessed on 8 Feb, 2005).

Yoshitaka, Mori. 2005. "Culture = Politics: The Emergence of New Cultural Forms of Protest in the Age of Freeter" *Inter-Asia Cultural Studies* 6: 17-29.

Young, Iris M. 1990. *Justice and the Politics of Difference*. Princeton, NJ: Princeton University Press.

Young, Iris.M. 2000. *Inclusion and Democracy*. Oxford: Oxford University Press.

Yuval-Davis, Nira. 2010. "Theorizing identity: Beyond the 'Us' and 'Them' Dichotomy" *Patterns of Prejudice* 44: 261-80.

Yuval-Davis, Nira. 2012. "Dialogical Epistemology-An Intersectional Resistance to the "Oppression Olympics" *Gender & Society* 26: 46-54.

Zimmet, Paul 2001. "Globalization, Coca-Colonization and the Chronic Disease Epidemic: Can the Doomsday Scenario be Averted?" *Journal of Internal Medicine* 249: 17-26.

Zinn, Howard. 2003. *A People's History of the United States: 1492-Present*. New York: Harper Collins.

CHAPTER 7

Humanism, Empathy, and Moral Progress in Global Trade

Randall Horton

INTRODUCTION

In April of 2011, the top executives of Transocean Ltd. announced they would donate their bonuses awarded for "safety performance" to the victims of the rig explosion that killed 11 workers in 2010.[1] This single event revealed both the moral myopia of the executives of a transnational corporation and the possibility of moral progress driven more by compassion than profit. I would like to report that after a short course in the humanities, these executives developed a profound and nuanced theory of morality and justice and applied this theory to their daily actions, resulting in greater concern for the well-being of the families of the explosion victims, but there is obviously no basis for such a claim. Alternatively, I would like to report that liberal public education in the humanities made it possible to create a groundswell of public support for the victims' families and condemnation of greedy executives. Although this alternative is slightly more plausible, I cannot claim it is the reason for the sudden moral awareness of Transocean executives.

I will claim, however, that the plight of the victims raised the moral awareness of the general public and that many people imagine vividly the suffering of these families that resulted from what was quite possibly a preventable accident. Because this accident happened in an affluent country and saturated the news, many people are able to imagine themselves in the place of the workers who were killed and of the families mourning their loss of a loved one and struggling with the loss of family income. Many corporate executives have become accustomed to acting in obscurity and anonymity as most people affected by oil spills, dangerous working conditions, and environmental degradation live in remote, developing countries. Precisely because we were able

---

[1] CNN Wire Staff, "Transocean executives donate safety bonuses to rig victims' families," *www.cnn.com*, April 6, 2011,
http://www.cnn.com/2011/US/04/05/gulf.spill.bonuses/index.html.

to imagine the voices of the victims and their families in this case as our own voices, we were moved to demand justice or at least respectful treatment of them.

This was a result of education from our own lived experience and not exclusively from education in the humanities, but it is education in the humanities and the efforts of humanistic enterprises that expand our ability to imagine ourselves in the position of a much greater variety of humans grappling with the conditions of humanity. Humanists, historically, have engaged in a public discourse hinged not only on rational argument but also on emotional persuasion. Humanists have employed art, poetry, drama, music, fiction, and argument in the effort to broaden the social imagination. This humanistic discourse thrives when education in the humanities is deep and broad but as humanities education withers, so the discourse dies.

As educators in the humanities struggle to demonstrate that providing courses in the humanities improves the moral behavior of students, it becomes increasingly evident that a society that does not value the humanities recedes in the race for moral advancement. My claim, then, is not that humanities courses produce moral individuals but that moral advancement is severely hindered in societies that neglect the humanities. Moral progress occurs gradually in both the intellectual and emotional cores of society. Reasoned arguments for human rights and justice are essential to advancement, but such arguments, no matter how compelling, are effective only when injustice becomes intolerable to the collective consciousness of a society.

Moral Progress

Moral progress does not occur as a natural outgrowth of human evolution. Moral progress requires a change both in behavior and in attitude. To effect change, an injustice must first be recognized as an injustice, and injustice is almost invariably the result of an abuse of power. Not surprisingly, those who hold power rarely sacrifice it voluntarily, so those who seek to correct an injustice must either convince those in power to change their behavior, convince those not in power to stand in solidarity against those in power to pressure them to change, or convince those not in power to take action, violent or non-violent, against the power holders. Assuming that violence is a last resort for most people, other forms of persuasion are necessary to affect relevant power structures and gain a foothold for justice. In this sense, the humanistic tradition in philosophy, art, literature, and cultural studies is necessary for advancing civil discourse.

In *The Honor Code: How Moral Revolutions Happen*, Kwame Anthony Appiah describes the process by which slavery became intolerable in British society. Appiah (2010, 134) notes that eventually, Britons responded against slavery because, "It rankled because they, like the slaves, labored and produced by the sweat of their brow." Just as many were able to imagine themselves in the position of the victims of the 2010 oil rig explosion, workers in earlier centuries were able to imagine themselves in the place of victims of slavery. Many conditions and activities led to the public turn against slavery, including church sermons, philosophical argument, and public dissent, but literature also played a role. In particular, Appiah mentions novels by Henry Mackenzie (*The Man of Feeling*) and Laurence Sterne (*A Sentimental Journey*). These works emphasized not the rational arguments against slavery but the compassion that all virtuous people should feel when confronted with great misery. The person who is indifferent to such suffering should feel shame. It is Appiah's claim that moral revolutions occur when taking action or not becomes a matter of honor, as it did for the executives of Transocean.

The slave trade, of course, was an earlier form of forced trade globalization; whether it was more or less coercive than today's global trade practices is a matter of debate. Nonetheless, slavery was profitable for a great many people, and ending the slave trade required a shift from concern for profit only to a concern for decency. The tension between profit and decency has plagued humanists for centuries, of course. In his second letter to Cicero, Petrarch laments, "They still are in existence, glorious volumes, but we of today are too feeble a folk to read them, or even to be acquainted with their mere titles. Your fame extends far and wide; your name is mighty, and fills the ears of men; and yet those who really know you are very few, be it because the times are unfavorable, or because men's minds are slow and dull, or, as I am the more inclined to believe, because the love of money forces our thoughts in other directions."[2] As we can see from Petrarch's words, education in the humanities has been in "crisis" for some time. As humanists argue for the value of the humanities, we are participating in a discussion as old as the humanities themselves. In 2010, Martha Nussbaum echoed the complaint of Petrarch, saying, "What we might call the humanistic aspects of science and social science—the imaginative, creative aspect, and the aspect of rigorous critical thought—are also losing ground as nations prefer to pursue short-term profit by the cultivation of the useful and highly applied skills suited to profit-making" (Nussbaum 2010, 2). When wealth is seen as the measure of greatness, the struggle to become more honorable, more admirable, and more virtuous withers and dies. The humanities help to awaken feelings of concern, shame, compassion, and nobility.

---

[2] Francesco Petrarch, "To Marcus Tullius Cicero (2 of 2)," trans. James Harvey Robinson, n.d., http://petrarch.petersadlon.com/read_letters.html?s=pet11.html. Accessed May 25, 2011.

The philosopher David Hume (2005) described the pursuit of justice as an "artificial virtue," growing by analogy from the "natural virtues" of caring and compassion for those closest to us, such as our children and members of our community. Morality, for Hume, arises from emotional responses to events and actions we observe, but our reasoning ability enables us to apply these emotional responses to imagined situations and develop moral rules by extension to others, including those we may not know. In this way, we are motivated to create a just society or even a just world. For Hume, justice is artificial in the sense that it arises not from natural emotional responses, but from a rational response to the world based on extrapolation from natural feelings of compassion, disgust, and so on. While moral codes vary from culture to culture, some initial emotional responses seem to occur throughout the world, though not in every individual. Most people are quite disgusted by the thought of seeing their own child murdered in front of them. As a result, we have no tolerance for people anywhere in the world who would murder their children. Indifference to injustice requires individuals to either be unaware of the injustice, to dismiss the moral standing of the victims of injustice, or to blame the victim for the injustice. It is humanists who help to remedy all three situations by exposing both the humanity and suffering of victims. In addition to compassion for victims, a sense of responsibility for their suffering can enhance the drive for moral change. Jeremy Bentham famously said we are driven by two masters: pleasure and pain; moral progress can be driven by a peculiar type of pleasure, honor, and a corresponding pain, shame.

Humanists, of course, participate in a long tradition of raising the specter of shame for the human race. A. Richard Turner (1994, 215) quotes Leonardo da Vinci's lament on the cruelty of man:

> Animals will be seen on earth who will always be fighting against each other with the greatest loss and frequent deaths on each side. And there will be no end to their malice; by their strong limbs we shall see a great portion of the trees laid low throughout the universe; and when they are filled with food, the satisfaction of their desires will be to deal death and grief and labour and fears and flight to every living thing; and from their immoderate pride they will desire to rise towards heaven, but the excessive weight of their limbs will keep them down. Nothing will remain on earth, or under the earth, or in the waters, which will not be persecuted, disturbed and spoiled, and those of one country removed into another. And their bodies will become the tomb and the means of transit of all the living beings they have killed.

As we read words such as these and recognize the truth of them, we may be motivated to do better and achieve feelings of honor, and, indeed, many humanists also give descriptions of the great honor humans can achieve. Da Vinci almost appears to predict of effects of trade globalization, but Turner avers that da Vinci was probably reacting to the horrors of war (in some respects the horrors resulting from global trade recall Thomas Hobbes's vision of universal war in a state of nature). The fact remains that the humanist reacts with disgust at the inhumanity of humanity. Given the ongoing cruelty of humans, the effort may seem pointless, but surely a world devoid of the mitigating force and light of compassion shown by humanists would be even more sorrowful than the world we currently inhabit.

James Nachtwey is a contemporary artist who highlights the horrors of war and famine through his photography.[3] Christian Frei's 2001 film, *War Photographer*, is a documentary of Nachtwey's work.[4] In a sense, the film poses a sort of double aesthetic; it is beautifully filmed and exposes the viewer to the achingly attractive photography of James Nachtwey. The aesthetic qualities of the film place the viewer in a bind, however, as the images are generally of horrific events of human cruelty and suffering. Nachtwey appears to assume that most of his viewers in affluent societies will feel it is inappropriate to witness preventable suffering and take no action to alleviate it. He enters no debate as to how much any one person should do; he merely attempts to make suffering visible and personal. He believes this is an action required of him by basic morality. In this sense, Nachtwey is both moral agent and ethicist. He is attempting to both act morally and to motivate others to adopt his moral position. Of course, affluent people may watch the images, comment on the beauty of the photography, praise the dignity of those suffering, cry a few tears, exhort others to view the images, and then go about their normal routine. However, if affluent citizens will respond to the suffering, they will be motivated by their knowledge of the suffering, and the disturbing images are likely to provoke at least some people to take positive action. In a sense, Nachtwey has made it easier for concerns of justice to become what Hume would label "natural" virtues.

In an essay on human-rights themed entertainment, Vivian Nun Halloran (2007) described works of popular culture that deal with political activism and the promotion of human rights. Halloran mentions a number of works that include film, television, and novels. What these works have in common are heroic health professionals who are Western or Westernized and have transnational affiliations

---

[3] James Nachtwey, "Witness: Photography of James Nachtwey", n.d., http://www.jamesnachtwey.com/.

[4] Christian Frei, *War Photographer*, Documentary (First Run Features, 2001).

through organizations such as the World Health Organization and Doctors Without Borders. She concludes by saying, "By illustrating how health care professionals strive to preserve the dignity of their patients or ward even in situations that threaten to deprive them of 'life,' 'security of person,' or 'health,' these outlets of low, popular, and high culture promote an image of health care professionals as moral arbiters and ethical agents in a corrupt world" (Halloran 2007, 111). These works of art, then, expand our conception of moral agency and nobility while simultaneously affirming the authority of affluent, Western professionals. What these works do not do, however, is give voice to the victims in developing countries, even while highlighting abuses against them.

Activists are beginning to highlight the voices of such victims. On May 25, 2010, I attended an event at Rice University in Houston, Texas titled "The True Cost of Chevron: Public Forum on Struggle and Success." For approximately two hours, I listened to the stories of people affected by environmental degradation they say is caused by Chevron. I heard the stories of people from the United States (including Alaska), Angola, Australia, Burma, Canada, Colombia, Venezuela, Ecuador, Iraq, Kazakhstan, Nigeria, and the Philippines. Many of the speakers were ill or had family members who had been ill or died. Their stories were moving and compelling. It was their intention to present these stories at the Chevron shareholders meeting on May 26, 2010. Although they had shareholder proxies, most of them were denied entry, and five were arrested.[5] One of the people arrested was author and activist Antonia Juhasz of Global Exchange (she is actually a shareholder, not a proxy holder as the others were). Although it would be a major overstatement to say activists are winning in their struggle with Chevron, Juhasz put a personal face on the suffering caused by pollution around the globe. Juhasz and her program, the Global Exchange, continue to appear at Chevron shareholder meetings.[6] The management of Chevron absolutely does not want the stories of these affected individuals shared. Powerful economists and policy makers at the WTO and other organizations may eventually implement regulations that will limit the damage corporations can do, but it is the people on the ground who will provoke sympathy and outrage at injustice, and that is the only force that will motivate true changes.

---

[5] "Chevron Management Hit Hard at Annual Meeting over Ecuador Liability $38 Billion in Shareholder Value Defies CEO John Watson," *Hot Indie News*, May 27, 2010, http://www.hotindienews.com/2010/05/27/1024646.

[6] Kari Paul, "Women Demand Environmental Justice from Chevron," *Ms. Magazine Blog*, May 25, 2011, http://msmagazine.com/blog/blog/2011/05/25/women-demand-environmental-justice-from-chevron/, accessed May 26, 2011.

Moral movement requires a loss of certainty, and educators in the humanities are uniquely positioned to bring doubt to their students. I once attended a faculty work session with educators in the sciences and mathematics. These educators were driven by what they called the "aha moment." They said they would explain a problem until they saw a look of recognition on the faces of the students. I told them that my job was quite the opposite as a philosophy instructor. Most students come to a philosophy class feeling rather sure of their answers to the questions I will pose. I know I have done my job when the students get a look of doubt or confusion on their faces. Some students make comments such as, "I thought I knew what a human was before I took your class." The humanist tradition forces us to recognize uncertainty but demands that we continue a search for truth. As we gain new knowledge, we carry it along with the weight of skeptical humility and continue the search. It is not that we believe there is no absolute truth in the universe; it is only that we recognize our own limitations in perceiving the absolute truth.

As such, the humanist enters public discourse with the goal of promoting truth and justice in a humble and sincere manner, and this is the method of rhetoric held in high esteem by humanists; it should not be confused with a cruder form of rhetoric aimed at manipulating audiences only to achieve some short-term goal. The virtuous rhetor will persuade audiences with a common search for truth and honor. The use of rhetoric, even the best rhetoric, cannot guarantee success, but it is the best option for motivating people to change their ideas and their behavior. Legal remedies or even brute force will not be effective if the majority of the public is not moved to a new understanding of morality.

Rhetors face their greatest challenges in cases of extreme power imbalances, deeply entrenched social values, or great cultural disparity. Rhetors opposed to slavery in the United States confronted such challenges and moved many people to oppose slavery but did not eliminate slavery without extreme and pervasive violence. The history of humanity is in some ways a history of extreme violence, but it is also filled with moral progressions. More and more people are now given full consideration as full members of the human community, and even non-human animals are beginning to earn the concern and compassions of their human cohabitants of the earth. It is the success of moral and intellectual change that should motivate the rhetor, even with the recognition that extremely painful or even deadly events are likely to continue to occur.

A valuable rhetor must not be complacent or self-assured of her or his own knowledge. The rhetor must possess skeptical humility and be open to both exposure and change. James Kastely (1997, 46) describes this quality eloquently:

> Rhetoric needs to make those who are unwilling to undergo suffering do so voluntarily. It needs to remind us that evil is not simply a problem of bad motives but that our languages inevitably limit whom we can see as human. And rhetoric needs to provoke all of us so that we do not rest content in the satisfaction of our good intentions. A philosophical rhetoric will continually seek to refute our understandings of ourselves and of others so that these understandings do not become fixed and thereby close us to the voices of others. If we cannot prevent ourselves from causing inadvertent injury, we can through a philosophical rhetoric open ourselves to claims that we have treated others unjustly.

In this passage, Kastely beautifully enunciates the required humility required to enter the public arena in search of just social arrangements.

William Bouwsma (1990) looks to Socrates and the Sophists for guidance as to what humanists and rhetors should strive for. Bouwsma notes that Protagoras held a "thorough skepticism" about the ability of humans to arrive at an immutable truth, a stated goal for Socrates and Plato (Bouwsma 1990, 387). Protagoras famously declared that man is the measure of all things. By this he meant that we cannot reach beyond our own experience to another world of immutable truth or ideal reality. Protagoras embraced the realm of human experience and rejected the goals of philosophy as conceived by Socrates and Plato (Bouwsma 1990). Bouwsma (1990, 388) points out, "Rhetoric, not philosophy, gave us the humanities. The position represented by Protagoras was further developed by Gorgias and other rhetoricians, converted into a more systematic pedagogy by Isocrates, transmitted to Rome by Greek teachers of rhetoric, and assimilated by Latin orators." Ironically, even among humanists, the contributions of the Sophists have been forgotten, and Socrates and his philosophy have been elevated to the point that "sophist" is now a term of opprobrium (Bouwsma, 1990).

Bouwsma (1990, 392) claims that humanists have embraced Socrates because "Socrates has allowed them—and us—to cherish the humanities and at the same time to lay claim to a wisdom infinitely more prestigious than anything in the more mundane tradition of Protagoras". It is our desire for authority, Bouwsma claims, that makes Socrates so appealing. He says, "There is a further problem for us in the latent influence of philosophy represented among us by Socrates; its authoritarianism. If human culture is a body of sublime insights derived by man's higher faculties from the heavens above, then its values must apply equally to all men in all times. This conception of what we have to offer puts us in the position of a kind of . . . priesthood." (Bouwsma 1990, 394f.).

Bouwsma points out that Socrates was both more and less than we generally perceive him to be. He is variously described as a poet, a dancer, a sculptor, and, of course, a rhetorician. Socrates can and should be recognized as part of the humanistic tradition, but we should also recognize the diversity of our ancient exemplars (Bouwsma 1990, 395f.).

For Gary Remer (2008, 22), humanist rhetoric is defined by its agonistic structure and denial of the possibility of certain knowledge. If there were certainty, he points out, there would be no controversy and no need for discussion. Similarly, Cicero stated that in judicial disputes, those that had no ambiguity would have no reason for being heard. For that reason, and possibly for others, skepticism is an inherent feature of the discussion (Remer 2008, 23). In the absence of absolute certainty, skeptical rhetoricians such as Cicero had to settle for probability (Remer 2008, 24). Cicero's notion of establishing the probable is similar to that of the academic skeptics, the philosophical school with which Cicero identified (Remer 2008, 25). In *Academica*, Cicero says,

> Nor is there any difference between ourselves and those who think that they have positive knowledge except that they have no doubt that their tenets are true, whereas we hold many doctrines are probable, which we can easily act upon but can scarcely advance as certain; yet we are more free and untrammeled in that we possess our power of judgment uncurtailed, and are bound by no compulsion to support all the dogmas laid down for us almost as edicts by certain masters. (Cicero 1933, 475).

The value of skepticism is its openness to inquiry and rejection of blind obedience to authority. When any point of view is open to revision, conversation among diverse groups of people is possible without giving over to a hopeless and unfettered relativism.

Writing in the sixteenth century, Montaigne refers to the skepticism of Cicero, saying, "It was without obligation to any party, following what seemed probable to him now in one sect, now in another, keeping himself always in Academic doubt." (Montaigne 1958, 370). Montaigne's embrace of skepticism was embedded in a call for humility, not for a radical denunciation of efforts to find truth. In "Apology for Raymond Sebond," Montaigne says, "To really learned men has happened what happens to ears of wheat: they rise high and lofty, heads erect and proud, as long as they are empty; but when they are full and swollen with grain in their ripeness, they begin to grow humble and lower their horns." (Montaigne 1958, 370). It is this humility that helps the humanist to advance both private and public discourse. This idea is echoed in "Of the Art of Discussion" where Montaigne declares, "When someone opposes me, he arouses my attention, not my anger. I go to meet a man who contradicts me, who instructs me. The cause of truth should be the common cause for both." (Montaigne 1958, 705).

Like humanists in the past, we live in a world of uncertainty with disparate voices constantly bombarding us. Globalization has created one world with many voices. Many have asked whether individuals should be citizens of one nation or citizens of the world, but this question has become increasingly meaningless. We live in a state of interdependence with people from nearly every part of the earth. Humanists traditionally have had many disagreements, but I am unaware of any who rejected a commitment to virtue and justice.

The humanist recognizes that we all share the experience of being human, and this shared humanity gives us shared needs, hopes, fears, and values. Humanists can help find these shared experiences in a number of ways, but an obvious way is through education, and many of us are educators. Martha Nussbaum makes an impassioned plea for education that makes us more sensitive to the needs of others, more compassionate, and more critical (Nussbaum 2010). She says the abilities we should be teaching include "the ability to think critically; the ability to transcend local loyalties and to approach world problems as a 'citizen of the world'; and, finally, the ability to imagine sympathetically the predicament of another person" (Nussbaum 2010, 7). I have said that globalization has made us interdependent. It would seem that this would engender contact and conversation between groups, but such contact must be facilitated, and that is the job of educators. Nussbaum (2010, 44) says, "A surrounding culture can teach children to see new immigrant groups, or foreigners, as a faceless mass that threatens their hegemony—or it can teach the perception of the members of these groups as individuals equal to themselves, sharing common rights and responsibilities". One way to help students understand the viewpoint of others is to have them participate in arguments in the humanist tradition.

Argument is central to philosophy, and she has special advice for philosophy teachers: "Teachers of philosophy betray Socrates' legacy if they cast themselves as authority figures. What Socrates brought to Athens was an example of truly democratic vulnerability and humility. Class, fame, and prestige count for nothing, and the argument counts for all" (Nussbaum 2010, 51). As students confront the arguments of others, they are more able to understand how others think, and this is a necessary skill to develop empathy. Of course, literature, music, the arts, history, and cultural studies all help students understand and appreciate the experiences of others. It is necessary for schools to give people skills to support themselves through gainful employment, but it is also essential that citizens be able to think critically and with sensitivity.

Conclusion

I said above that humans share the experience of being human. In *Cosmopolitanism*, Kwame Anthony Appiah (2006) holds out hope that we can find shared values. He does not promise perfection by any means. He says, "Another aspect of cosmopolitanism is what philosophers call *fallibilism*—the sense that our knowledge is imperfect, provisional, subject to revision in the face of new evidence." In spite of this skepticism, he sees hope for nearly universal agreement on certain values such as kindness. It seems unlikely that anyone would not want to be treated kindly. He says, "The concept of kindness, or cruelty, enshrines a kind of social consensus. An individual who decides that kindness is bad and cruelty good is acting like Lewis Carroll's Humpty-Dumpty, for whom a word 'means just what I choose it to mean—neither more nor less." (Appiah 2006, 28). Our human experience makes it possible to understand what others might be feeling in some circumstances. Learning about the differences between people is likely to reveal even more similarities. Appiah (2006, xxi) says,

> There are some values that are, and should be, universal, just as there are lots of values that are, and must be, local. We can't hope to reach a final consensus on how to rank and order such values. That's why the model I'll be returning to is that of conversation—and, in particular, conversation between people from different ways of life.

Like Nussbaum, he urges us to engage in conversation with the people who share our globe. If we fail to do so, we remain isolated and insensitive to others. In addition to not understanding them, we prevent them from understanding us.

When we remove ourselves from others, we risk injustice and violence. We fail to recognize others as fully human, and they fail to recognize us as fully human. If we want to create a just society, we must come into contact with the joy, but especially the pain, of others. As Kastley (1997, 121) says,

> The problem of justice is the problem of just response, and the philosophical force of this problem arises because bureaucratic structures allow individuals to inure themselves from the pain of others by disavowing any personal responsibility for their actions or omissions. The ethical problem for such a world is not primarily to avoid doing evil, for evil will come, since the world is not completely under one's control; rather, it is to deal with the unbidden evils in such a way that justice can live.

Humanists have both the skills and the obligation to create the conditions for justice to thrive.

The problems facing the world now are not new. Wars, pollution, and poverty have been with us for centuries. But these same problems are now acute, chronic, and critical. It is easy to despair at our lack of progress, but Martha Nussbaum reminds us that progress has been made. In *Frontiers of Justice*, she says, "Racial hatred and disgust, and even misogynistic hatred and disgust, have certainly diminished in our public culture, through attention to the upbringing of children and their early education. The careful attention to language and imagery that some pejoratively call 'political correctness' has an important public purpose, enabling children to see one another as individuals and not as members of stigmatized groups." (Nussbaum 2006, 413)

As humanists, we cannot solve the world's problems, but we can choose to contribute to moral progress and promote greater care and understanding for one another, regardless of how many people join us along the way. The Transocean executives changed their behavior because the public identified with the victims of the tragedy of 2010. Humanists can help expand the moral imagination to include the victims of human rights abuses globally. Rational arguments for human rights and changes in policy must be coupled with emotional appeals that enable us to convert our natural virtues, in Hume's words, to a concern for global justice. Without the humanities, only profit is left to guide our moral journey.

REFERENCES

Appiah, Anthony. 2006. *Cosmopolitanism: Ethics in a World of Strangers*. New York: W.W. Norton.

Bouwsma, William. 1990. *A Usable Past: Essays in European Cultural History*. Berkeley/Los Angeles: University of California Press.

Cicero, Marcus Tullius. 1967. *De Natura Deorum. Academica* . Cambridge, MA: Harvard University Press.

Cicero, Marcus Tullius. 1933. *Academica*, translated by H. Rackham. Cambridge, MA: Harvard University Press. (online available at http://www.loebclassics.com/view/marcus_tullius_cicero-academica/1933/work.xml)

de Montaigne, Michel. 1958. *Complete Essays*. Stanford, Calif: Stanford University Press.

Francesco Petrarch, "To Marcus Tullius Cicero (2 of 2)," translated by James Harvey Robinson, n.d., http://petrarch.petersadlon.com/read_letters.html?s=pet11.html. Accessed May 25, 2011.

Frei, Christian, 2001. War Photographer, Documentary (First Run Features).

Hume, David 2005. *A Treatise of Human Nature*, edited by David Fate Norton and Mary J. Norton, 307-311. Oxford, UK: Oxford University Press.

Kastely, James. 1997. *Rethinking the Rhetorical Tradition: From Plato to Postmodernism.* New Haven: Yale University Press

Kwame Anthony Appiah. 2010. *The Honor Code: How Moral Revolutions Happen*. New York: W. W. Norton..

Nachtwey, James Nachtwey, "Witness: Photography of James Nachtwey", n.d., http://www.jamesnachtwey.com/.

Nun Halloran, Vivian. 2007. "Health Professionals, Truth, and Testimony: Witnessing in Human Rights-Themed Entertainment,", The Journal of the Midwest Modern Language Association 40: 97-114.

Nussbaum, Martha C. 2006. *Frontiers of Justice: Disability, Nationality, Species Membership*. Cambridge: The Belknap Press.

Nussbaum, Martha C. 2010. *Not For Profit: Why Democracy Needs the Humanities*. Princeton: Princeton University Press.

Remer, Gary. 2008. *Humanism and the Rhetoric of Toleration*. University Park: Penn State Press.

Turner, Richard A. 1994. *Inventing Leonardo*. Berkeley: University of California Press.

CHAPTER 8

Collective Responsibilities: New Principles for Order in the 21st Century

Elizabeth Edmondson

INTRODUCTION

Climate change impacts present a series of escalating political ramifications for states and the broader array of actors who comprise the contemporary world. Responding to specific climate change impacts, such as rising atmospheric temperatures and sea levels, loss of agriculturally productive land, redistributions of water resources, increased storms and severe fires, demand new forms of action from political actors and organizations (Human Development Report 2007/2008). These changes will impose new responsibilities upon political, economic and social actors, including those who remain reluctant to accept the new levels of authority and collective action demanded of them (Eckersley 2004; Matthew 2007). The rather limited outcomes of the Copenhagen Summit in 2009 demonstrated the extent to which government leaders continue to clutch at historically developed rights based concepts of sovereign authority, prosperity, harmony, order and international influence.

In spite of mounting evidence to the contrary, states continue to cling to hopes that their interdependent geophysical systems will prove amenable to independent political and economic management. They demonstrate ongoing reluctance to re-structure their industries, economies and the globalised market places in which they conduct their dealings (Hoffman, and Hoffman 2008). At present, states regard their rights to exercise independent political authority as more important than addressing global climate change. This drives their reluctance to set meaningful greenhouse gas emissions targets and underpinned their ineffectual 'let's see what others do first' meanderings at the Copenhagen Climate Summit in 2009.

The Need for Change

The experiences of protracted and less than effective international greenhouse emissions targets over the last decade suggest that continuing business-as-usual approaches to international political negotiations and bargaining are unlikely to prove timely in their completion. Neither are they be likely to provide effective contexts for collective goal setting or agreement implementation because states that might display political leadership will instead wait to see what others set as targets and avoid unilateral actions. Currently, these behavioural patterns jeopardize effective potential responses, however, they could be redirected to facilitate emerging collective responsibilities by amending the relative importance of rights and responsibilities as attributes of states as sovereign entities. As Hoffman (1997, ix) argues, "[w]hat threatens us is... an imbalance between the supreme legitimate authority' of states, and the 'feeble authority of collective institutions dealing with problems that transcend the states, or exceed their capacities". At present, states often struggle to translate their collective goals into international achievements, such as comprehensive policies to mitigate climate change, or to achieve collective strategies to redistribute adaptive technologies that might support changed industrial practices, even when they can agree on general goals.

Climate change poses new and complex problems for a broad array of political and economic actors, ranging from those in high order international activities to small scale enterprises grappling with altered regulatory environments. The political consequences of these global climate change impacts are likely to challenge the abilities of governments to ensure the social and economic wellbeing of their people and to preserve their security (Young 2002; Dow, and Downing 2007; Matthew 2007). In the immediate future, the sites of economic and political activity that are expected to be most directly affected by climate change impacts include agriculture, manufacturing and energy production (Dow, and Downing, 2007; Human Development Report 2007/2008). These industries also characterize sites of social and political vision concerning progress and prosperity, wherein the political and economic aspirations of peoples and their governments find expression.

Present inaction suggests that many states are acting out of expectations that global climate impacts are likely to remain largely external problems experienced elsewhere affecting the wellbeing of others. However, as social, economic and political actors experience successive 'predictable surprises', they are likely to seek to influence the development of international and domestic climate change mitigation and adaptation strategies (Ellwood 2009). Changing economic policies within particular locations are likely to achieve what sustained efforts by an array of scientific and other experts could not in altering visions and expectations of governmental responsibilities. Their challenges include dealing with changing production inputs and new market sensitivities which are likely to become subject to greater unpredictability (Kjéllen 2006; Parry, Canziani, Palutikof, van der Linden, and Hanson 2007).

As global climate change impacts upon their political and economic capacities, states and the people on whose behalf they act will revise their values concerning the features and benefits of well-ordered societies and generate new political visions and structures for achieving their fullfilment (DiMento, and Doughman 2007; Eckersley 2004; Eckersley 2005; Edmondson 2008; Kütting 2000). Consequently, the sources and forms of authority that people create and shape as core political institutions are likely to be affected by various direct and indirect climate change consequences (Young 2002). Changes in seasonal temperatures, rainfalls and sea levels, for instance, will directly affect the human habitability of populated regions and present a series of indirect impacts upon 'liveability factors', such as housing and water costs, insurance and banking markets (Human Development Report 2007/2008; Stern 2009). The regulatory and justice related challenges these present to states, intergovernmental organizations and other actors will ultimately alter their opportunities and capacities to assert themselves as authoritative agents (Haas, Keohane, and Levy 1993; Roberts, and Parks 2007).

ORDER, AUTHORITY AND RESPONSIBILITIES

The political ramifications of global climate change extend to the need for new understandings of the roles, rights and responsibilities that characterize states because the contemporary international political community has been formed on the basis of ideas concerning states as primary sites of political authority. As holders of sovereign authority, states have collective responsibilities for preserving international political institutions that enable the development and implementation of global climate change responses (Archibugi 2001; Gupta 2005). These are expressed in various multilateral environmental treaties and agreements achieved over several decades and supported by numerous international organizations, including implementing agencies (Biermann 2005; O'Neill 2009). Effective responses will only be achieved in the 21st century through collective agreements and agencies that reflect these behavioural norms and conform to emergent international customary law (Haas, Keohane, and Levy 1993; Paterson 2000; Postiglione 2001). Their orientation towards mitigation and adaptation will also demand appropriate attention to the distribution of relative costs and equitable burden sharing among parties (Human Development Report 2007/2008; Roberts and Parks 2007).

In the 21st century, global climate change will require new political practices among states and other actors, including redistributions of political and regulatory authority. The Copenhagen Summit demonstrated just how difficult this will be if democratic and cooperative procedures remain integral components of the international community's response. To date, the differentiated interests of states have thwarted attempts by climate change actors, such as the IPCC, and have limited the implementation of joint government and non-government organizational initiatives, such as the EU/Greenpeace Clean Energy strategy (Greenpeace 2009). Breakthroughs that galvanize rapid and fundamental changes will remain rare unless individual states adopt leadership roles that include unilateral initiatives and recognize collective responsibilities for global responses.

Addressing climate change requires the autonomy of statehood to be mediated by internationally articulated and environmentally responsible parameters. Increased accountability can be achieved through new strengthened mechanisms for global governance and/or the expectations of informed citizens (Eckersley 2005; Human Development Report 2007/2008; Kütting 2000; Young 2002). If the lessons of the past can be relied upon to predict the future, we might then expect these new political dynamics to transform the prerogatives and privileges of statehood, triggering a further evolution in what is understood as state sovereignty (Philpott 1999). Already, sovereign states cannot be considered bounded spaces, and their decisions are only rarely taken without regard for global interests that have been incorporated into their institutional demeanor. Achieving predictable and orderly constraints depends upon effective leadership within the international political community and the states that constitute its primary components.

If the members of the international political community are to create and implement meaningful mitigation and adaptation strategies, they will be required to engage with global, regional, and localized climate change consequences (Adger, Lorenzoni, and O'Brien 2009; O'Neill 2009). This will require their acceptance of increased levels of responsibility for developing and implementing mitigation and adaptation strategies. Effective responses will require organizational flexibility and collective recognition of their authoritative status to enable responses that extend states' spheres of accountability in sharing collective responsibilities for global climate change and its uneven impacts (Eckersley 2005; Nelson 2009; Young 2002). These dynamics will alter the nature of sovereignty preferred and sought by states as their pre-occupations with prosperity are replaced by more fundamental concerns with stability and order.

As a result, global climate change will lead states and other political actors to establish a new range of legitimate activities as they construct new sites of political interaction that reflect their interdependent and contingent collective responsibilities.

ACHIEVING COLLECTIVE RESPONSIBILITIES

New norms that recognize states as holding inherent collective responsibilities and new structures to support these goals will require the abandonment of states' individuated rights-based claims to sovereign independence. Even at this early stage of witnessing an array of direct and indirect threats to human survival arising from climate change consequences, it is apparent that these cannot be isolated to their impacts upon the interests of individual states. Adopting a new model of statehood premised upon common responsibilities would establish new political visions, institutions and structures suited to alleviating the risks arising from global climate change impacts such as loss of habitable and arable land, and redistributions in freshwater resources. Effective global climate change responses must also take account of the likely incidence of resource related conflicts in the 21st century. Among other things, responsibilities-based statehood would support the introduction of stronger compliance and monitoring mechanisms in states' international dealings.

This might seem a rather ambitious blueprint for those who perceive the international political community as inherently anarchical, emphasizing the spaces between states as primary sites of international order. However, the ability to exercise reason, hope and confidence is central to the nature of states – and these features arise from their inherent moral and legal standing as sovereign authorities (Bonanate 1995). It should then be possible, under the changed conditions of the 21st century, to achieve norms of political leadership that take account of inherent geophysical environmental interdependencies between states and to perceive their implications for the possible lifestyles and forms of political association that might be sustained (Achterberg 2001; Kütting 2000; O'Neill 2009). Even the most determinedly isolationist and independent state can no longer perceive itself as autonomous given its reliance upon the presence of a broader international political community. While states hold ubiquitous interests in self-preservation, they also hold responsibilities arising from these interests and their accommodation of them.

As global climate change challenges increasingly dislocate people from their former homelands and alter the relationships between people and their states, alongside changing patterns of economic production, states' abilities to claim, delineate and reiterate their specific interests will become increasingly subject to contestation (Human Development Report 2002/2008; Paterson 2000). States' abilities to claim uncontested political authority will be diminished as specific climate change impacts become more easily identified in local contexts and thereby challenge their central political institutions. However, internal responsibilities to maintain orderly societies give states collective obligations to preserve their people and territories even when they might resist the collective responsibilities that are implicit to statehood (Archibugi 2001). As global climate change presents new demands for political order states are likely to reassert their superiority over other political entities, conceding to their collective responsibilities as they seek to continue to exercise authority through privileged political status (Paterson 2000; Archibugi 2001).

Throughout the 20th century, liberal democracies showed particular sensitivity towards the importance of exerting influence over the international political community. These states displayed international political leadership in adopting collective security arrangements, and structuring the international political community to support order (Edmondson, and Levy 2008). In the latter decades of the 20th century, these principles were extended to include humanitarian intervention, which in some respects provides a template for recognizing collective responsibilities for developing and implementing climate change mitigation and adaptation strategies.

An important feature of the contemporary international political context is that to some extent, the liberal democracies perceive themselves as guardians or trustees of order and security (Eckersley 2005; Roberts, and Parks 2007). These states are most engaged in developing shared recognition of collective responsibilities among states in relation to extending universal human rights and protecting citizens from various threats even when they continue to reassert their rights to economic independence (Eckersley 2006; Edmondson, and Levy 2008; Kütting 2000). These features and sensitivities might now enable their pursuit of international leadership in developing climate change mitigation and adaptation strategies, if they can perceive the benefits of attributing priority to their collective responsibilities (Edmondson, and Levy, 2014).

Climate change consequences are widespread, only partly predictable in their patterns of occurrence, and overwhelmingly disruptive of contemporary societies (Human Development Report 2007/2008; Ellwood 2009; Stern 2009). They cannot be isolated to groups of states or political coalitions, or even to particular economic sectors across the world. While this observation might seem self-evident, it often remains implicit, at best serving a background role in international political negotiations concerning global climate change. However, it also reflects some of the fundamental geophysical interdependencies that are part of the political, economic and social realities experienced and constructed by states and inter-governmental organizations.

Territories, Markets, Communities

This necessitates a considerable reconfiguration of power relations because in the modern world, the authority of states rests upon their capacities to make and implement laws within the territories they claim. States claim territory and exercise authority by enacting and implementing laws, and recognizing the rights of other states (Bonanate 1995). This relationship between territory-authority-sovereignty establishes states' rights and underpins their abilities to exercise jurisdiction over defined – and recognized – territories (Edmondson, and Levy 2008; Kütting 2000; Matthews 1991). In very practical ways, states claim and exercise their rights of sovereignty through their supreme authority within a jurisdiction by creating laws within territorial limits that provide legal boundaries and separate different sovereign entities (Herz 1957).

The nature of sovereignty will inevitably be affected in the 21st century as climate change consequences impact upon the territorial possessions of states and efforts to reduce greenhouse gases and other industrial emissions alter their economic activities and structures (Bearce, Floros, and McKibben 2009; Human Development Report 2007/2008). It will become necessary to reconsider the nature of states as political entities with rights to claim exclusive use of resources within their territories through their capacities to claim the rights and responsibilities of representing their citizens' interests. Climate change is likely to challenge these attributes of contemporary states. As some states lose territory to rising sea levels and others lose rivers as rainfall patterns change, they will expect to find support from their peers as they attempt to provide ongoing security for their citizens.

Throughout the modern international political community, sovereign states have outlined and utilized common rules of mutual recognition which have allowed them to relate to each other as equals (Edmondson, and Levy 2008). Their mutual recognition as states has enabled them to function as autonomous actors, holding independent jurisdiction over their territory and control over domestic issues (Kegley Jnr., and Raymond 2005, 47). When states have taken unilateral actions they have often justified these through the principle of sovereignty which, in the 20th century, was regularly invoked to reaffirm the autonomous authority of states. These foundations of international political behavior exacerbate the challenges of achieving collective agreements among states and increase the importance of effective political leadership in achieving climate change adaptation and mitigation strategies (Matthews 1991; Paterson 2000; Young 1994).

Increased communication, migration and trade have added layers of complexity to state relations that renders traditional thinking about the rights and authority of states too simplistic in contemporary global politics. Statehood, in part, relies upon states demonstrating that their internal actions comply with universal values. It is possible to imagine a not-too-distant future in which such measures might extend to encompass climate change and water distribution issues. In such a future, if states did not contribute positively to alleviating climate change, then their status as legitimate actors could be called into question.

The expanded array of political actors and voices that seek to influence international climate related decisions can extend collective responsibilities among states by creating new sites of collective responsibilities. For instance, monitoring international sea level increases and agreements to regulate and limit the production of ozone-depleting chlorofluorocarbons, positively contribute to new forms of global economic endeavor. Securing human wellbeing can become a new central goal shared among international political actors (Kütting 2000; Biermann, and Bauer 2005). Empowering these new sites of political authority can secure the survival of vibrant and harmonious human communities into the future, but doing so will demand considerable political leadership. Specifically, these changes will require re-setting the balance between political and economic actors to privilege global commons principles.

PRESERVING THE FUTURE

Reconsidering sovereignty and the nature of states is necessary for developing effective responses to climate change because sovereign statehood provides the central norms and ordering mechanisms of the international community. Sovereign states constitute the principal forms of political association and it seems likely that at least some of these might lose their abilities to provide physical and social security and maintain territorially based jurisdictional capacities (Edmondson 2009; Human Development Report 2007/2008; Roberts, and Parks 2007; Young 2002). Although some states may be in a position to exercise leadership in responding to climate change and water challenges, it seems inevitable that others will lack adaptability, struggle to demonstrate timely responsiveness to information, or wilfully resist attempts to pursue responses under the leadership of others. Hence, it is now necessary to consider the roles that might be played by states that are unable or unwilling (for reasons of ideology or capacity) to make meaningful contributions to international climate change responses (Edmondson, and Levy, 2014).

States that share common interests in self-preservation can revise their conceptions of authority and establish new means of identifying, incorporating and acting in support of their collective responsibilities (Bearce, Floros, and McKibben 2009; Bonanate 1995; Edmondson 2008). By forming and maintaining international institutions, organisations and agencies to implement international agreements, states recognise their mutual rights and responsibilities to protect national interests (Archibugi 2001; Bonanate 1995). The institutions they create and maintain reflect their interdependencies and underlying common interests among states. They also highlight the importance that states attribute to their privileged authoritative status (Hurrell 1995).

Like the effects of global climate change, international order transcends the security and economic interests of individual states that are concerned with the conditions that preserve their peaceful coexistence (Kütting 2000; Eckersley 2005). When states collectively ensure security for their citizens, protecting them from violence, invasion, government by foreigners and the imposed interests of foreigners, they also conceive of themselves as bound by a common set of rules and the workings of common institutions (Bull 2002).These and other dynamics of international order enhance states' prospects of self-preservation. They produce forms of behavior among states that alter their established identities and produce new orderly relations among them.

Rule structures create order in international society. States and inter-governmental organizations create formal and informal rules that offer symbolic representations of their shared values and beliefs, construct order and provide them with opportunities to lead collective responses to challenges that impact upon all of their members (Adger, Lorenzoni, and O'Brien 2009; Stern 2009). Ensuring the livelihood of their citizens and maintaining social and political order will require states to accept their collective obligations to support adaptation and mitigation policies that prioritize global wellbeing and the survival of human societies into the future. Accepting economic challenges and relinquishing hopes of never ending economic growth and industrial expansion will be central factors for effective international climate change responses (Gallagher 2009).

CONCLUSION

States are experiencing increasing pressure to take responsibility for developing and implementing climate change mitigation strategies in order to justify their continuing rights to claim sovereign authority and to preserve their state structures (Paterson 2000; Nelson 2009). States are not only responsible for domestic environmental practices and solving climate change issues in relation to their own territory. They must also participate in constructing, applying and adhering to global solutions to an inherently global problem. For meaningful political authority to be exercised through sovereign states and the international political community, states are now required to acknowledge the responsibilities that arise from their sovereign rights (Archibugi 2001; Bonanate 1995; Postiglione, and Kütting 2000).

The diverse rights, responsibilities and perceptions of common good that exist among states can be utilized by the international political community to support mitigation and adaptation policies (Bonanate 1995; Najam 2005). Although physical interdependencies among states do not of themselves make it easier to achieve international agreement, their impacts upon sovereign authority can be harnessed to re-configure power relations, privileging collective responsibilities over individuated rights based interests (Young 2002; Edmondson and Levy 2013). As global climate change unfolds, it is now timely to engage with the manner in which the political challenges posed by these changes raise new questions regarding the nature of rights and responsibilities, and their distribution among states and other international actors.

REFERENCES

Achterberg, Wouter 2001. "Environmental Justice and Global Democracy" In *Governing for the Environment: Global Problems, Ethics and Democracy*, edited by Brendan Gleeson and Nicholas Low, 183-195. Houndmills: Palgrave.

Adger, W. Neil, Irene Lorenzoni, and Karen L. O'Brien. 2009. 'Preface' In *Adapting to Climate Change: Thresholds, Values, Governance*, edited by W. Neil Adger, Irene Lorenzoni, and Karen L. O'Brien, 1-22. Cambridge: Cambridge University Press.

Archibugi, Daniele. 2001. "The Politics of Cosmopolitan Democracy" In *Governing for the Environment: Global Problems, Ethics and Democracy*, edited by Brendan Gleeson and Nicholas Low, 196-210. Houndmills: Palgrave.

Bearce, David. H., Katherine. M. Floros, and Heather. E. McKibben. 2009. "The Shadow of the Future and International Bargaining: The Occurrence of Bargaining in a Three-Phase Cooperative Framework." *The Journal of Politics* 17: 719-732.

Biermann, Frank. 2005. "The Rationale for a World Environment Organization" In *A World Environment Organization: Solution or Threat for Effective*

International Environmental Governance?, edited by Frank Biermann, and Steffen Bauer, 117-144. Aldershot: Ashgate.

Biermann, Frank, and Steffen Bauer. 2005. "The Debate on a World Environment Organization: An Introduction." In *A World Environment Organization: Solution or Threat for Effective International Environmental Governance?,* edited by Frank Biermann, and Steffen Bauer, 1-26. Aldershot: Ashgate.

Bonanate, Luigi. 1995. *Ethics and International Politics*. Cambridge: Polity.

Bull, Hedley. 2002. *The Anarchical Society: A Study of Order in World Politics*. Basingstoke: Palgrave.

DiMento, Joseph. F. C., and Pamela Doughman. 2007. "Climate Change: How the World is Responding" In *Climate Change: What it Means For Us, Our Children and Our Grandchildren*, edited by Joseph. F. C. DiMento and Pamela Doughman, 149-226. Cambridge: MIT Press.

Dow, Kirstin, and Taylor Downing. 2007. *The Atlas of Climate Change: Mapping the World's Greatest Challenge*. Berkeley: University of California Press.

Eckersley, Robyn. 2004. *The Green State: Rethinking Democracy and Sovereignty*. Cambridge: MIT Press.

Eckersley, Robyn. 2005. "Greening the Nation-State: From Exclusive to Inclusive Sovereignty" In *The State and the Global Ecological Crisis*, edited by John Barry, and Robyn Eckersley, 159-180 . Cambridge, M.A.: The MIT Press.

Eckersley, Robyn. 2006. "Communitarianism" In *Political Theory and the Ecological Challenge*, edited by Andrew Dobson and Robyn Eckersley, 91-108. Cambridge: Cambridge University Press.

Edmondson, Elizabeth, and Steward Levy. 2013. *Climate Change and Order: The End of Prosperity and Democracy*. Houndmills: Palgrave Macmillan.

Edmondson, Elizabeth, and Steward Levy. 2008. *International Relations: Nurturing Reality*. Frenchs Forest: Pearson Education.

Edmondson, Elizabeth. 2008. "Global Order: Accommodating Diversity in the 21st Century." *The Global Studies Journal* 1: 25-34.

Edmondson, Elizabeth. 2009. "The Impossible Dream: Consensus-Based International Climate Change Responses." *The Global Studies Journal* 2: 1-14.

Edmondson, Elizabeth. 2001, "The Intergovernmental Panel on Climate Change: Beyond Monitoring?" In *Governing for the Environment: Global*

Problems, Ethics and Democracy, edited by Brendan Gleeson, and Nicholas Low, 44-60. Houndmills: Palgrave.

Ellwood, David. T. 2009. "Foreword" In *Acting in Time on Energy Policy*, edited by Kelly S. Gallagher, vii.Washington D.C.,:The Brookings Institution Press.

Gallagher, Kelly. S. 2009. "Acting in Time on Climate Change" In *Acting in Time on Energy Policy*, edited by Kelly. S. Gallagher, 12-38.Washington D.C.:The Brookings Institution Press

Greenpeace 2009. *Clean Energy Solutions*.

Gupta, Joyeeta. 2005. "Global Environmental Governance: Challenges for the South from a Theoretical Perspective" In *A World Environment Organization: Solution or Threat for Effective International Environmental Governance?*, edited by Frank Biermann, and Steffen Bauer, 57-83. Aldershot: Ashgate.

Haas, Peter M., Robert O. Keohane, and Mark A. Levy ,eds.1993. *Institutions for the Earth: Sources of Effective International Environmental Protections*. Cambridge: MIT Press.

Hoffman, Jane and Michael Hoffman. 2008. *Green: Your Place in the New Energy Revolution.* Houndmills: Palgrave Macmillan.

Hoffman, Stanley. 1997. "Foreword" In *State Sovereignty, Change and Persistence in International Relations*, edited by Sohail H. Hashmi. Pennsylvania: Pennsylvania State University Press.

Kjéllen, Bo. 2006. "Foreword" In *The Atlas of Climate Change: Mapping the World's Greatest Challenge*, edited by Kirstin Dow, and Taylor E. Downing. Berkeley: University of California Press.

Kütting, Gabriela. 2000. *Environment, Society and International Relations: Towards More Effective International Environmental Agreements*. London: Routledge.

Matthew, Richard. 2007. "Climate Change and Human Security" In *Climate Change: What it Means for Us, Our Children, and Our Grandchildren*, edited by Joseph. F. C. DiMento, and Pamela. Doughman, 161-180. Cambridge, MA: MIT Press.

Mathews, Jessica. T., ed. 1991. *Preserving the Global Environment: The Challenge of Shared Leadership.* New York: W.W. Norton.

Najam, Adil. 2005. "Neither Necessary, Nor Sufficient: Why Organizational Tinkering Will Not Improve Environmental Governance." In *A World Environment Organization: Solution or Threat for Effective*

International Environmental Governance?, edited by Frank Biermann, and Steffen Bauer, 235-256. Aldershot: Ashgate.

Nelson, Donald R. 2009. "Conclusions: Transforming the World" In *Adapting to Climate Change: Thresholds, Values, Governance,* edited by W. Neil Adger, Irene Lorenzoni, and Karen L. O'Brien, 491-500. Cambridge: Cambridge University Press.

O'Neill, Kate. 2009. *The Environment and International Relations*. Port Melbourne: Cambridge University Press.

Parry, Martin L., Osvaldo Canziani, Jean Palutikof, Paul van der Linden and Clair Hanson (eds.). 2007. *Climate Change 2007: Impacts, Adaptation and Vulnerability. Contribution of Working Group II to the Fourth Assessment Report of the Intergovernmental Panel on Climate Change*. Cambridge: Cambridge University Press.

Paterson, Matthew. 2000. *Understanding Global Environmental Politics: Domination, Accumulation and Resistance*. New York: St. Martin's Press.

Postiglione, Amedeo. 2001. "An International Court of the Environment" In *Governing for the Environment: Global Problems, Ethics and Democracy*,edited by Brendan Gleeson and Nicholas Low, 211-220. Houndmills: Palgrave.

Roberts, J. Timmons, and Bradley C. Parks. 2007. *A Climate of InJustice: Global Inequality, North-South Politics and Climate Policy*. Cambridge: MIT Press.

Thompson, Janna. 2001. "Planetary Citizenship: the Definition and Defence" In *Governing for the Environment: Global Problems, Ethics and Democracy*, edited by Brendan Gleeson, and Neil Low, 135-146. Houndmills: Palgrave.

United Nations Development Program. 2008. Human *Development Report 2007/2008*.

Vogler, John. 2005. "In Defense of International Environmental Cooperation" In *The State and the Global Ecological Crisis,* edited by John Barry, and Robyn Eckersley, 229-254. Cambridge: MIT Press.

Young, O. 1994. *International Governance: Protecting the Environment in a Stateless Society*. Ithaca: Cornell University Press.

Young, Oran. 2002. *The Institutional Dimensions of Environmental Change: Fit, Interplay and Scale.* Cambridge: MIT Press.

CHAPTER 9

Reorientating the Focus on Responsibility to Protect to a Responsibility to Prevent

John Janzekovic

INTRODUCTION

The need to prevent violence and to protect people from the excesses of their governments has been argued by many but serious societal, operational and structural strategies that help prevent the ultimate need for protection are significantly more theory than practice. Prevention and protection have a complementary relationship but it is the prioritization of prevention that is lacking in much of the discourse. When the need to protect arises then prevention has failed to protect those most at risk and protection, if it occurs at all, becomes a rearguard action to prevent an already calamitous situation from becoming even worse. The progression of Responsibility to Protect (R2P) from concept to principle to formal ratification by most states at the 2005 UN World Summit has been a very difficult one with a great deal of disagreement over the validity of R2P as a substantive or even a formative norm in international affairs. The disagreement is not that protection and prevention are unimportant nor is it that the international community does not have some sort of responsibility to try to stop extreme human rights violations. The disagreement is primarily about how fine sounding principles in R2P are supposed to work in practice and of what possible use such 'principles' are when governments and policy makers continue to ignore the basic premise of responsibility to protect. This is not just a theoretical debate and it is not only about semantics or use of terms, although both are evident in the proliferation of literature on this topic.

This is a debate that is about the fundamental obligations of a civil and moral society and how the international community should or even could protect peoples who are at extreme risk of deliberate violence. If one can accept the fundamentals of the R2P then there is another hurdle to overcome. That is, how do we pre-empt or prevent the need to protect and does a preventative responsibility have any real meaning when protection is itself so difficult? The contention again is not about the value of prevention rather it is about how we practically implement preventative strategies to lessen the need for protection as a final response.

The term Responsibility to Protect was popularized in the international lexicon following the 1994 genocide in Rwanda and the 1998-99 war in Kosovo. The events in Rwanda and in Kosovo were catalysts in the formulation of the idea that the international community had at least some sort of overarching responsibility to protect peoples who were at extreme risk from the excesses of their governments, and that a collective responsibility also existed to prevent such events in the future. In Rwanda, between 500 000 and 1 million people were killed in 100 days mostly by Hutus wielding clubs, machetes, stones and iron bars. When it was clear that the genocide had started, the UN Secretary-General proposed a small intervention force of 5 500 troops to be sent to Rwanda but the United States actively campaigned to dissuade the African countries who were prepared to participate in such a force from intervening. The United States Administration still had fresh and painful memories of the UN-sponsored 1992 and 1993 US peacekeeping intervention disaster in Somalia (Operation Restore Hope).

In Kosovo, during the summer of 1998 events reached a flashpoint when Albanians mounted mass protests against Serbian rule, and Serb police and army reinforcements were sent in to crush the protesters who were supported by the Kosovo Liberation Army (KLA). The first major massacre occurred in the spring of 1998 in the Drenica region when 51 civilians were killed by Serb forces in retaliation for a KLA provocation. Open conflict between Serbian military and police forces and Kosovar Albanian forces during 1998 resulted in the deaths of over 1 500 Kosovar Albanians and forced 400 000 people from their homes. In January 1999 there were further massacres of Kosovo civilians by Serb forces in the village of Racak. The UN was incapable of deciding what to do in Kosovo and on 24 March 1999 NATO began its 11 week air war against the Serbs in the Federal Republic of Yugoslavia (FRY) without explicit UN approval.

In the aftermath of the Rwandan genocide and the events in Kosovo, all members of the Security Council proclaimed that they would 'never again' fail to respond to genocide. Unfortunately the Security Council and the international community have not lived up to this promise and the crisis in Dafur in western Sudan is only one example. Dafur continues to be a major humanitarian disaster with an estimated 2.7 million people displaced, more than 240 000 people forced into neighbouring Chad, and an estimated 450 000 people killed since 2003. On 31 August 2006, Security Council Resolution 8821 (2006) adopted UN Resolution 1706 by directly applying the R2P principle to a particular context for the first time when it called for the deployment of UN peacekeepers to Darfur. The UN authorized the United Nations Mission in Sudan (UNMIS) to use 'all necessary means' to protect civilians under threat of physical violence. In mid-2007 the U.N. Security Council passed Resolution 1769 (2007), authorizing the deployment of 26 000 peacekeepers (currently there are 22 000 in country) from the African Union to Darfur. Trevor Salmon (cited in Galbraith, 2008, p. 134) argues that the presence of these under resourced and ill prepared peacekeepers has not brought peace or even managed to limit the violence in the Dafur.

The notion of R2P has evolved since the 1990s as a response by the wider international community struggling to deal with individual, collective, and state responsibilities regarding immediate human security issues. Kofi Annan, the 1994-1999 Carnegie Commission on Preventing Deadly Conflict, the International Commission on Intervention and State Sovereignty (ICISS), and the UN High-Level Panel on Threats, Challenges and Change all attempted to articulate R2P as a formative concept with the idea that it should develop into a new type of responsive norm regarding how the international community should react to serious human rights violations. The Carnegie Commission in its 1999 final report, Preventing Deadly Conflict, identified three aims of preventative action. Firstly, prevent the emergence of violent conflict. Secondly, prevent ongoing conflicts from spreading. Thirdly, prevent the re-emergence of violence. The Commission proposed three fundamental principles underpinning effective prevention strategies; early reaction to signs of trouble; a comprehensive, balanced approach to alleviate the pressures, or risk factors, that trigger violent conflict; and an extended effort to resolve the underlying root causes of violence. No one would disagree that these are important prerequisites to the protection ethos but the report does not address the critical questions or strategies about how all or any of these were to be practically implemented. The report proposes merely that prevention is either 'operational or structural' in nature. Operational prevention is focused on addressing and responding to the immediacy of conflict whilst structural prevention is aimed at identifying and responding to the underlying causes of conflict. However, as Bellamy et al. (2010, 155) point out structural, preventative initiatives currently exist more in theory than in practice.

In September 1999, UN Secretary-General Kofi Annan delivered a major statement to the UN General Assembly emphasizing the equal importance of individual and state sovereignty principles. Annan's approach was to reiterate support for the fundamental principle of protecting human security within states but also that this support required the direct engagement and involvement (meaning forcible intervention as a final option) from the wider international community. His statements were primarily a response to the international community and particularly the UN's failure to act before or during the genocide in Rwanda and to the Security Council's open disagreements about what to do regarding the war in Kosovo after the end of the war in Bosnia. Annan's statements motivated Lloyd Axworthy, Canada's Foreign Minister (1996–2000) and the Canadian government to establish the ICISS in September 2000 in order to consider ways in which a new international consensus may be achieved regarding the 'principles of protection and responsibility'. The Commission sought to develop a new formative framework in response to Annan's plea that the UN avoid future Rwandas where the UN was united but ineffective, and future Kosovos where the UN was divided and where a collective of states acted without explicit UN Security Council authorisation. The ICISS, co-chaired by Gareth Evans and Mohamed Sahnoun, provided the impetus for the 2005 UN World Summit initiatives and outcomes regarding international responsibilities of protection and prevention. The 2001 ICISS Report The Responsibility to Protect claimed a 'new approach'; R2P that underlines and reinforces much of its content and argument. The 2001 Report states that, "Prevention is the single most important dimension of the responsibility to protect." (Evans, and Sanhoun 2001, p. xi), and that the responsibility to protect embraces three specific responsibilities: the responsibility to prevent, the responsibility to react, and the responsibility to rebuild. Juan Garrigues (2007) proposes that the responsibility to protect implies a significant empirical and normative progression, and that it has existed since 2001 when the ICISS presented its report and created the term.

> "R2P as a norm reasserts the responsibility or the obligation of states to protect their citizens, both within and beyond their national borders, under the umbrella concept of the common heritage of mankind in international law." (Chatawa, 2007, p. 195)

Teresa Chataway (2007) and Chris Abbott (2005) claim that the concept of R2P is a distinct development in the history of human rights since the adoption of the Universal Declaration of Human rights, and that it is comprised of the following three key elements; (a) Responsibility to prevent aims to address both the root and direct causes of internal conflict and other man-made crises that place populations at risk. (b) Responsibility to react aims to respond to situations of compelling human need with appropriate measures, which may include coercive measures like sanctions and international prosecution, and in extreme cases military intervention. (c) Responsibility to rebuild aims to provide, particularly after military intervention, full assistance with recovery, reconstruction and reconciliation, and to address the causes of the harm the intervention was designed to halt or avert.

On 3 November 2003, the UN Secretary General appointed a High-Level Panel on Threats, Challenges and Change in response to the serious, destabilizing events such as the attacks against the United States on September 11, 2001, and the escalating wars in Iraq and Afghanistan. On 2 December 2004 the Panel published its report, A More Secure World: Our Shared Responsibility. A central theme of the report was the responsibility to protect civilians from large-scale violence that incorporated the 'responsibility to protect' as a fundamental principle. The Panel reiterated the emphasis on conflict prevention and post-conflict reconstruction.

In September 2005 at the UN World Summit, the governments of Australia, New Zealand, South Africa, Rwanda, Argentina, Tanzania, Mexico, Singapore, Canada, Chile, Peru, Japan and all the European governments strongly supported the proposed agreement to enshrine their responsibility to protect civilians and stop mass killings. However, the governments of the Russia, Egypt, USA, India, Malaysia, Cuba, Pakistan, Iran, Syria, Venezuela and Brazil stalled and attempted to weaken the agreement over a range of concerns about the practicality and the implementation of the various principles stated in the ICISS report. Despite nearly one hundred and ninety states committing themselves during the Summit to the idea that the rule of non-intervention was not sacrosanct under particular circumstances (for example, a government committing genocide and ethnic cleansing within its borders) the UN's endorsement of this evolving norm did not address the basic question of what to do if the Security Council could not or would not mandate forcible intervention to protect populations at extreme risk. In paragraphs 138 and 139 of the Outcome Statement, R2P was included as an "emerging norm" in international affairs but there was little else substantial in the document that canvassed how or when this new norm should be implemented.

There are at least three fundamental limitations on the principles of responsibility to protect. Firstly; there is the problem of political will generally. If there is no general consensus between political entities about when or if they need to act to protect populations at risk then the question over who has the responsibility to act barely rates on the agenda. Unless this vexing problem is addressed then the issue of obligation or responsibility will not be confronted. The very selective nature of past interventions and the myriad issues that they have raised coupled with the aggressive posture and behaviour of the West in places such as Iraq and Afghanistan do not bode well for a more coherent substantiation of the glacially evolving protection norm. Even in Kosovo the Security Council made no reference to the protection needs of the Serbian and minority populations in Kosovo nor did it address the problem of how to promote the peaceful co-existence of Kosovo's ethnic communities. Addressing this second problem lies squarely in the realm of prevention. The issue of protection was, in mid-June 1999, seen to be a critical and immediate issue only with regard to the Kosovo Albanian population.

The second major problem is what to do if the Security Council cannot or will not agree on a response to address serious humanitarian issues. One option is for a state or a collective of states to act but this may create even further problems with perceptions (real or otherwise) of other agendas, self-interest or imperial expansionism. A third issue is that the world's most powerful military superpower, the United States, rejects the fundamental concept of any limitations to its capacity and capability to use its military power whenever and wherever it chooses. This is a serious constraint on the progression of the protection thesis. Finally, the fundamental notion of prevention was essentially sidelined by the many difficult and still unresolved questions relating to protection. Even the role of the UN Peace Building Commission established in December 2005 by General Assembly Resolution 60/180 (2005) is expressly limited to post conflict situations. Steven Toope et al. (1998, 9) argue that as the Peace Building Commission has no mandate for early warning or intervention, "how then will the preventative aspect of the responsibility to prevent play itself out?". The overall difficulty is that states may sign up to the principle of the responsibility to protect but disagree over its application in particular cases or even generally.

The notion of "direct support" involving the intervention by external states or parties into the affairs of a sovereign state remains hugely problematic as a normative response to manmade humanitarian disasters. Not only is there no clear understanding, much less an agreement, about when or under what circumstances forcible intervention should occur but the violation of state sovereignty continues to be seen either as imperial expansionism and the forcible imposition of foreign values and ideals or as some other external agenda that has little to do with the principles of humanitarianism. The majority of the lengthy discussions, meetings, reports and press releases about the development of R2P focused on proposing 'a new direction' in the sovereignty norm. This new direction placed much more emphasis and responsibility on the state and on the international community generally to deal with serious human security issues. It also attempted to qualify many complex and difficult questions about the legitimacy of external intervention into the affairs of a state that violates its fundamental obligations to its citizens. These discussions culminated in the UN Summit Report after the 2005 UN World Summit but the Report did not qualify any particulars about prevention. Toope et al (1998, 7) maintain that the progression of R2P as a formative norm is still significant despite many setbacks, constraints and limitations to the development of R2P since the 1990s.

> Given the history of debates around humanitarian intervention, and the possible implications of the concept of responsibility to protect for sovereignty, non-intervention and so-called 'friendly relations' it's inclusion in the Summit Outcome document is astonishing. The norm of responsibility to protect has now been articulated, and at least formally endorsed.

Ann-Marie Slaughter (2005, 627) also claims that the redefinition of sovereignty was, "a tectonic shift, reinterpreting the very act of signing the Charter in ways that will create a new legal and diplomatic discourse about member states' obligations to their own people and to one another." Others such as Louise Arbour (2008) say that the responsibility to protect presents itself with intellectual clarity and political usefulness, and it is now a norm that is part and parcel of a new vision of human security.

Despite these and similar optimistic views the implementation of R2P from the theory and evolving norm development stage into actual practice remains hugely problematic. Such a transition requires consensus, political will and a great deal of leadership none of which are evident today in the ongoing crisis in Iraq, Afghanistan, the Sudan, and in many other places. There are two fundamental reasons for this as Thelma Ekiyor and Mary Ellen O'Connell (2007) point out. Firstly, there is the critical impasse in the conversation about the interpretation, or perhaps the ongoing reinterpretation, of R2P. That is; who is responsible, what does protection mean, how do we go about practically responding to human crisis, and how does the prevention thesis fit into the picture. How should we deal with human security issues before they develop into human catastrophes that may invoke the protection paradigm? The second major problem is that R2P is focused on the reaction pillar, and in particular the application of forcible intervention. The threshold for military intervention is very high and it includes war crimes, ethnic cleansing and crimes against humanity but what is needed is a much more pre-emptive, preventative ethos in dealing with human security issues long before they reach a stage of criticality. Emphasis must be placed on strengthening and promoting the prevention ambit which includes a commitment to promoting good governance and democratization fostered by appropriate diplomatic, humanitarian and other peaceful means.

A Responsibility to Prevent (R2Prevent) ethos must be contextualized to a people, a state or a region and different preventive strategies are appropriate to different places, different times and different situations. There is no one simple solution but this does not mean that there are no solutions at all. There are a number of viable and practical preventative approaches that make an endgame need for protection much less likely but before preventative action can occur there is the fundamental problem of conceptualizing what prevention actually means. A preventative strategy requires a great deal of contextual understanding and, most importantly, foresight in order to deal with situations that potentiality have a high risk of escalating out of control. A protective strategy is also very complex but most people can identify the basic requirement to protect when the media and other news sources stream shocking pictures of extreme violence directly into our sitting rooms. When Kuwait was attacked by Iraq in the early 1990s the protection response was based on violation of state sovereignty. Despite all the talk about the increasing importance of globalization and transnationalism, state sovereignty remains sacrosanct and people respond instinctively when a state is under threat. When Coalition Forces invaded Iraq after September 11 the protection response was concern over Weapons of Mass destruction (WMDs) falling into the hands of extremists. The international community may argue about the validity or otherwise of the protection response but they understand the simple rationale behind the need for protection. Prevention and preventative action is much less tangible. Emma Rothschild (1995, 72-73) argues that,

> [o]ne of the distinctive characteristics of prevention is that it takes place under conditions of imperfect information… Without good information, anticipatory actions are always likely to be too late… One does not know that one cares about something, or reflect on what one has it in one's power to do, until one knows about some particular injustice or crisis..

Therefore, the prevention thesis is much more complicated because it relies on the international community being proactive. Prevention means strong states showing practical and moral leadership by not supporting despotic regimes, not selling vast quantities of military equipment particularly to states that have little or no interest in their citizen's human security needs, and not providing diplomatic or political support to states that abuse their own citizens. The regime in Iraq was directly and indirectly supported by many Western powers for decades prior to the first Gulf war despite its dreadful human rights record and its aggressive actions in the region. The rapid militarization of Iraq and the lack of international response to the violent activities of the Iraqi regime contributed to the Iraqi invasion of Kuwait until the very selective 'protection' of Kuwait by a UN sponsored Coalition force seemed to be the only final option. Strong states in particular have a special obligation to act responsibly in their behavior towards others. If powerful states only pay lip service or ignore entirely important international humanitarian conventions then there is little point in hectoring weaker states to change their behavior. Leadership and compassion in this area is seriously lacking.

For 'prevention' to be effective the following criticalities must be addressed: First, a reorientation from traditional state security paradigms to grass roots human security embracing R2Prevent strategies. Few can argue that in the end, and in the beginning, the best protection is prevention. Second, the international community has a moral and legal responsibility to prevent the escalation of extreme violence and serious human deprivations. This responsibility must be embraced early and directly to ameliorate human suffering. Third, serious attention to the notion of prevention before the need for protection has a greater chance of success in the reduction of serious wants and in the reduction of fear for citizens and states at risk. Fourth, the sheer waste of precious lives and the scarce resources of would be interventionists and citizens at risk alike are the usual outcomes when protection becomes a priority in desperation. A focus on prevention is future orientated and it does not rely on diplomatic or military outcomes that ultimately fail to protect those most at risk.

The prevention of conflict begins and ends with the promotion of human security and human development. However, when policy makers, researchers, and norm entrepreneurs talk about 'prevention' they usually frame the discussion through the lens of protection as the primary point of reference. The problem is that conceptualizing prevention in this way is extremely limiting. To do very little or nothing at all to ameliorate the condition of populations at risk and then to aim to instigate "preventative measures" in order to "protect" such populations when events spiral out of control does not address the wider potentiality of what prevention could and should mean. The fundamental idea of the R2Prevent approach is that human security issues must be addressed preemptively and, most importantly, before an overwhelming need for immediate protection presents itself.

Conclusion

State responsibility in the area of human security and protection remains very important but in an increasingly violent and complex world prevention must come first. The international community may occasionally directly intervene in an effort to protect those already subject to widespread and extreme levels of violence but when a situation has deteriorated to such a level then prevention efforts, if they have occurred at all, have mostly been too little and too late. A general criticism against the human security approach particularly in the area of 'prevention' is that these themes are to many people incomprehensible in a meaningful and practical sense. That is, what does human security really mean, why and how is prevention different to protection (is it different), and is the idea about prevention and all the talk about grass roots human security needs just fine words and a lot of theorising? The problem of context is a serious one and it affects both R2P and R2Prevent. What may or may not work in one area or circumstance may or may not work in another.

When critics of the prevention thesis ask the question, how can one seriously talk about prevention in places such as Afghanistan when people need immediate and direct protection from extreme violence, they are asking a valid question but the context is wrong. This is a protection question. The prevention question to ask long before an invasion and the beginning of the 10 year war should have been, how can we prevent conflict and war in Afghanistan from happening? We need to re-orientate our perceptions of what protection and prevention means to the wider human community because a myopic focus on the state-centric protection paradigm is much too limiting in our increasingly globalized world. The need for homeland protection is not in contention regarding national security matters nor is the need to prevent extremists from planning or carrying out their dreadful acts against civilians and non-combatants. We all accept the necessity for this type of protection. The problem is that limiting protection and prevention in this way is not making us safer nor is it reducing the levels of fear in many parts of the world today. Prevention must come first in an effort to pre-empt the need to protect.

REFERENCES

Abbott, Chris. 2005.'"Rights and Responsibilities: Resolving the Dilemma of Humanitarian Intervention". (Accessed 24 April, 2015). http://www.oxfordresearchgroup.org.uk/sites/default/files/rightsresponsibilities.pdf

Annan, Kofi. 1999." Two Concepts of Sovereignty" Press Release GA/9595, *The Economist*, 18 September 1999: 49-50.

Annan, Kofi. 2000. "Sustaining the Earth in the New Millennium: The UN Secretary-General Speaks Out" *Environment* 42: 20-30.

Annan, Kofi. 2000. *We the Peoples: The Role of the United Nations in the 21st Century*, 20-30. New York: United Nations.

Arbour, Louise. 2008. "The Responsibility to Protect as a Duty of Care in International Law and Practice" *Review of International Studies* 34: 445-458.

Bellamy, Alex. 2008. "Conflict Prevention and the Responsibility to Protect" *Global Governance* 14: 135-156.

Bellamy, Alex, Paul Williams, and Steward Griffin. 2010. *Understanding Peacekeeping*. Cambridge: Polity Press.

Benjamin, Dave. 2009. "Last Resort: Bridging Protection and Prevention" *International Journal on World Peace* 26: 37-62.

Carnegie Commission on Preventing Deadly Conflict. 1997. *Preventing Deadly Conflict: Final Report with Executive Summary*. Washington.

Carsten, Stahn. 2007."'Responsibility to Protect: Political Rhetoric or Emerging Legal Norm?" *The American Journal of International Law* 101: 99-120.

Chataway, Teresa. 2007. "Towards Normative Consensus on Responsibility to Protect'" *Griffith Law Review* 16: 193-224.

Crocker, Chester, Fen O. Hampson, and Pamela Aall 2007. *Leashing the Dogs of War : Conflict Management in a Divided World.*. Washington: United States Institute of Peace Press.

Dagne, Ted. 2010. *CRS Report to Congress* (RL33574) *Sudan: The Crisis in Darfur and Status of the North-South Peace Agreement*, Washington.

Danish Ministry of Foreign Affairs, 2004. *Evaluation: Humanitarian and Rehabilitation Assistance to Kosovo, 1999-2003*. Copenhagen, Denmark.

Ekiyor, Thelma, and Mary E. O'Connell. 2007. *International SEF Symposium 2007, 29-30 November*. Bonn: The Development and Peace Foundation.

Evans, Gareth, and Mohamed Sahnoun. 2001. *The Responsibility to Protect: Report of the International Commission on Intervention and State Sovereignty*. Ottawa: International Commission on Intervention and State Sovereignty.

Galbreath, David. 2008. "International Regimes and Organisations". In *Issues in International Relations*, edited by Trevor Salmon, and Mark Imber., 121-135. London ; New York: Routledge.

Gareth, Evans. 2004."'Rethinking Collective Action: The Responsibility to Protect and a Duty to Prevent" *Proceedings of the Annual Meeting of the American Society of International Law*. (Accessed 24 April, 2015) http://www.crisisgroup.org/en/publication-type/speeches/2004/the-responsibility-to-protect-rethinking-humanitarian-intervention.aspx<

Garrigues, Juan. 2007. *The Responsibility to Protect: From an Ethical Principle to an Effective Policy*. Madrid: The Fundación para las Relaciones Internacionales y el Diálogo Exterior (FRIDE).

Piiparinen, Touko. 2010. *The Transformation of UN Conflict Management: Producing Images of Genocide from Rwanda to Darfur and Beyond*. London: Routledge.

Rothschild, Emma. 1995. "What is Security?" *Daedalus* 124: 53-98.

Slaughter, Anne-Marie. 2005. "Security, Solidarity, and Sovereignty: The Grand Themes of UN Reform" *The American Journal of International Law* 99: 619-631.

Thakur, Ramesh C. 2006. *The United Nations, Peace and Security: From Collective Security to the Responsibility to Protect*. Cambridge: Cambridge University Press.

Toope, Stephen, E. Theis, J. Anaya, and H. Charlesworth. 1998. "Contemporary Conceptions of Customary International Law." *Proceedings of the 101st Annual Meeting.of the American Society of International Law* 92: 37-41.

Totten, Samuel, Paul Bartrop, and Steven Jacobs. 2008. *Dictionary of Genocide*. Westport: Greenwood Press.

UN General Assembly. 2005. A/RES/60/180 *The Peacebuilding Commission*. United Nations, 30 December, New York: United Nations.

UNHCR 1998. 'UN Doc. No. A/52/87-S/1998/318 *Report of the Secretary-General on the Work of the Organization: The Causes of Conflict and the Promotion of Durable Peace and Sustainable Development in Africa*'.

United Nations General Assembly, 1999. *Implications of International Response to Events in Rwanda, Kosovo Examined By Secretary-General, in Address to General Assembly*, Press Release GA/9595. New York: United Nations.

United Nations General Assembly. 2005. United Nations General Assembly (A/60/L.1*) 2005 World Summit Outcome*. New York: United Nations.

United Nations. 2004. *United Nations Report of the High-level Panel on Threats Challenges and Change, 2004, A more Secure World: Our Shared Responsibility*. New York: United Nations.

United Nations Security Council. 2006, *Security Council Resolution S/RES/1706 (2006). Adopted by the Security Council at its 5519th meeting, on 31 August 2006*. New York: United Nations.

United Nations Security Council. 2007. *Security Council Resolution S/RES/1769 (2007) Adopted by the Security Council at its 5727th meeting, on 31 July 2007, United Nations, 24 October*. New York: United Nations.

CHAPTER 10

Mitigating Globalization with Basic Human Rights

M. Raymond Izarali

INTRODUCTION

It need hardly be said that globalization has been quite a controversial subject and concept. But equally so, it need hardly be said that globalization has been a continuously evolving process. This is so because there are social dimensions to globalization (which may include culture, communication, internet forums, international travels, etc.) as well as economic dimensions. Following David Held (2004), we may also say there are political as well as justice related aspects to globalization, as evident in global movements for democracy and human rights and institutions like the International Criminal Court (Held 2004). Of course, there are security aspects to globalization as well (Barnett 2004). But the globalization that has dominated social and political debates in contemporary times is economic globalization.

This inference seems a reasonable one given the types of discussions, studies, and decisions taken at the United Nations and the World Bank, and from debates among key stakeholders - political units, corporations, and communities. Such debates and discussions imply that economic globalization is arguably one *key* issue to matters of social justice in the present time. That said, discussions on globalization are at times polarized, with insufficient focus given to how we may be able to harness its strengths and circumvent its harms. My aim presently is to develop an outline of a mitigated globalization by constraining the practices of corporations with some very basic human rights to protect basic human needs, in the form of a subset of a minimal ethics (a corporate code of ethics). A more developed theory would extend beyond the scope of this paper.

GLOBALIZATION: THE DEBATE

Economic globalization may be viewed as a process of integrating the economies of the world through a global system of free markets and free trade so as to establish one global union in which we may do commerce. Naturally, such a process makes for heated debates. In principle, some might see it as a positive, clear-cut matter that perhaps has some moral good. Adam Smith certainly saw, in 1776, the system of free trade as a moral and economic good when he wrote the *Wealth of Nations*; for him, it increases cooperation and interaction among nations, which, in his view, can be useful in times of disasters, and helps to dismantle local monopolies (Smith, 1819). John Stuart Mill also considered free trade as a good for the world when he wrote in his voluminous *Principles of Political Economy* that:

> ...it may be said without exaggeration that the great extent and rapid increase of international trade, in being the principal guarantee of the peace of the world, is the greatest permanent security for the uninterrupted progress of the ideas, the institutions, and the character of the human race (Mill 1961, 582).

He saw it as bringing the community of nations into greater contact, and organizing production on a global level. Mill adopted and refined David Ricardo's concept of comparative advantage, claiming that whatever allows for a greater quantity of anything to be produced in one place tends to augment the productive powers of the world (Mill 1961, 581). Thus in his memorable essay, *On Liberty*, he claims:

> ...it is now recognized, though not till after a long struggle, that both the cheapness and the good quality of commodities are most effectually provided for by leaving the producers and sellers perfectly free, under the sole check of equal freedom to the buyers for supplying themselves elsewhere. This is the so-called doctrine of "free trade," which rests on grounds different from, though equally solid with, the principle of individual liberty asserted in this essay. Restrictions on trade, or on production for purposes of trade, are indeed restraints; and all restraint, qua restraint, is an evil; but the restraints in question affect only that part of conduct which society is competent to restrain, and are wrong solely because they do not really produce the results which it is desired to produce by them (Mill 1978, 94).

These thinkers are highlighted to illustrate how far back the issue resonates. No doubt it is arguable that globalization itself, in its broadest terms, predates these thinkers.

In the contemporary context, the issue of globalization is taken up by a wide range of eminent scholars, but the issue has not been a clear-cut one. Some thinkers see globalization as an evil that threatens the dignity of human life because of the exploitation of labour that has accompanied it, the disproportionate level of harm it is said to exert on the poor, the deleterious impact it implies for the natural environment, and the political hegemony it affords to rich countries. Criminologist David Friedrichs talks about crimes of globalization in light of the structural approaches of the World Bank and other MLIs in effecting poverty and harms to communities and entire societies across the globe that impinge on their human rights (Friedrichs and Friedrichs, 2002). Crime according to him need not be understood simply as a violation of state law. According to Friedrichs, the World Bank is known to have a record for making money available to "ruthless military dictatorships (engaged in murder and torture)" and denying money to democratic regimes that are in need (Friedrichs, and Friedrichs 2002, 16). So conceived, he tells us:

> ...if the policies and practices of an international financial institution such as the World Bank result in avoidable, unnecessary harm to an identifiable population, and if these policies lead to violation of widely recognized human rights and international covenants, then crime in a meaningful sense has occurred, whether or not specific violations of international or state law are involved (Friedrichs, and Friedrichs 2002, 17).

Similar arguments have been advanced by John McMurtry, in his *Unequal Freedoms* (McMurty 1998) and his *Value Wars* (McMurty 2002).

It must be said that many of the thinkers who make such claims are not necessarily closed to the idea that globalization can have benefits; rather, many argue that certain harms are a result of the reckless and uneven manner in which globalization is carried out in practice (Giddens 1999). In their view, the global expansion of capital and free markets implies extensive freedom for transnational corporate entities. They see globalization in its current guise as, essentially, a globalization of property rights at the expense of communities, countries, and their resources and other rights. Thus, many critics argue that the global proliferation of capital is taking place at the expense of important variables to human society. Shiva, for example, sees globalization as a regime that replaces all values with commercial values (Shiva 1999). McMurtry sees globalization in its current form as an absolutist force that works exclusively for the benefit of corporations.

Proponents of globalization argue that globalization is a good way to achieve a greater range of human happiness. For them, reducing the state's involvement in the market implies more freedom for agents of the market. Thinkers in this camp are however mixed in their views. Some are more zealous about having markets and property rights free of state intervention. Libertarians such as Jan Narveson certainly champion this view, arguing that the idea of regulation is contradictory to the idea of free market. For Narveson (1988, 190), "defense of the market is defense of private property".

There are proponents, too, who argue that there is much to be gained from a globalized economy through free markets and free trade, but that this is no reason to eschew regulations or constraints. Economist Joseph Stiglitz (2002) and philosopher Thomas Pogge (2002) are two such proponents who argue that we need to approach globalization in a responsible and fair way. In other words, we should not leave moral considerations and social responsibility at the wayside in the name of economics and its attendant values as Milton Friedman would have us; rather, there are normative dimensions that should not be ignored – among them:

- serious environmental harms which in turn impact on human lives
- the struggles of poor countries;
- an acceleration of vested interests;
- the adjustment process required to transform to a different economic model; and
- exploitation of human labour and society.

Ultimately, it comes down to a question of how we address globalization.

Globalization: Defensible Aspects

From a pragmatic/pragmatist point of view, it is more plausibly said that there are some important considerations raised by both sides of the debate, and there is much room to accommodate perspectives from both poles while pushing for a more equitable form of globalization. A responsible approach certainly should consider issues raised by the various stakeholders. To begin with, a position in favour of globalization may be defended on the basis of some of its benefits. If carried out in an equitable way, the benefits *may* include:

- higher levels of employment
- alternative supply sources of goods to meet constant domestic demands
- access to a greater range of markets to purchase a broader scope of goods and services
- access to a greater range of markets to sell one's goods and services, which facilitates higher levels of income, which can increase GDP

- a broader geographical flow of technology on the basis of the transfer of technological resources, such as automated machines and computerization, that tends to accompany the movement of capital across border

It is not unreasonable to suppose that these benefits may generate benefits of other kinds through the funds that taxation on increased transactions makes possible. For example, increased economic transactions may help the state to develop infrastructures for social goods such as education, pensions, proper roads, and health care, on account of the public revenue such transactions generate. From this point of view, one can argue from a utilitarian perspective that globalization benefits human society by facilitating greater happiness for a larger number of people.

THE HARMS OF GLOBALIZATION

At the same time, it would be naïve to treat globalization as being without shortcomings or harm. As a 2004 report by the World Commission on the Social Dimensions of Globalization notes: "Global markets have grown rapidly without the parallel development of economic and social institutions necessary for their smooth and equitable functioning" (WCSDG 2004). Of course, Jean-Bertrand Aristide, former president of Haiti, certainly gave us a clear sense of the atrocious impact of globalization on the Haitian economy in his *Eyes of the Heart*; he laments the way globalization has been managed to advance the greed and gains of rich countries, notably the United States (Aristide 2000). In his view, it deepened Haiti's impoverishment.

Vandana Shiva (1999) reported cases involving reckless exporting of hazardous wastes to India and Third World countries. According to Shiva, toxic wastes – among them lead, cyanide, mercury, and arsenic – were/are shipped to India under the guise of "recyclable waste," despite the fact that India lacks both the demand and proper facilities to process such wastes (Shiva 1999, 57/58). Surely, there are other problems in the way globalization has been carried out.

The Bhopal Disaster

An amalgam of these issues have perhaps long been underscored by the Bhopal Disaster of 1984 involving the Union Carbide Corporation, where about 500,000 people were exposed to a leaked fatal gas named methyl isocyanate (MIC), resulting in over 7000 deaths and some 100,000 people who continue to suffer serious long term injuries (Eckerman 2005; Amnesty International 2004;

Morehouse, and Subramaniam 1986). Despite safety warnings from internal company audits on the need to properly service its equipment routinely according to the company's safety manual and despite complaints from employees at the Bhopal plant, the Union Carbide Corporation carried out its operations recklessly in attempt to cut costs. The safety of the workers and the community were compromised; the environment was badly contaminated, as the air was unbreathable, plants and the grass were discoloured and destroyed, and herds of cattle and other animals were likewise killed. In fact, the runaway MIC gas terminated human beings like flies, as people were fatally collapsing while rushing to the hospitals (Eckerman 2005, 85). The groundwater source remains contaminated. Bannerje describes the state of the environment at the time in Bhopal: "What was once a lush-green lawn had turned sickly yellow. It's as if someone had put a herbicide into an acetylene torch and fired it at every form of plant life there" (Banerjee 1986, 57).

The situation at the Bhopal plant was far from an isolated one. There were many smaller leaks of phosgene gas in the preceding years, where workers were seriously affected. Moreover, despite the toxicity of the chemical agents typically used at the plant in the production process, workers were often inadequately trained, some not even trained at all, to handle the materials - an aspect of cost cutting that became second-nature (Chouhan 1994). The Bhopal disaster remains the worst industrial disaster in history. At the heart of it was a gross disregard for people's basic human rights – the employees and those of the communities around the factory. For all the fatalities, pain, suffering, and destruction, Union Carbide brokered a settlement of a meagre sum of $470 million to address all constituents involved, though it never accepted legal responsibility for the tragedy (Eckerman 2005, 132).

In the current times, we see harms, though in a more subtle form, of corporate activities on communities and the natural environment in the Gulf of Mexico with the oil spill by BP Corporation. But, surely, from the time of the Bhopal disaster to now that has not been the only one.

The Search for a Middle Ground

Looked at from these angles, it must be said that there are some important concerns raised by both sides of the globalization debate that should be taken seriously. For stability and feasibility in business activities, private property must be protected. But equally so, for human flourishing and well-being, people's lives and environments must be respected and protected, even in the absence of globalization. There have been a number of philosophers who have called for caution and urged us to move in the direction of a middle ground. These thinkers include Peter Singer, Onora O'Neill, John Bishop, and Leo Groarke. Singer's (2004) *One World* addresses issues regarding the environment, genocide, the economy, and the need for us to see ourselves as a world community. He illustrates the subtle ways in which we fatally harm more people than the 9/11 tragedy through toxic exhaust emissions and other pollutants, and the ways in which adjudication of trade disputes at the WTO are slanted in favour of rich, powerful countries. In his view, globalization presents us with new challenges but with new opportunities as well, and we will not gain much by investing our energies to denounce it *ad nauseum* (Singer 2004). He claims that the outcome of globalization will ultimately depend on how we respond to globalization itself.

Onora O'Neill (2002) analyzes some of the deficiencies in existing accounts of justice in considering the idea of transnational justice and emphasizes the poverty of an account of human needs. John Bishop (2000) provides a detailed, illuminating assessment of arguments supporting and critiquing capitalism, of misconceptions of capitalism, and distinguishes the different categories of regulations. He argues that a moral capitalism will be a regulated one. Thus, if globalization can be interpreted as a global expansion of capitalism, then the only morally acceptable form is a regulated one (Bishop 2000).

Leo Groarke delineates what are good and beneficial about capitalism and some of its harms, noting that the harms could be exacerbated with globalization if capitalism is not mitigated (Groarke 2000). He highlights the benefits to its competitive nature such as lowering prices and inspiring innovation; the abundance of goods it fosters; the incentives it extends through our inherent drive to maximize our self-interests; threats to the environment; the exploitation of labour that it precipitates; and the exacerbation of the conditions of the poor. He argues that we seriously need a mitigated capitalism if capitalism is to be sustained.

Fruitful as these analyses are, none of these philosophers have outlined a plan of action that can be translated in a concrete form. An equitable form of such a plan should consider the salient elements raised by both sides of the debate and should include the most basic human elements that transcend cultural geography and wealth. This could be achieved through a subset of a general minimal ethics in the form of a corporate code of ethics to constrain the practices of corporate entities. Corporations are, in many ways, the vehicles of globalization, and at the end of the day economic globalization is tantamount to a global expansion of property rights. This claim certainly seems evident in the actions taken by the World Trade Organization. Property rights are not in and of themselves bad (for they provide the basis by which we can carry out business affairs, the way authors and inventors can claim entitlement to their own production, etc.); but property rights are too limited in scope to serve exclusively as the basis of human affairs. The social structure and people's lives encompass more than just property rights and are embedded in a wide range of human variables. Thus, a world order that emphasizes only property rights will have failed to address the human condition. With hundreds of millions of people already living on less than a dollar a day – many to be found in the 35 LDCs in sub-Saharan Africa – and with the rich developed countries enjoying about 80% of the world's wealth, a property rights regime alone will be injurious to much of the world's poor.

Property rights do not, as Groarke points out, help us to deal with people and issues who/which are not part of the market – such as the poor, orphans, children, the elderly, the environment. One might claim as libertarians do that one has property rights in oneself; but if so, such rights may also clash with the property rights of corporations, in which case we would be faced with a situation of having to determine which should override the other. One's life or community may also be undermined by an entity whose property rights give it tremendous influence over others on the basis of quantitative differences in property value. Simply put, the poor could be grossly disadvantaged by the well-off.

Basic Human Needs

What is required as a starting point for an equitable globalization is an enforced accompanying globalization of a more substantive set of rights to mitigate the globalization of property rights so as to protect people's ability to meet their basic needs. Basic human needs transcend culture and geography. Every human being has certain basic requirements such that if they are not met, he or she will be significantly diminished in organic capabilities (such as to move, think, and feel – to build on John McMurtry's work) or they may even die. We all have certain barebone requirements – need for food and water, clean air, clothing, and shelter; excretion; proper sanitation and hygiene; adequate sleep and rest; liberty of person, expression, and conscience; and security against standard threats and mental abuse. The idea is that globalization can have no moral value if it tramples on the most basic requirements that we have as human beings, particularly if globalization is meant to advance the human condition. Being able to meet basic needs is a first-principle in exercising self-determination, for as Will Kymlicka points out, contrary to the libertarians, self-determination extends beyond the scope of mere self-ownership (Kymlicka 1990).

Without food and water people's lives would be compromised to the point of biological demise. Without adequate clothing and shelter to guard against nature's elements, one's life could be seriously imperilled. Inhalation of poor quality of air on a continual basis could result in respiratory harms and death. Not having the freedom and proper environment to excrete the body's natural waste could induce severe harms to the body. Lack of adequate sleep and rest could make one seriously dysfunctional at a mental level in a way that critically affects one's cognitive abilities and one's ability to have a sound quality of life, a concern which had preoccupied Marx in his discussion on alienation. Human beings after all are not designed to function like robots.

Liberty of person, expression, and conscience are essential needs for one to live as a person free of bondage and slavery, to exercise that freedom in expressing discontent or satisfaction among other things, and to live in accordance with one's understanding of the metaphysics of one's being (for a great many people see their existence and path to the good as determined by God whereas others see their existence as stemming from other factors). The lack of liberty of conscience could seriously impair one's organic abilities, as in the case of many Aboriginal elders in Canada who are still struggling to overcome their experience in Canadian residential schools, wherein the Canadian Government tried to forcibly Christianize them and rid them of their Indiannes at a mental level; a European conception of life and education was forced upon them as the good life [1], something not unlike the experience of many people who were colonized in Africa, the West Indies, and elsewhere. In significant ways, the need for these types of liberties distinguish us as a species, something which John Rawls recognizes and treats as "urgent rights" we must have to them (Rawls 1999). In fact, in Rawls' view, people need a certain/sufficient degree of freedom of conscience, thought, and religion.

The need to prevent the spread of disease is an epidemiological one, for harmful disease can itself debilitate one's ability to meet other basic needs and could be fatal. Bodily excretion is inherent to living creatures and in the case of the human species, human feces and urine can be fertile elements for disease, from the stench and harmful bacteria and through contamination of our consumption goods like water (as was evident in the cholera outbreak in Zimbabwe recently). Given this consideration, there is a need for proper hygiene and sanitation. This need is both an individual and a public health issue.

The need for security against what Henry Shue (1980) calls "standard threats," to which I add mental abuse, is critical like the other needs. Standard threats include rape, assault, and murder, concerns that pervade all human societies. In fact, as Hobbes has painstakingly pointed out, there is an individual and a social aspect to it. We are social creatures as human beings and without

---

[1] Annett, Lawless, and O'Rorke, *Unrepentant: Kevin Annett and Canada's Genocide*, Documentary, 2006.

adequate safety for one's person, one's property, and one's family, one's ability to interact will depend on muscles, might, and our inventory of armaments. The strong would be able to exercise some liberty while the not-so-strong would be in a kind of open incarceration. Human well-being would be undermined and social progress would come to a halt. As Hobbes (1992, 89) puts it:

> Whatsoever therefore is consequent to a time of Warre, where every man is Enemy to every man; the same is consequent to the time, wherein men live without other security, than what their own strength, and their own invention shall furnish them withal. In such condition, there is no place for Industry; because the fruit thereof is uncertain; and consequently no Culture of the Earth; no Navigation, nor use of the commodities that may be imported by Sea; no commodious Building; no Instruments of moving and removing such things as require much force; no Knowledge of the face of the Earth; no account of Time; no Arts; no Letters; no Society; and which is worst of all, continually fear, and danger of violent death...

The need for security against standard threats is thus vital for human flourishing. In a similar way, the need for security against mental abuse is essential, as mental health defines the soundness of one's quality of life and one's ability to attain self-actualization. Safeguards are thus required to militate against a life of mental abuse by others.

The needs outlined above do not exhaust the full scope of human needs, but they capture the barebones as are relevant to individuals and corporate entities. One can outline a host of other needs such as education, health care, social assistance to the poor, and companionship, but it is not clear that such elements are enforceable on corporations. They would appropriately align with a more general minimal ethics. While they are important, we must be cautious not to generate too long a list as a starting point, since one of the goals is to get corporate entities to accept and enforce the subset proferred.

The concept of need is perhaps best identified in a formulaic form advanced by John McMurtry (1998, 164), namely: "N is a need if and only if, and to the extent that, deprivation of N always leads to a reduction of organic capability". By organic capabilities McMurtry has in mind one's ability to move, think and feel. Certainly there are more needs that could be outlined from what I have listed, and Martha Nussbaum's (1992) "*Human Functioning and Social Justice*" and David Braybrooke's (1987) *Meeting Needs* are excellent in outlining various categories of human needs. Nussbaum's philosophical outline of the human form of life elucidates with majestic clarity the nature and needs of human beings as social, sentient beings with rational capacities. As I am concerned with developing only a subset of a minimal ethics, I focus on the most basic needs from what they have outlined.

BASIC HUMAN RIGHTS

The question now is how do we protect these basic needs. There are some options such as the Capability Approach advanced by Amartya Sen (1993), but for practical purposes, there seems to be more value in a rights-based approach, specifically human rights, to constrain the practices of corporate entities to respect basic human values. The Capability Approach is useful in a number of respects and can attend to micro matters in different contexts in enabling people with better functionality; but it also has limitations in that it is difficult to apply and manage in broad settings. A rights-based approach has normative weight, is enforceable, and can be broadly applied, particularly since human rights have broad appeal in contemporary times. Rights themselves, and claim-rights (Becker 1982) in particular, can be seen as justifiable moral demands we may make of others, to use the language of Henry Shue (1980). That is, claim-rights have correlative duties in that others have a duty to respect my rights (Orend 2002). Moreover, a human rights approach in the form of an enforced corporate code of ethics allows us a basis to integrate corporate entities with basic human values that transcend culture and geography. Certainly that is what the Universal Declaration of Human Rights was meant to be; the power exercised by corporate entities were, as Sumner B. Twiss (2004) tells us, not envisioned by the architects of the human rights instruments. Human rights capture the core elements of morality and human happiness; this characteristic is evident in struggles throughout history to have such contents/objects respected as fundamental elements to human life (Ishay 2004; Sen 1997). Some that are vague may be debated, but others that are basic and essential may not.

We need to derive a concrete set of basic rights that can address the basic needs outlined above, and to enforce them on the basis of a principle of "non-interference," as a starting point. That is, one is not asking that corporate entities provide food, shelter and the sort to people but that the activities of corporate entities ought not to violate or undermine people's ability to achieve them. Thus corporate entities have to be accountable to at least a set of basic human rights. Such a set of rights can be arrived at through a concrete interpretation of particular Articles of the Universal Declaration of Human Rights (UDHR) – namely, Articles 3,4,5,10, 18, 19, 23(3), and 24. The list of needs I argue for to protect from the infringement of capital are:

A List of Concrete Basic Human Needs

- Need for adequate food, clean drinking water, clean air, clothing, and shelter
- Need to excrete
- Need for proper sanitation and hygiene to prevent harm from the outbreak and spread of disease
- Need for adequate sleep and rest
- Need for liberty of person (i.e., freedom from slavery and bondage), expression, and conscience
- Need for security against standard threats and mental abuse

The list of basic rights that can protect them are:

A List of Concrete Basic Human Rights

1. Everyone has the right to food, shelter, clean drinking water, and clean air.
2. Everyone has the right to proper excretion.
3. Everyone has the right to proper sanitation and hygiene.
4. Everyone has the right to adequate sleep and rest.
5. Everyone has the right to liberty of person, expression, and conscience.
6. Everyone has the right to humane treatment and freedom from harm.
7. Everyone has the right to a living wage in their employment.
8. Everyone has the right of full equality to due process and fair adjudication in addressing grievances and defending their character against allegations.

The particular articles from the Universal Declaration of Human Rights (UDHR) from which the set of basic rights above have been derived are:

Article 3

Everyone has the right to life, liberty and security of person.

Article 4

No one shall be held in slavery or servitude; slavery and the slave trade shall be prohibited in all their forms.

Article 5

No one shall be subjected to torture or to cruel, inhuman or degrading treatment or punishment.

Article 10

Everyone is entitled in full equality to a fair and public hearing by an independent and impartial tribunal, in the determination of his rights and obligations and of any criminal charge against him.

Article 18

Everyone has the right to freedom of thought, conscience, and religion; this right includes freedom to change his religion or belief, and freedom, either alone or in community with others and in public or private, to manifest his religion or belief in teaching, practice, worship and observance.

Article 19

Everyone has the right to freedom of opinion and expression; this right includes freedom to hold opinions without interference and to seek, receive and impart information and ideas through any media and regardless of frontiers.

Article 23(3)

Everyone who works has the right to just and favourable remuneration ensuring for himself and his family an existence worthy of human dignity, and supplemented, if necessary, by other means of social protection.

Article 24

Everyone has the right to rest and leisure, including reasonable limitation of working hours and periodic holidays with pay.

What I have essentially done is concretely interpret the basic human rights I have outlined previously from the specific articles of the UDHR just noted, in a way that the specific articles may be understood and put in practice on the ground. It may draw some attention that I have enumerated six sets of basic needs and eight sets of basic rights. Enumeration seven emphasizes the right to a living wage and eight emphasizes procedural justice. These rights are vital if the subset of a minimal ethics is to have value. For example, the right to food and other necessities are immaterial if one works for a daily wage that cannot even purchase a basic meal. Similarly, the preceding rights outlined will have little value if there is not a mechanism to address violations of the rights. A mechanism for conflict resolution is necessary in other words. Such rights are important in so far as they are part of a body of rights designed to achieve a certain goal. Of course, there may be criticisms focusing on the relative nature of a living wage from one society to another. This need not be an issue, since what is crucial is comparing one's wage with the cost of living in one's society and indices associated with the basics to enjoy a minimally decent life.

Conclusion

There has been much debate about the value of globalization and whose interests it benefits. Ardent proponents take a laissez-faire approach while more broadly focused proponents argue for a responsible and fair approach. Critics may be discouraged by the perils they see implied in globalization and thus argue that it has been carried out in a one-sided manner that benefits the rich developed countries. Polarities in positions taken on globalization overlook the prospect of mitigating globalization in such a way to secure its benefits and circumvent its harms. This paper has argued that, as a starting point, a mitigated globalization could be achieved through a subset of a minimal ethics that applies basic human rights to protect basic human needs. Basic human needs transcend human geography and culture and must be met before one can entertain any conception of the good life. Applying basic human rights derived from the Universal Declaration of Human Rights is an effective way to protect such needs, as human rights have universal currency, normative weight, and are enforceable in broad settings.

References

Amnesty International. 2004."Clouds of Injustice: Bhopal Disaster 20 Years On – Summary," *Amnesty International Report ASA 20/015/2004.*

Annett, Kevin, Louie Lawless, and Lori O'Rorke. 2007. *Unrepentant: Kevin Annett and Canada's Genocide.* Documentary, directed by Louie Lawless, and Annett-Lawless.
(Accessed at www.hiddenfromhistory.org)

Aristide, Jean-Bertrand. 2000. *Eyes of the Heart: Seeking a Path for the Poor in the Age of Globalization*, edited by Laura Flynn. Monroe, ME: Common Courage Press.

Banerjee, Brojendra Nath. 1986. *Bhopal Gas Tragedy: Accident or Experiment.* New Delhi: Paribus.

Barnett, Thomas P.M. 2004. *The Pentagon's New Map: War and Peace in the Twenty-first Century*. New York: G.P. Putnam's Sons.

Becker, Lawrence C. 1982. "Individual Rights." In *And Justice for All*, edited by Tom Regan and Donald Van DeVeer, 197-216. New Jersey: Rowman & Allanheld.

Bishop, John Douglas. 2000. "Ethics and Capitalism: A Guide to the Issues." In *Ethics and Capitalism*, edited by John Douglas Bishop, 3- 48. Toronto: University of Toronto Press.

Braybrooke, David. 1987. *Meeting Needs*. Princeton: Princeton University Press.

Chouhan, T.R. 1994. *Bhopal: The Inside Story. Carbide Workers Speak Out on the World's Worst Industrial Disaster*. New York: The Apex Press.

Eckerman, Ingrid. 2005. *The Bhopal Saga: Causes and Consequences of the World's Largest Industrial Disaster*. Hyderabad: Universities Press.

Friedrichs, David O., and Jesica Friedrichs. 2002. "The World Bank and Crimes of Globalization: A Case Study." *Social Justice,* 29: 13-36.

Giddens, Anthony. 1999. *Runaway World*. London: Profile Books.

Groarke, Leo. 2000. "Can Capitalism Save Itself: Some Ruminations on the Fate of Capitalism." In *Ethics and Capitalism*, edited by John Douglas Bishop, 196-217. Toronto: University of Toronto Press.

Held, David. 2004. *Global Covenant: The Social Democratic Alternative to the Washington Consensus*. Cambridge: Polity Press.

Hobbes, Thomas. 1992. *Leviathan*. Edited by Richard Tuck. New York: Cambridge University Press.

Ishay, Micheline R., ed. 2004. *The History of Human Rights: From Ancient Times to the Globalization Era*. Los Angeles: University of California Press.

Kymlicka, Will. 1990. *Contemporary Political Philosophy: An Introduction*. Oxford: Clarendon Press.

McMurtry, John. 1998. *Unequal Freedoms: The Global Market as an Ethical System*. Toronto: Garamond Press.

McMurtry, John..2002. *Value Wars: The Global Market Versus the Life Economy*. London: Pluto.

Mill, John Stuart. 1978 [orig. 1848]. *On Liberty*. Indianapolis: Hackett Publishing.

Mill, John Stuart. 1961 [orig. 1848]. *Principles of Political Economy With Some of Their Applications to Social Philosophy,* edited by Sir W.J. Ashley. New York: Augustus M. Kelley.

Morehouse, Ward, and M. Arun Subramaniam. 1986. *The Bhopal Tragedy: What Really Happened and What it Means for American Workers and Communities at Risk.* New York: Council on International and Public Affairs.

Narveson, Jan. 1988. *The Libertarian Idea.* Philadelphia: Temple University Press.

Nussbaum, Martha. 1992. "Human Functioning and Social Justice: In Defense of Aristotelian Essentialism." *Political Theory* 20: 202-246.

O'Neill, Onora. *Bounds of Justice.* 2002. New York: Cambridge University Press.

Orend, Brian. 2002. *Human Rights: Concept and Context.* Peterborough: Broadview.

Pogge, Thomas. 2002. *World Poverty and Human Rights.* Cambridge: Polity.

Rawls, John. 1999. *The Law of Peoples.* Cambridge: Harvard University Press.

Sen, Amartya. 1993. "Capability and Well-Being." In *The Quality of Life*, edited by Amartya Sen, and Martha Nussbaum, 30-53. Oxford: Oxford University Press.

Sen, Amartya. 1997. "Human Rights and Asian Values." Sixteenth Morganthau Memorial Lecture on Ethics & Foreign Policy. New York: Carnegie Council on Ethics and Public Affairs, 1997. Available online at: http://www.cceia.org/media/254/_sen.pdf (Accessed 9 September, 2008).

Shiva, Vandana. 1999. "Ecological Balance in an Era of Globalization." In *Global Ethics & Environment*, edited by Nicholas Low, 47-69. London: Routledge.

Shiva, Vandana. 1999. "Food Rights, Free Trade and Fascism." In *Globalizing Rights: The Oxford Amnesty Lectures 1999*, edited by Matthew J. Gibney, 87-108. Oxford: Oxford University Press.

Shue, Henry. 1980. *Basic Rights.* Princeton: Princeton University Press.

Singer, Peter. 2004. *One World: The Ethics of Globalization.* New Haven: Yale University Press.

Smith, Adam. 1819. *An Inquiry Into the Nature and Causes of the Wealth of Nations*, edited by J.R. M'Culloch. Edinburgh: Stirling and Slade.

Stiglitz, Joseph. 2002. *Globalization and its Discontents.* London: W.W. Norton & Company.

Stiglitz, Joseph. 2008. "Making Globalization Work – The 2006 Geary Lecture." *The Economic and Social Review* 39: 171-190.

Twiss, Sumner B. 2004. "History, Human Rights, and Globalization." *Journal of Religious Ethics* 32 (1): 39-70.

World Commission on the Social Dimension of Globalization (WCSDG). 2004. *A Fair Globalization: Creating Opportunities for All*. Geneva: International Labour Organization (ILO).

CHAPTER 11

Accountants and Human Rights: Extending the Boundaries of Accountability

Susan Wild & Edwin Mares

INTRODUCTION

Accounting as a practice is integral to all aspects of business operations, and in recent decades has facilitated the rapid expansion of multinational corporations and international trade and commerce. With the growth of globalized business, the negative impacts of corporate activity on human rights, particularly in developing countries, has become a significant concern for governmental regulatory bodies, legal representatives, non-governmental organizations and other civil society groups (see, for example: Ruggie, 2006-2010; Human Rights Watch; Clapham, 2008; UNDP, 2009).

Traditionally, the accounting profession has claimed that its practice represents a set of technical and specialist skills that are ethically and politically neutral, and that are conducted in the public interest (refer, for example, to the International Federation of Accountants (IFAC) Code of Ethics for Professional Accountants). However, while the ethical codes of the international accounting bodies studied in this paper include references to members' obligations to observe specific rights of particular groups (in particular, property rights of clients and employers) they contain no reference to members' responsibilities regarding human rights observance.

While there exists a significant literature on the role of state governments in protecting human rights, and on the international legal aspects of human rights protection, there is little on the responsibility of the accounting profession in regard to the human rights obligations of its members. This paper considers essential issues underlying questions pertaining to the appropriate role of the accounting profession, and to the nature and extent of the profession's accountability to society in general. It contributes towards addressing the present gap in the literature relating accounting practice to issues of human rights.

BACKGROUND: INTERNATIONAL HUMAN RIGHTS AND GLOBAL BUSINESS

The modern concept of specific and enforceable international human rights was established in the 1945 United Nations Charter, and reinforced in subsequent decades in a range of international declarations, treaties, covenants and conventions. In 2000, the United Nations Global Compact (GC) was established with the aim of aligning corporate values with the GC's policies of social and environmental responsibility, including its human rights principles. Membership of the GC comprises governments, national and multinational corporations, labour organizations and civil society groups. The GC's stated aim is to encourage the adoption of sustainable and socially responsible business practices, with its key objectives set out in its 'Ten Principles', including to 'support and respect the protection of internationally proclaimed human rights' (GC website).

A series of recent reports commissioned by the United Nations Human Rights Council (UNHRC) - the 'Ruggie' Reports[1] - address the problematic issue of human rights observance by transnational corporations and other business enterprises, and aim to establish a framework for addressing corporate human rights abuses.[2] The first of the reports[3] assessed the nature and extent of the problem, and established the project's terms of reference and methodologies. In March 2007 the second report was presented to the Council's General Assembly on the subject of business and human rights.[4] A supplementary report in the following year focused further on the establishment of an international policy framework for the achievement of such human rights goals. The most recent reports, presented in 2009 and 2010, outline detailed strategies for achieving Ruggie's business and human rights goals and objectives in the medium term.[5]

The reports express concerns as to the extent of 'social harms caused by markets',[6] in particular the 'costs [imposed] on people and communities – including corporate-related human rights abuses' resulting largely from increasing globalization. While recognizing that state governments bear primary responsibility for ensuring human rights observance within national borders, the reports emphasize that governments 'need to be joined by other social actors and

---

[1] Named after the John Ruggie, the central author of the reports, as a special representative to the UNHRC.

[2] Ruggie (2007), Introduction, 3.

[3] Ruggie (2006)

[4] Ruggie (2007)

[5] Ruggie (2009, 2010)

[6] Ruggie (2007), Section 1.

to utilize other social institutions to achieve this goal … within their sphere of influence'[7].

Professional accounting bodies exert significant authority within the milieu of business and commercial activity both nationally and internationally. All exhort their members to uphold a high level of ethical conduct in their practice and mandate a requirement to 'serve the public interest', as proclaimed in their various published documents including codes of ethics and rules of professional conduct.[8]

However, an analysis of the text of these publicly available documents, reveals that there exists in their scope significant limitations as to the responsibilities of the accounting profession regarding its wider obligations towards the wellbeing of the society within which it operates, particularly as to its members' relationship of influence over the ethical conduct of clients. Within these documents the term 'public interest' commonly limits members' ethical responsibilities only to specific stakeholders within a narrow range of commercial interests, so as to exclude any obligation of accountability towards wider society. The documents also very narrowly define the concept 'ethical conduct', generally limiting this to specific issues of malfeasance. Some accounting bodies, at most, impose upon their members only a minimal obligation to comply with 'relevant laws and regulations and avoid any action that may bring discredit to the profession'.[9]

UN 'Ruggie Reports' and the Global Compact

Since the affirmation in 1948 of the United Nations Universal Declaration of Human Rights (UDHR) and the subsequent adoption of an array of other international treaties and conventions focused on issues of human rights and sustainability of the natural environment, there has been a growing acceptance among nations and civil society groups of a range of legally enforceable standards for individual accountability in regard to these globally important ethical issues. Over recent decades this development has extended further into expectations of higher standards of ethical conduct in regard to corporate responsibility and greater business accountability in relation to national and international crimes and civil violations,[10] including those of complicity.[11]

---

[7] Ibid, Section 4.

[8] Refer to list of organizations in appendix.

[9] IFAC Code of Ethics for Professional Accountants, Section 150.

[10] Ruggie (2007), Section 33.

[11] Defined in Ruggie (2008), Sections 73-81.

In response to increasing public concern regarding the nature and extent of human rights abuses by business entities, and to new complexities confronting states in regard to their 'duty to protect',[12] resulting largely from a substantial increase of globalized business operations, the UN Human Rights Council (UNHRC) commissioned the series of 'Ruggie' reports to assess the scope of the problem and to propose potential solutions.

The reports assert that a framework of enforceable legal rules in a regulated society is an essential precondition for the efficient and sustainable operation of the market, both in national and international contexts, and, further, that these rules include those relating to observance of human rights[13]. The reports further assert that among the institutional parameters generally assumed to be essential for the operation of a successful market is included the ethical necessity of 'curtailing individual and social harms imposed by markets', due to their potential to create inefficiencies in the market which may become 'socially unsustainable' in the long-term.

The 2007 Ruggie report, Business and Human Rights: Mapping International Standards of Responsibility and Accountability for Corporate Acts, provides an analysis of the 'standards and practices governing corporate "responsibility" (the legal, social, or moral obligations imposed on companies) and "accountability" (the mechanisms holding them to these obligations)'. It considers the effectiveness of existing structures for constraining business behaviour, from 'the most deeply rooted international legal obligations [to] voluntary business standards'. The particular areas under examination within the reports' terms include 'corporate responsibility and accountability for international crimes', and 'corporate responsibility for other human rights violations under international law'. [14]

A significant general observation is made that, regardless of the nature of particular business entities, their governance and ownership structures, industry area, or the geographical location of their operations, there exists a

> fundamental institutional misalignment ... present between the scope and impact of economic forces and actors, on the one hand, and the capacity of societies to manage their adverse consequences on the other. This misalignment creates the permissive environment within which blameworthy acts by corporations may occur without adequate

---

[12] Ruggie (2007), Section 10.

[13] Ibid.

[14] Ibid, p4.

> sanctioning or reparation. For the sake of the victims of abuse, and to sustain globalization as a positive force, this must be fixed. [15]

Ruggie asserts, in a consideration of the nature and extent of corporate accountability for human rights practices, and of a general duty to comply with the UN's directives in this regard, that 'the baseline responsibility of companies is to respect human rights … [i]n addition to compliance with national laws'. [16] Further, 'the broader scope of the responsibility to respect is defined by social expectations – as part of … a company's social licence to operate … [and] exists independently of States' duties'.[17]

THE CODES OF ETHICS OF THE PROFESSIONAL ACCOUNTING BODIES

Accounting bodies, which are supported in many countries by the force of law, enable, control and endorse the activities of their members through a range of mechanisms, including the application of technical and other standards, but also through the imposition of their ethical codes (which assume the role of guiding rules of professional conduct). These codes have mandatory status for members, and outline the ideals of the profession.

However, an analysis of the public codes of ethics of all the major European-oriented accounting bodies internationally reveals a significant ethical gap in the doctrines encompassed within the codes, in that they make no reference to human rights issues. In every case the codes evidence within their texts only a very narrowly-defined interpretation of ethical concepts, and specify only a very limited group of stakeholders towards whom responsibility and accountability are requisite.

A common feature of the public assertions of professional accounting bodies internationally is the uniformity in their proclamations as to their adherence to and promotion of high ethical status, evidencing this with a codified set of ethical requirements to which adherence is mandatory for their membership, and which are publicly available as an integral part of their promotional literature. [18] All provide details of disciplinary procedures which may be invoked for breaches of the conduct standards specified in the codes. Most of the national accounting bodies have aligned the content of their own codes of conduct (or equivalent

---

[15] Ibid, Section 3.

[16] Ibid, 2007, 55.

[17] Ruggie (2008), Section 54.

[18] See for example the websites of IFAC, NZICA, et al.

documents) with that promulgated in the Code of Ethics for Professional Accountants of the International Federation of Accountants (IFAC).

An analysis of the ethical codes of all the major accounting bodies internationally, including that of IFAC, reveals, however, that, none includes within its description of specifications for compliance with the requirements for ethical conduct of its members any reference to human rights obligations (nor towards other matters of international ethical concern such as environmental issues). In addition, none refers to any matter of ethical obligation towards society in general.

New Zealand Institute of Chartered Accountants (NZICA) Code of Ethics

The published ethical code of the New Zealand Institute of Chartered Accountants (NZICA) is typical in its text and basic principles of those of the other major accounting bodies internationally. NZICA's currently applicable Code of Ethics, which was effective from 1 July 2003 (with amendments effective from October 2006 in accordance with revisions to the IFAC Code), is prescribed by the Institute's Council as being binding on all its members. The Code has legislative force pursuant to Section 7 of the Institute of Chartered Accountants of New Zealand Act 1996, and contains within its parameters specifications for the enforcement of its observation, and disciplinary procedures for non-compliance.

The New Zealand Code confirms that it is based closely upon the promulgations of the IFAC Code, and states that it is comparable also with the Australian Certified Practising Accountants (CPA) Code of Professional Conduct (CPC), so that '[t]he fundamental principles in all three codes are identical'. The New Zealand Code therefore 'is consistent in all material respects with the IFAC Code and the CPC', and it is further asserted that in relation to the former, the New Zealand Code 'is substantially different in structure but not content ...'[19] Common to all the codes is that they 'outline the objectives of the accountancy profession and the four basic needs (credibility, professionalism, quality of services and confidence) to be met by the accountancy profession in order to meet the objectives identified' [20]. A substantive difference between the texts of the documents in that while the NZICA Code specifies and delimits in its Section 16 the particular groups that fall within its purview of those comprising the 'public interest', the IFAC Code does not.

---

[19] NZ Institute of Chartered Accountants, Code of Ethics, Appendix 3, p55.

[20] Ibid.

The NZICA Code states inter alia that it is 'based on a number of Fundamental Principles that express the basic tenets of ethical and professional behaviour and conduct' to which all members must abide 'at all times'. The Code avers that '[o]bservance of these Fundamental Principles is central to the public interest'.[21]

Section 15 of the Code further defines 'the public interest' as comprising 'the collective wellbeing of the community of people and institutions the profession serves'. However, the Code then further delimits the scope of this section by defining the 'accountancy profession's public' as being restricted to that group encompassed within 'clients, governments, employers, employees, investors, creditors, the business and financial community, and others who rely on the Objectivity and Integrity of members for sound financial accounting and reporting, effective financial management and competent advice on a variety of business and taxations matters'. The Code, therefore, requires of accountants no general obligation in regard to ethical conduct, including human rights observance, that is extended towards the wider social environment within which the profession and its client or employing organizations operate.

The five Fundamental Principles of the NZICA Code are specified as those that 'express the basic tenets of ethical and professional behaviour and conduct' for accountants, comprising qualities of 'Integrity', 'Objectivity and Independence', Competence', 'Quality Performance', and 'Professional Behaviour'.[22] These qualities are further defined, so that beyond the mere application of essential skills and professional competence, 'integrity' is required in 'all professional and business relationships', and this 'implies not merely honesty but fair dealing and truthfulness'; members must at all times be 'fair, impartial and intellectually honest, and must not allow prejudice or bias, conflict of interest or influence of others to override Objectivity'; further, the duty of members to demonstrate 'professional behaviour' requires that they must 'act in a manner consistent with the good reputation of the profession and refrain form any conduct which might bring discredit to the profession'. While leaving open a definition of what activities may constitute 'discredit' in this context, the Code does acknowledge in Section 7 that 'public opinion' may be a contributory factor in its determination. This requirement falls well short of any requirement for members to proactively influence and support ethical conduct, including human rights observance, in their client entities, and is justificatory rather than exhortatory in its emphasis.

---

[21] Ibid, 3.

[22] Ibid, 3.

The Code asserts that 'Integrity' is a 'quality of overriding importance for all members' and 'implies not merely honesty but fair dealing and truthfulness'; it is this quality of 'integrity' that 'allows the public to derive their trust in the accountancy profession'. In addition to proscribing dishonesty and 'deceit', the quality of integrity 'cannot accommodate ... subordination of principles, values and standards'. Essentially, 'Integrity is measured in terms of what is right or just'.[23] However, the observance of this quality of 'integrity' in the accountant's professional dealings is restricted in scope so as to demarcate its applicability only towards those specified within the Code's limited definition of 'public interest', and not beyond those interest groups, suggesting that members have no further accountability towards others upon whom the activities of the member or the member's client organization might impact.[24]

The Code suggests only a minor extension of this restriction pertaining to 'professional conduct', in its Rule 14 edict that members 'must conduct themselves with courtesy and consideration towards all they come into contact with during their professional work, including clients, other members, employers, staff, third parties and the general public', although again the Code does not define the extent of those to be included in this latter group. When considering the 'application of the rules', the Code's Section 23 directs that members 'do not lend their names or their professional status to an enterprise which ... may bring discredit to those associated with the enterprise.'

In the outline of the 'applicability of the code of ethics' set out in its Appendix 1, there is some consideration of 'members' responsibility for the conduct of others'. However, this responsibility is limited to 'persons associated with the member in the practice of Chartered Accountancy, who are either under the member's supervision or are the member's partners or fellow directors in a corporate practice'[25] and extends to no further parties. With regard to a member's obligations for ethical conduct for 'services outside New Zealand', the member is required to observe at the 'strictest' level, the 'relevant ethical requirements' of '(a) the International Federation of Accountants' (IFAC) Code of Ethics; (b) the ethical requirements of the country in which the work is being performed; and (c) the Institute's Code of Ethics'.[26]

In the case where a member is unable to comply with the Code's requirements to uphold its required standards of ethical conduct, the accountant is required to disengage from the client entity. The provides that where a member is

---

[23] Ibid, Section 16.

[24] Ibid, Section 15.

[25] Ibid, Appendix 1, Section 4.

[26] Ibid, Appendix 1, Section 6.

confronted with 'threats to compliance with the Fundamental Principles' emanating from 'the nature of engagements and work assignments', so that the member's ability to act with 'Integrity' may be compromised, the member 'should decline or discontinue the specific professional service involved, or ... resign from the client or the employing organization'. [27]

The New Zealand Code, in common with its IFAC parent document, requires of its member accountants no general obligation in regard to ethical conduct, including human rights observance, towards the wider social environment within which the profession and its client organizations or employers operate. As in the case of the IFAC Code, and in the equivalent documents of all the other national and international accounting bodies included in this analysis, no reference is made in the New Zealand Code to any general ethical responsibility or obligation, such as those regarding human rights observance; nor does it specify any ethical obligation towards any societal group other than those specifically identified within the Code's terms.

There is, for example, no reference in the text of the NZICA Code to any commitment towards members' obligations regarding the rights of New Zealand's indigenous Māori people encompassed within the scope of the Treaty of Waitangi. These rights were initially established in 1840 in the text of the Treaty between representatives of the major Māori tribes and of the British Crown, and subsequently ratified in legislation in the Treaty of Waitangi Act 1975.[28] They are further supported by international agreements on the rights of indigenous peoples, including the UN Declaration on the Rights of Minorities (1992). While the NZICA Code makes no reference to the obligations of the Treaty of Waitangi, these rights are specifically noted in the ethical codes of a number of other professions in New Zealand.[29]

CONCLUSIONS

A responsibility for the accountancy profession to promote the observance of human rights obligations, nationally and globally, both in the practice of its own discipline and in that of the individuals and entities falling within its 'sphere of influence', is located in the general requirement for 'social institutions' (as

---

[27] Ibid, Section 10A.

[28] A copy of the text (in both English and Māori languages) of the Treaty of Waitangi, and a description of its scope, legal effects and application, is located at the Waitangi Tribunal website.

[29] See, for example, the ethical codes of the Royal Society of New Zealand (RSNZ), and the Institute of Professional Engineers New Zealand (IPENZ).

outlined in the Ruggie Reports) to comply with the terms of the United Nations Universal Declaration of Human Rights (UDHR). Such an obligation, however, also exists within the general consequentialist ethical requirement for professions to act in the public interest, in order that they maintain their social legitimacy.

The series of 'Ruggie Reports' to the United Nations Human Rights Council address the current problematic issue of failures in human rights observance by transnational corporations and other business enterprises.[30] The reports emphasize that in order to mitigate the 'social harms caused by markets'[31], in particular 'corporate-related human rights abuses' deemed to result largely from increasing globalization, '[governments] need to be joined by other social actors and to utilize other social institutions to achieve this goal ... within their "sphere of influence"'[32]. This definition therefore encompasses the professional accounting bodies within its range.

Developments in international human rights law since the mid-twentieth century have extended the scope of responsibilities well beyond a focus on national governments, so as to encompass other entities including national and multi-national corporations, other social institutions, and individuals. These developments have significant potential litigation risk implications for accountants, particularly in their roles as agents and advisors for corporations engaged in a range of global trade and commerce, as well as ethical implications.

The professional status of accounting bodies accords them extensive powers to influence, direct and control business activity. Such status also imposes major obligations to utilize those powers in the service of the wider society which accords them their legitimacy. The codes of ethics of the professional accounting bodies establish guidelines as to the expectations and requirements of those bodies regarding notions of 'ethical conduct' and the 'public interest'. However, in their present form, none of those bodies sets minimum standards regarding the expectations they hold regarding their members' obligations in regard to human rights obligations. A particular deficit exists in regard to the codes of ethics of the professional accounting bodies based in those nations with a colonial history, in that they make no reference to members' ethical obligations towards the specific human rights pertaining to their indigenous peoples.

While all the accounting bodies overtly exhort their members to maintain a high level of ethical conduct in their practice and mandate a requirement to 'serve the public interest', as proclaimed in their published codes of ethics or rules of professional conduct, an analysis of these publicly available documents reveals

---

[30] Ruggie Report 2007, Introduction, 3

[31] Ibid, Section 1.

[32] Ibid, Section 4.

that the term 'public interest' is commonly limited to specific stakeholders, so as to exclude any accountability towards wider societal groups. The documents also very narrowly define the concept 'ethical conduct', limiting the scope of the term to specific acts and responsibilities towards specified parties. At most, the accounting bodies impose a minimum obligation on their members to comply with 'relevant laws and regulations and avoid any action that may bring discredit to the profession'.[33]

This very constrained interpretation of ethical responsibilities strongly contrasts with that of some other professional bodies, including those of engineers, architects, scientists, doctors, and lawyers, all of which promote generally a much wider perspective of their obligations towards the society within which they operate, and a significantly more extensive set of accountabilities for their members.

It is the conclusion of this paper that the professional accounting bodies are included within the compass of the Ruggie Reports' terms 'relevant actors' and 'other social institutions', upon which particular responsibilities for human rights obligations are imposed. Further, the paper concludes that these bodies should proactively extend their role in influencing and promoting improved corporate behaviours towards human rights observance through the medium of extending the requirements of their mandated codes of ethical conduct for their members.

REFERENCES

American Institute of Certified Public Accountants website. Retrieved 5 January 2009, from http://www.aicpa.org/about/code/index.html

Association of Chartered Certified Accountants website. Retrieved 7 January 2009, from http://www.accaglobal.com/

Business & Human Rights Resource Centre, accessible at http://www.business-humanrights.org/Gettingstarted/UNSpecialRepresentative

Clapham, Andrew. 2008. "Extending International Criminal Law beyond the Individual to Corporations and Armed Opposition Groups" *Journal of International Criminal Justice* 6: 899-926

CPA Australia, *Code of Ethics for Professional Accountants*. Retrieved 12 January 2009, from http://www.cpaaustralia.com.au/cps/rde/xchg/cpa/hs.xsl/index.html

Freedom House, 2008. *Combined Average Ratings: Independent Countries.* Washington, US. Retrieved 22 May 2010 from:

[33] IFAC Code of Ethics for Professional Accountants, Section 150.

www.freedomhouse.org/template.cfm?page+410&year=2008

Global Accounting Alliance (GAA) website. Retrieved 7 January 2009, from http://www.gaaaccounting.com/home.aspx

HRCA (2009). Human Rights Council of Australia. *Submission to the National human Rights Consultation on the Protection and Promotion of Human Rights*, 15 June 2009. Retrieved 22 May 2010, from:http://www.hrca.org.au/wp-content/uploads/2009/06/nhrc-submission.pdf

Human Rights Watch website, http://www.hrw.org/

Institute of Chartered Accountants in England and Wales (ICAEW) website. Retrieved 7 January 2009, from http://www.icaewfirms.co.uk/section.asp?catid=24

International Federation of Accountants (IFAC) Public Interest Oversight Board (PIOB). Retrieved 7 January 2009, from http://www.iasplus.com/ifac/piob.htm

International Federation of Accountants (IFAC), *Code of Ethics for Professional Accountants*. Retrieved 12 January 2009 from http://www.ifac.org/

New Zealand Institute of Chartered Accountants (NZICA), *Code of Ethics*. Retrieved 12 January 2009, from http://www.nzica.com/Technical%20and%20business/Ethical%20and%20professional/~/media/NZICA/Docs/Tech%20and%20Bus/Ethical%20and%20professional/Standards%20and%20Guidance/Ethical%20Standards/CodeofEthics_Oct06_.ashx

Ruggie, John G. *Interim Report of the Special Representative to the Secretary General*, 22 February 2006; '*Business and Human Rights: Mapping International Standards of Responsibility and Accountability for Corporate Acts'*, 28 March 2007; '*Protect, Respect and Remedy: A Framework for Business and Human Rights'*, 7 April 2008. Retrieved 13 November 2008, from http://www.reports-and-materials.org/Ruggie-docs-list-8-Jan-2009.pdf '*Business and human rights: Towards operationalizing the "protect, respect and remedy" framework'*, 22 April, 2009. Retrieved 15 July 2009, from http://www2.ohchr.org/english/bodies/

hrcouncil/docs/11session/A.HRC.11.13.pdf '*Business and Human Rights: Further steps toward the operationalization of the "protect, respect and remedy" framework,* 9 April 2010. Retrieved 22 May 2010, from: http://198.170.85.29/Ruggie-report-2010.pdf.

United Nations (1992). UN Rio Declaration on Environment and Development (1992). Retrieved 7 January 2009, from http://www.unep.org/Documents.Multilingual/Default.asp?documentid=78&articleid=1163

United Nations (2001). Report of the High-Level Panel on Financing for Development appointed by the United Nations Secretary-General, United Nations General Assembly, 55th Session, Agenda item 101, 26 June 2001, A/55/1000, 3. Retrieved 13 January 2009, from www.un.org/esa/ffd/a55-1000.pdf

United Nations Charter. Retrieved 5 December 2008, from http://www.un.org/aboutun/charter/

United Nations Development Programme (UNDP) (2009). *Human Development Report 2009 – HDI rankings.* New York, US: United Nations. Retrieved 22 May 2010 from: http://hdr.undp.org/en/statistics/

United Nations Global Compact. Retrieved 7 January 2009 from http://www.unglobalcompact.org/AboutTheGC/index.html

United Nations: Summary of United Nations Agreements on Human Rights. Retrieved 5 December 2008, from http://www.hrweb.org/legal/undocs.html

Universal Declaration of Human Rights (UDHR). Retrieved 5 December 2008, from http://www.un.org/Overview/rights.html

Organizations Included in Analysis

IFAC	International Federation of Accountants
ACAUS	Association of Chartered Accountants in the US
ACCA	Association of Chartered Certified Accountants
AICPA	American Institute of Certified Public Accountants
CICA	Canadian Institute of Chartered Accountants
CIPFA	Chartered Institute of Public Finance and Accounting
CPA	Australia Certified Practising Accountants Australia
GAA	Global Accounting Alliance
ICAA	Institute of Chartered Accountants in Australia
ICAEW	Institute of Chartered Accountants in England and Wales
ICAS	Institute of Chartered Accountants of Scotland
NIA	National Institute of Accountants (Australia)

NZICA	New Zealand Institute of Chartered Accountants
SAICA	South African Institute of Chartered Accountants

CHAPTER 12

Spinoza's Ethics in a Global World

Lydia Amir

> Spinoza is the noblest and most lovable of the great philosophers. Intellectually, some have surpassed him, but ethically, he is supreme. (Bertrand Russell, *A History of Western Philosophy*, 1979, 559)

INTRODUCTION

Ethics plays a central role in problems raised by globalization. Implicit in the term globalization is the idea that we are moving beyond the existing conception of the nation-state. This needs to be reflected at all levels of our thought, especially in our thinking about ethics. Peter Singer begins his *One World* by emphasizing that

> the newly interdependent global society, with its remarkable possibilities for linking people around the planet, gives us the material for a new ethic that will serve the interests of all those who live on the planet in a way that no previous ethic has ever done... How well we come through the era of globalization will depend on how we respond ethically to the idea that we live in one world. (Singer 2001, 12-13)[1]

The ethics of the seventeenth-century philosopher Benedict Spinoza is highly relevant to the challenge a global world represents for moral theorizing. Its importance has been recognized by philosophers of ecology, but ignored by ethicists and business ethicists. I suggest that Spinoza's ethics is important for business ethics and especially for global business ethics.[2] I explain its relevance

[1] For the role of ethics in globalization see also Kessler 2000.

[2] Apart from the 2001 lecture on "Virtue, Happiness and Management – A Spinozistic-Nietzschean Approach," I delivered at the 1st Conference on Philosophy in Management, St. Anne College, Oxford, England, I am unaware of discussions in congresses or in the literature of the suitability of Spinoza's ethics for the business setting or for global

to deep ecology, and conclude that Spinoza's philosophy may prove especially helpful for businessmen with ecological concerns.

SPINOZA AND BUSINESS ETHICS

The past twenty years witnessed a dramatic resurgence of philosophical interest in the virtues. The advantage of virtue ethics is both the enriching of moral description and the enrichment of moral life. Virtue theory argues that the aim of the moral life is to develop the general dispositions we call the moral virtues, and to exercise and exhibit them in the many situations that life sets before us. This approach to ethics is now recognized as a viable alternative to act-and principle-centered and consequentialist theories.

Few business ethics textbooks refer to virtue ethics.[3] John Dobson believes, however, that virtue ethics is creating "something of a paradigm shift" in the business setting (Dobson 1994, 73). Robert Solomon eloquently describes the need this shift answers; he believes business ethics is lacking an adequate account of the personal dimension in ethics:

> Much of business ethics today focuses on questions of policy – those large questions about government regulation and the propriety of government intervention, e.g., in failing industries and affirmative action programs, and in very general business practices and problems, e.g., pollution control, opacity and lying in advertising, employee due process and the social responsibilities of companies to their surrounding communities... traditional theories of ethics... have been called in to support one or another concern beyond or contrary to the bottom line.

---

business ethics. For the reasons of the contemporary neglect of Spinoza's ethics, see Amir 2010. Although the subject of this essay is different than the present article, parts of the essay have been helpful here, especially the possible solution to the ethnocentrism of virtue ethics that Spinoza's ethics represents (section 2 above).

[3] The following are a few examples extracted from repeated editions of major business ethics textbooks: John Boatright allocates a few pages to virtue ethics, mentioning Aristotle and Robert Solomon (Boatright 1993, 65-71); William Shaw does not mention virtue ethics at all and refers to "virtue" once (Shaw 2002, 72); Manuel Velasquez allots only nine pages out of 528 to virtue ethics in which he surveys the views of Aristotle, Thomas Aquinas, Alastair MacIntyre and Edmund Pinkoff (Velasquez 2002, 132-41). Jennifer Jackson (1996), who defends virtue ethics for businessmen and Robert Solomon (1992; 1997), who endorses an Aristotelian-based virtue ethics, are notable exceptions to the preference of act- and principle-centered and consequentialist theories over virtue ethics in business ethics books.

> But what gets left out of these well-plumbed studies and arguments is an adequate sense of personal values and involvement. (Solomon 1997, 208)

Policy disputes do not have much to say to the ordinary manager or executive, and even less to the ordinary business student. Thus, an adequate account of the personal dimension in business ethics is needed, and can be supplied by virtue ethics.

Which virtue ethics should we choose? Most contemporary virtue ethicists choose Aristotle. Yet his paganism and aristocratic values are considered problematic by contemporary standards.[4] Moreover, Aristotle's denigration of commerce stands out as being at odds with business ethics. Being the first economist, Aristotle had much to say about the ethics of exchange and so might be called the first (known) business ethicist as well. But Aristotle distinguished two different senses of economics: "*oecinomicus*" or household trading, which he approved of and thought essential to the working of any even modestly complex society, and "*chrematisike*," which is trade for profit. Aristotle declared the latter activity wholly devoid of virtue and called those who engaged in such purely selfish practices "parasites." His view of what we call "business" was that it was a trade, and that all trade was a kind of exploitation. I do not think that Aristotle's view of business should be brushed away,[5] especially if other virtue ethicists, who can provide the business area with the ethics it needs, do not share his view.

When Aristotle is not taken as the prime model of virtue ethics, the Classical philosophers generally are.[6] Martha Nussbaum, for example, sees a resemblance

---

[4] For reasons why Aristotle's paganism and aristocratic virtues can be at odds with contemporary ethics, see Casey 1990. Another difficulty experienced by Aristotelian scholars is the adoption of some more or less Aristotelian notion of human flourishing without committing to Aristotle's metaphysics, and without abandoning the search for an alternative to utilitarianism (see Wallace 1978, 34; MacIntyre 1985, 187-9). Others (Taylor 1985; Nussbaum 1988) seem willing simply to endorse Aristotle's claim that our function is a life of rational activity despite whatever metaphysical difficulties may attend it. Martha Nussbaum attempts to present Aristotle as a source of non-relative virtues (1988), an attempt that bears similarities to my proposal.

[5] Notwithstanding Aristotle's denigration of commerce, which Robert Solomon acknowledges, Solomon endorses Aristotle's view of ethics and goes as far as to maintain that "almost all of Aristotle's virtues are recognizable as business virtues" (Solomon 1997, 222). For a fuller exposition of Solomon's views on Aristotle, see Solomon 1997; 1992; 1999.

[6] Thomas Morris, for example, urges business to follow the teachings of the classical philosophers and not Aristotle alone (Morris 1997).

between our times and Antiquity. At least, she explains, "our vices are, in some ways, Roman vices: excessive money making, excessive attachment to honor, and excessive anger" (Nussbaum 2000, 41). She finds, therefore, that Roman philosophers' views are relevant to our workplace. Apart from Ancient philosophies, sources of influence on business practices can be found in other pre-Christian civilizations and Eastern philosophies. Indeed, one of the consequences of the postmodern criticism of Western civilization and the New Age movement's criticism of established Christianity is the positive evaluation of pre-Christian and non-Western civilizations and philosophies (Amir 2009). The theories that together make up the "New Age movement" urge us to find in these civilizations the inspiration for better organizational and managerial practices.[7]

None withstanding the undeniable importance and interest of both Ancient philosophies and non-Western and Pre-Christian cultures, I believe that their applicability to a contemporary business environment is problematic. The reason is that most Westerners are post-Christians in a way that is similar to their being post-Freudian. That is, whether or not they have been Christian, they are part of a civilization that is heir to the Christian world. Westerners are profoundly influenced by Christian values. This may be the reason for the revival of interest in the Christian philosopher Thomas Aquinas. Aquinas added to Aristotle's list of the moral virtues the Christian virtues of faith, hope, charity, and humility.[8]

I suggest, however, that Spinoza's ethics is better suited to answer contemporary needs in moral theory and business environment than the philosophies mentioned above, for the following reasons:

A. Spinoza's ethics is better suited to our times than Greek and Roman ethics because his ethics combines the virtues of Antiquity, such as those of Platonism, Aristotelianism and Stoicism,[9] with a profound Christian influence.[10] This is

---

[7] For the New Age characteristics, see Hanegraaff 1998; Heelas 1996; York 1995.

[8] For the revival of interest in Aquinas' ethics, see Casey 1990; Ramsey 1997, 177, n. 1, and *passim*.

[9] A number of Ancient influences are evident in Spinoza's ethical theory. From Plato, he accepts a conception of ethics as concerned with the conflict between reason and the passions, and the distinction between understanding the eternal, on the one hand, and sensing or imagining the merely durational, on the other. From Aristotle, he takes a conception of ethics as concerned with virtue and a kind of human flourishing whose highest expression lies in the life of active reason. From the Stoics, he appropriates the ideal of an internal freedom found in reconciling oneself to the necessities of nature. His own ethical theory, however, is distinctive, and not reducible to any of these influences. For Aristotle's and the Stoics' influence on Spinoza, see Wolfson 1934, chapter 9.

important inasmuch as most Westerners are profoundly influenced by Christian values.

B. Although similar influences can be found in Thomas Aquinas' philosophy, Spinoza, unlike Aquinas, is a post-Judeo-Christian, who rejects from both religions features that may alienate non-religious persons.[11] It is important that a viable contemporary ethics should not be tied to a particular established religion.

C. One of the outcomes of Spinoza's rejection of established religions is a worldly-oriented philosophy, which is another reason for preferring Spinoza in a business setting to Aquinas.[12]

D. Spinoza's experience of commercial and worldly affairs constitutes a *prima facie* edge in comparison with Aristotle and other less worldly-oriented virtue ethicists. Spinoza worked as a businessman from the age of seventeen to twenty-four, first together with his father, and then, when his father died (1654), together with his brother Gabriel in the firm "Bento y Gabriel Despinoza" (Klever 1996, 15). Even afterwards, when he devoted himself wholly to learned pursuits, he practiced the trade of lens grinding, which he had learned earlier and which

---

[10] Spinoza's biography can account for the notable Christian influence in his writings. Although Spinoza's parents reverted to Judaism before his birth, his family was "marano". The "maranos" were Spaniard Jews forced to convert to Christianity but who kept the Jewish religion and traditions secretly. They were nonetheless expelled with all Jews from Spain in 1492 and fled to Portugal. Expelled again from Catholic Portugal, they traveled through the south of France to Amsterdam, where they initiated a new Jewish community of Sefarad or "Spanish" Jews. Spinoza was born there in 1632 to a family that had been strongly influenced by Christianity for many generations. Spinoza's relationship with Judaism seems simpler than his relationship with Christianity. He abandoned the Jewish religion quite early in his life and was excommunicated from the Jewish community at the age of 24. There is a controversy regarding the extent of the influence of Jewish thought on his philosophy. For Spinoza's biography, see Nadler 1999. For Jewish influences on Spinoza, see Yovel 1988, vol. 1; Nadler 2001.

[11] Spinoza's attitude to the Judeo-Christian moral tradition is complex. He endorses the Christian view that hate is to be overcome by returning love to those who hate us (E IIIPP43-44, E IVaP11). He rejects Christian asceticism and guilt, however, and maintains that such central Christian virtues as humility, repentance, and pity are not virtues at all but evils, because they are all species of sadness and hence indications of lack of power. Moreover, Spinoza's God is very different from the Christians' God, as the former does not issue commands nor desires that human beings should live well.

[12] For an interesting comparison of Aquinas and Spinoza, see Byrne 1994, 121.

enabled him to earn a bare sufficiency. True, his interest was scientific, rather than economical, but still he earned a living (ibid., 18). Spinoza had also been involved in lawsuits, not only in connection with commercial debtors, but also later with his own step-sister, when she attempted to exclude him from his patrimony on the pretext of his heretical views.

E. Spinoza's view of the role of money in life is another *prima facie* edge in comparison with other philosophers. At first, it seems as if money is not important for Spinoza because he shares with Aristotle and other Greek and Roman philosophers the view that happiness is not to be obtained through wealth. His philosophical inquiry begins with this remarkable sentence: "after experience has taught me that all things which commonly occur in life are vain and futile…" (EI, 1);[13] two paragraphs below he explains that "most things which present themselves in life, and which, to judge from their actions, men think to be the highest good, may be reduced to these three: wealth, honor, and sensual pleasure" (EI, 3).[14]

Yet, Spinoza's appreciation of the power of money is clear from the following passage of the *Ethics*:

> To achieve these things the powers of each man would hardly be sufficient if men did not help one another. And indeed, money has provided a convenient instrument for acquiring all these aids. That is why its image usually occupies the Mind of the multitude more than anything else. For they can imagine hardly any species of Joy without the accompanying idea of money as its cause. (E IV A XXVIII)

Thus, the pursuit of money is not wrong; it is a vice "only in those who seek money neither from need nor on account of necessities, but because they have learned the art of making money and pride themselves on it very much" (E IV A XXIX); nor is there anything wrong in other worldly pursuits: "I saw that the acquisition of money, sensual pleasure, and esteem," Spinoza writes, "are not

---

[13] The following list of abbreviations of Spinoza's works will be used: EI stands for *The Emendation of the Intellect*; E, for the *Ethics*; and ST, for the *Short Treatise on God, Man and his Well-Being*. Roman capitals refer to parts (e.g., E V refers to the *Ethics*, part V, ST II refers to the *Short Treatise*, part II), followed in the *Short Treatise* by chapter number in Roman capitals and section number in Arabic numerals; in the references to the *Ethics*, P stands for proposition, C for Corollary, S for Scholium, D for Demonstration and A for Appendix.

[14] See also Spinoza, ST II, V, 6; Aristotle, *Nichomachean Ethics*, I, 4.

obstacles at all. On the contrary, they will be of great use in attaining the end on account of which they are sought…" (EI, 11). I suggest, then, that Spinoza's relatively balanced view of money gives him a *prima facie* edge in the business arena over other virtue ethicists.

F. Some of the tenets of Spinoza's philosophy may be especially appealing for businessmen, such as those involving activity, self-preservation, power, egoism, and a realistic view of human nature. Indeed, Spinoza's philosophy is a philosophy of *activity* whose explicit goal is to improve action and minimize passivity. It is a philosophy of *self-preservation*, wherein psychological and moral consequences follow from the physiological conatus or vital impulse to persevere in one's being. It is a philosophy of *power* or successful self-perseverance that is also identical with virtue. Both a psychological and ethical *egoist*, Spinoza crafted a philosophy that is *realistic* about human nature and illuminates the causes of human behavior without condemning it.

Enlightened by his experience of commerce and the usefulness of money, Spinoza's realistic and worldly-oriented egoistic philosophy of activity – by which he understands successful self-preservation or power – may prove to be more kindred to businessmen than other philosophies.

G. But there should be more to a choice of business ethics than its *prima facie* attractiveness for businessmen. Additional characteristics of Spinoza's philosophy contribute into making his ethics particularly relevant to contemporary trends of thought. His philosophy emphasizes the *body* as much as the mind, for it considers them identical.[15] It is a philosophy that promotes *health*, both physical and psychological. It allots *emotions* a crucial role in determining our well-being. It is a *naturalistic* philosophy of *immanence*: while there is a God in Spinoza's philosophy, he is not a personal God who issues decrees; rather he is identical with nature, which means that the human being who is part of nature is also necessarily part of God.

Spinoza devises an ethic which would satisfy the *altruist*'s nonretributivism. In Spinoza's ethics morality is not submission to an alien rule, but is *determination by the law of one's nature*, which is universal and objective. It is an ethics which *inverses* the traditional relationship between happiness and virtue: contrary to the views of traditional morality and various religions, which consider virtue the road to happiness, Spinoza maintains that it is because we are happy

---

[15] Spinoza holds an interesting view of human nature according to which the body and the mind are two aspects of a sole reality. For Spinoza's resolution of the mind-body problem, see Harris 1992, chapter 5.

that we can be virtuous (E VP42). It is a philosophy that sees the highest good as *self-love*, which is identical with liberty, happiness and peace of mind.

In order to help us fulfill the highest good Spinoza bothers with specifics: his philosophy offers *remedies* against the passions that plague and paralyze us. Though very ambitious in its goal, it is a philosophy whose path towards it is *gradual* and never fully completed. It is a philosophy that is *feasible*, as testified by Spinoza's concluding sentence in his *Ethics*: "If now the way, which I have shown leads to this, seems very difficult, yet it can be found… for all excellent things are as difficult as they are rare" (E VP42S).

It is a *practical* philosophy. Spinoza saw ethics as the knowledge of "the right way of living."[16] He sought primarily to improve the character of human beings – both himself and others – by improving their self-understanding. Spinoza sought improvement of the intellect, and, specifically, his own, not merely as a theoretical exercise, but chiefly as a remedy against three ethical hindrances, the overvaluing of wealth, fame, and sensual pleasure, and as an instrument for distinguishing, appreciating, and achieving the one true and eternal practical good – liberty, which is identical to happiness and peace of mind.

A detailed discussion of Spinoza's ethics as embedded in his metaphysics is beyond the scope of the present article, but recent publications have contributed to make its notorious difficulty more accessible.[17] It is worth the effort, Don Garrett maintains, first, because Spinoza's ethics is "despite the brevity of its presentation, one of the most important ethical theories of the modern era." Second, in its naturalism, its practical rationalism, its asymmetrical conception of moral freedom and responsibility, its nonretributivism, its emphasis on virtue as well as consequences, and its close relation to social and political theory, Spinoza's ethics is "a forerunner of, and of special relevance to, contemporary trends in ethical theorizing" (Garrett 1996, 269, 308).[18] One of those

---

[16] The phrase is from the first paragraph of the appendix to *Ethics* part 4; it also appears in the preface to part 3.

[17] Although self-preservation first appears in the *Ethics* as a tendency towards temporal duration, the achievement of adequate understanding – which is the highest virtue – brings a participation in the eternal that is itself a kind of perseverance in one's being. Accordingly, the highest virtue is not merely a means toward self-preservation; it is itself a kind of self-preservation. That is, the very consequence at which Spinoza's consequentalism aims is also, at least in its most important manifestation, a state of character.

[18] For a fuller exposition of Spinoza's ethics, see Wolfson 1934; Curley 1973; Bennett 1984; Llyod 1994. For understanding the practicability of Spinoza's ethics, even more helpful than these illuminating interpretations is Neil Grossman's recent monograph,

contemporary trends is globalization. I surmise that Spinoza's ethics is particularly relevant to the challenge a global world represents for moral theorizing.

SPINOZA AND GLOBAL BUSINESS ETHICS

When faced with the variety of moral theories that we encounter through globalization processes, it seems that the only viable morality for all is moral relativism. According to this theory, the only criterion for judging whether one's action is morally right or wrong is the norm applying to the action in one's culture. Yet, moral relativism raises insuperable problems. Among the problems such a position raises are the impediment of a dialogue between representatives of different moralities and the impossibility of criticizing one's own morality (Singer 2004, 139-40; Amir 1999). These problems make moral relativism untenable.

What kind of morality should we choose instead of moral relativism in a global era? Virtue ethics seems to be a good candidate, but provinciality and ethnocentricity risk plaguing it.[19] Alastair MacIntyre attempts to solve the problem virtue ethics creates by arguing that in addition to the notion of virtue as tied to historically and culturally situated roles, there is a notion of virtue which is tied to a human *telos* applying to all human beings.[20] Yet this universalistic claim has been criticized for being incompatible with MacIntyre's historicism.[21] Daniel Statman explains that the problem of universality is connected to the problem of justification, because,

> If we could anchor the virtues in some general theory of human flourishing, we could thereby grant them universal application, assuming that such a theory would apply, more or less equally, to all human beings. Since, however, such an anchor is not available, we are left with

---

which introduces the philosophy of Spinoza adapted for a new age and with exercises (Grossman 2003).

[19] Referring to Aristotle's defense of slavery in his *Politics*, Robert Solomon writes that "the problem with virtue ethics is that it tends to be provincial and ethnocentric" (Solomon 1997, 212).

[20] See MacIntyre 1985, chapter 15, and Postscript, 272-78.

[21] See Putman 1987, and the sources he mentions in note 8, p. 99.

> changing intuitions about virtues and vices, upon which no universal claims can be made. (Statman 1997, 20)[22]

I suggest that Spinoza's ethics can supply an anchor for the virtues for the following reasons. First, Spinoza is no relativist: although he believes that the terms "good" and "bad" used in current moralities denote only our desires, he is also persuaded that there is an absolute good towards which we strive when our thinking is not confused (Harris 1992, 8-9). Second, Spinoza's philosophy can supply the required anchor because the virtues that Spinoza advocates may be more congenial to a wide variety of persons from different cultures than virtues proposed by other virtue theorists. The current need for "a set of values and patterns at the world level," to use James Mittelman's definition of global order (Mittelman 2011, 1), calls for ethical theories that appeal to persons with different cultural background.

Spinoza's philosophy may do just that. Apart from its Classical and post-Judeo-Christian features, Spinoza's philosophy has affinities with Buddhist, Japanese and Chinese thought.[23] With the possible exception of Schopenhauer, Spinoza is the most Eastern philosopher of the West. Due to its creative mixture of Classical and Christian influences and to its Eastern affinities, Spinoza's ethics may prove to be more suited to the contemporary global challenge in ethics than each of these traditions separately.

If MacIntyre is right in asserting that there must be some non-relative virtues which are essential in all societies, albeit with local variations and interpretations, such as courage, honesty, generosity, congeniality, Spinoza's ethics may be a good source for non-relative virtues. It may thus be an answer to the problem of ethnocentricity and provinciality that virtue ethics faces. Spinoza's ethics may thus prove helpful in solving ethical problems raised by globalization, such as the need for non-relative virtues that do not solely or even primarily reflect Western values.

---

[22] For a recent attempt to anchor the virtues in a general theory of human flourishing, see Kraut 2007.

[23] For a study of the affinity between Spinoza's and Buddhist thought, see, for example, Wetlesen 1972, 1977; Naess 1978. For his affinity with Chinese thought, see Hu-Shih 1977, and with Japanese thought, see Saito 1977. For his affinity with Eastern thought in general, see Hessing 1977.

SPINOZA AND DEEP ECOLOGY

Not only is Spinoza's ethics particularly relevant to the challenge a global world represents for moral theorizing, Spinoza is central to the Environmentalists' search for a unifying metaphysics that would provide the basis of a new ethics. Since Arne Naess first used Spinoza's philosophical framework to ground "deep ecology" – a term he coined in a paper given in Bucharest in 1972 – others have followed in championing Spinoza as the main ecological philosopher.[24]

Deep ecology sets itself up as the substantial basis for a philosophy of ecology as distinct from an environmental ethics.[25] Deep ecologists aim to show how a harmonious relationship with nature can be made available through extending care from the human to the non-human world. They are united in holding that the environmental crisis is not a technical problem that can be solved by the application of the appropriate technology. Nor do they believe its ultimate solution to be found in political or economic reforms.[26] A change of

---

[24] Naess 1973; 1975; 1977; 1980; 1993, inter alia. Other thinkers who have adopted Spinoza as the main deep ecology philosopher are George Sessions 1977; Freya Matthews 1991; Eccy de Jonge 2004.

[25] Not only do deep ecologists reject environmental ethics with its "shoulds" and "oughts" (De Jonge 2004, ix), they also eschew the tradition of virtue ethics although it is centered on character rather than on actions (Elliot 2001, 190; Van Wensveen 2000, 19, n. 17). For the reasons that account for the rejection of virtue ethics by deep ecologists and for a rebuttal of these reasons, see James 2004, 59-60. For a defense of the usefulness of virtue ethics for deep ecology, see Fox 2000. Warwick Fox defends virtue ethics by equating it with self-realization because he believes that the development of the virtues can help us develop a love for the good in ourselves, which will lead to recognizing intrinsic values in nature.

[26] The relation between deep ecologists and political activism should be clarified. We can view deep ecology in four different ways: as a deep questioning of the relationship between human beings and nature; as a metaphysics of ethics rather than an environmental ethics; as a political movement whose premises are both descriptive and normative; and as an activist movement approach to dealing with the ongoing destruction of natural entities. For the differences between these four meanings of deep ecology, see de Jonge 2004, 2-5. An additional difficulty in defining deep ecology and its attitude towards politics lies in the relation of the movement to the eight principles for a Deep Ecology Platform, or DEP, that George Sessions devised with Arne Naess in 1984, and published a year later by Sessions and Bill Devall (Devall and Sessions 1985, 70). The eight principles of the DEP were adopted by the Deep Ecology Movement: an agreement with these principles authorized its supporters to be known as "deep ecologists" – a demand Naess retracted from later on (Naess 1995, 220). The movement as interpreted by activists is a call to take direct action against governments and corporations in order to save the earth from ecological

consciousness, a new way of seeing the natural world and our relation to it is called for. In explaining what deep ecology is, Simon James emphasizes that it is not (or not only) "a call to revise our intellectual understanding of what the world is; it is a call for us to change the way we actually experience the world" (James 2004, 28).

Although the phrase "deep ecology" was originally conceived as an umbrella term to encompass a variety of thoughtful responses to environmental issues, over the years, it has become associated with a particular position on environmental matters and a specific conception of what it means to see the world aright. On this conception, the goal of deep ecology is to foster "Self-realization," an ideal that is based on a holistic conception of the self: just as we ultimately depend on the whole of nature, so there exists a particular mode of consciousness in which one identifies with nature a whole. This is said to be the consciousness of one who has realized his or her mature Self, and the process by which this is achieved is said to be one of "Self-realization".

In articulating what sort of experience is required to conceive the world aright, deep ecologists turn to a variety of sources. Apart from the prominent role that Spinoza holds in this movement, other sources include Martin Heiddeger; the worldviews of indigenous peoples, such as the Native Americans; writers and poets, such as Henry Thoreau and Robinson Jeffers; reflective environmentalists, such as the American forester Aldo Leopold; and Eastern philosophies, such as Hinduism, Buddhism, Zen Buddhism, and Taoism.

Spinoza holds a prominent role in the deep ecology movement as a philosopher who can provide the frame of thought it needs. Arne Naess, Spinoza's chief proponent, admits to reconstructing his thought and emphasizes Spinoza's affinities with Eastern thought while doing so.[27] Especially important

---

catastrophe. But Naess is a follower of Gandhi's principle of non-violence, and himself a practitioner of non-violent direct action. It is highly unlikely, therefore, that Naess would support any acts which would harm life, whether human or non-human. Due to the links between the deep ecology movement and ecoterrorist groups, Warwick Fox (1990) and others have chosen to distance themselves from the movement while remaining sympathetic to a philosophy of ecology – a philosophy which seeks to ground environmental theory in ecology rather than in ethics.

[27] Naess admits to reconstructing Spinoza's thought (in Naess 1993, 7). For Naess' emphasis on Eastern features in Spinoza's philosophy, see Naess 1978. Arne Naess also refers sympathetically to the Hindu philosophy Advaita Vedanta in articulating his position and so encourages the idea that realizing one's Self is to realize one's identity with some metaphysical absolute (Naess 2001, 151-3; 1975, 98). He acknowledges the Zen

for the fate of Spinoza's philosophy in the hands of deep ecologists is Naess' change of the Spinozistic notion of "self-perseverance" into "self-realization" (Naess 1975, 97; 1977, 48-9; 1993, 12-13). Self-realization has since become the heart of deep ecology (de Jonge 2004, 35; Mathews 1988, 349), its deepest idea or esoteric core: the self is recognized as being intimately connected with the rest of nature through a meta-ontology that supporters of the deep ecology movement regard as a non-anthropocentric position. Naess also reconstructs Spinoza's views of non-human animals and of our relations with them along non-anthropocentric lines (Naess 1977, 49, n. 6; 52-3, n. 9). There are additional reconstructions of Spinoza's philosophy that Naess justifies by appealing to philosophers' creative use of other philosophies (1993, 7-8). Naess does not impose Spinoza as the sole articulator of deep ecologists' basic attitudes; rather, he recommends that other sources of inspiration be found, including poetic sources (ibid., 2).

Among Naess' followers – thinkers who share his project of grounding deep ecology in Spinoza's metaphysics – Eccy de Jonge's work is noteworthy for rectifying misappropriations of Spinoza by Naess, Freya Mathews, and George Sessions, while nevertheless grounding deep ecology, through its key concept of self-realization, in Spinoza's philosophy (de Jonge 2004). Although Spinoza's monistic substance "Nature or God" denotes a very different notion of nature from the one subscribed to by deep ecologists – nature for Spinoza is infinite, not composed of parts and, therefore, not descriptive of non-human forms of life[28] – Spinoza can provide the philosophical basis for two tenets of deep ecology: non-anthropocentrism and ecological holism (ibid., 73-83).

Self-realization in Spinoza's worldview means recognizing ourselves holistically, as a modification or aspect of God or Nature. The humility that comes with that realization – that God or Nature is the efficient cause and not "I" – is that which makes the Spinozistic self non-anthropocentric. The purpose of self-realization is to recognize ourselves as part of a greater whole in order to extend care to that whole. Through Spinoza's metaphysics, we recognize the inter-connectedness of beings as modifications of the same substance. We can thus care for the eco-systems as a whole without requiring an environmental ethics.

The rigorous approach to Spinoza exemplified in de Jonge's book makes a much stronger case for grounding a philosophy of ecology in Spinoza's metaphysics and ethics. De Jonge's work also fills a lacuna in grounding self-realization in Spinoza's political requirements for fulfilling this ideal. This is a

---

philosopher Dögen as a major inspiration as well (Curtin 1996, 241). For a criticism of Naess' Eastern reading of Spinoza's self-realization, see de Jonge 2004, chapters 2-3.

[28] For a good explanation of Spinoza's monistic substance, see Della Roca 2002.

theme generally ignored by deep ecologists, who sometimes hold an opposite view of politics to Spinoza's.

However, in order to choose Spinoza as a philosopher of deep ecology, we need more than de Jonge's emphatic, and Naess' systematic, choice of Spinoza (de Jonge 2004, 85; Naess 1977, 54; 1993, 2). We need to rule out other contenders that provide comprehensive worldviews, such as Eastern philosophies. While many in the deep ecology movement do turn to these philosophies,[29] groundbreaking thinkers on the source of Western civilization's relation to the environment, such as Lynn White and John Passmore, maintain that turning east is not a viable option. We need a new religion, White believes, but Zen Buddhism, for example, is as deeply conditioned by Asian history as Christianity is conditioned by the experience of the West; this makes Zen Buddhism's viability among us dubious (White 1967; Pojman 2001, 18). In contradistinction to White's search for a new religion, Passmore sees a danger in looking to the East because he considers Eastern religions as essentially mystical and, therefore, as opposed to the Western tradition of rational criticism and science (Passmore 1980, 173-6). Science seeks to dispel mystery and understand the world (ibid., 175), and it is science, not mysticism, that will eventually provide the solutions to the environmental problems the world faces.

I share White's and Passmore's concerns about turning east. I suggest that Spinoza's philosophy can provide the "new religion" White is seeking, and can satisfy Passmore's appeal to science to solve environmental problems because Spinoza's philosophy has been proven compatible with contemporary science (Amir 2010). I thus believe that a philosophy of ecology can definitely be grounded in Spinoza's metaphysics and ethics.

CONCLUSION

Spinoza's philosophy may supply the frame of thought necessary for both a global ecology and a global business ethics. This is important because we cannot consistently hold two ethics at the same time, as some businessmen and lawyers seem to believe, by compartmentalizing professional and personal life. By turning to Spinoza's ethics, a businessman with ecological concerns can adopt an ethic that supplies a realistic framework for activity, egoism, and power, as well as the prospect of self-realization, which, in Spinoza's worldview, means recognizing ourselves holistically as a modification or aspect of God or Nature. Using

---

[29] For deep ecologists that look into Eastern philosophies to ground their worldview, see, for example, Aitken 1985; Chapple 2001; Curtin 1994, 1996; James 2004; and the essays in Badiner 1990; Tucker and Williams 1997; Kasa and Kraft 2000.

Spinoza's ethics in the business setting connects business ethics not only with ecological responsibility, but also with the prospect of personal happiness: it is because we are happy that we can be virtuous. Human happiness for Spinoza lies not in accumulating material goods, or in being superficially popular, but in developing our own inner worth, free of pain, towards ultimate joy – a path whose description lies beyond the scope of this article.

REFERENCES

Aitken, Robert. 1985. "Gandhi, Dögen and Deep Ecology". In *Deep Ecology: Living as if Nature Mattered*, Bill Devall and George Sessions (eds.), 232–5. Salt Lake City: Peregrine Smith Groups.

Amir, Lydia B. 1999. "One of Us at Least Is Wrong: An Argument Against Relativism". Lecture delivered at the 30th Annual Israeli Sociological Association, The College of Management, Israel.

Amir, Lydia B. 2001. "Virtue, Happiness and Management – A Spinozistic-Nietzschean Approach". Lecture delivered at the 1st Conference on Philosophy in Management, St. Anne College, Oxford, England.

Amir, Lydia B. 2009. "Rethinking Philosophers' Responsibility". In *Creating a Global Dialogue on Value inquiry: Papers from the XXII World Congress of Philosophy*, Jinfen Yan and David Schrader (eds.), 21–56. Lewiston, NY: The Edwin Mellen Press.

Amir, Lydia B. 2010. "The Value of Spinoza's Ethics in a Changing World". *Journal of Axiology and Ethic*s 1: 301–20.

Aristotle, 1984. *Nicomachean Ethics. The Complete Works of Aristotle*. Jonathan Barnes (ed.). Princeton, NJ: Princeton University Press.

Badiner, Allan H. 1990. (ed.). *Dharma Gaia: A Harvest of Essays in Buddhism and Ecology*. Berkeley: Parallax Press.

Bennett, Jonathan. 1984. *A Study of Spinoza's "Ethic"*. Indianapolis, IN: Hackett.

Boatright, John R. 1993. *Ethics and the Conduct of Business*. New Jersey: Prentice Hall.

Byrne, Laura. 1994. "Reason and Emotion in Spinoza's Ethics: The Two Infinities". In *Spinoza: The Enduring Questions*, Graeme Hunter (ed.), 113–25. Toronto: University of Toronto Press.

Casey, John. 1990. *Pagan Virtue: An Essay in Ethics*. Oxford: Clarendon Press.

Chapple, Christopher K. 2001. "Jainism and Buddhism". In *A Companion to Environmental Philosophy*, Dale Jamieson (ed.), 52–66. Oxford: Blackwell.

Curley, Edwin. 1973. "Spinoza's Moral Philosophy". In *Spinoza: A Collection of Critical Essays*, Marjorie Grene (ed.), 354–74. Garden City: Doubleday/Anchor Press.

Curtin, Dean. 1994. "Dōgen, Deep Ecology, and the Ecological Self". *Environmental Ethics* 16, 195–213.

Curtin, Dean. 1996. "A State of Mind Like Water: Ecosophy T and the Buddhist Traditions". *Inquiry* 39: 239–53.

De Jonge, Eccy. 2004. *Spinoza and Deep Ecology: Challenging Traditional Approaches to Environmentalism*. Aldershot: Ashgate.

Della Roca, Michael. 2002. "Spinoza's Substance Monism". In *Spinoza: Metaphysical Themes,* Olli Koistinen and John Biro (eds.), 11–37. Oxford & New York: Oxford University Press.

Devall, Bill and George Sessions. 1985. *Deep Ecology: Living as if Nature Mattered.* Salt Lake City: Peregrine Smith Groups.

Dobson, John. 1994. "Theory of the Firm: Beyond the Sirens". *Economics and Philosophy* 10: 73–89.

Elliot, Robert. 2001. "Normative Ethics". In *A Companion to Environmental Philosophy*, Dale Jamieson (ed.), 177–91. Oxford: Blackwell.

Fox, Warwick. 1990. *Toward a Transpersonal Ecology*. Boston: Shambhala.

Fox, Warwick. 2000. "Deep Ecology and Virtue Ethics". *Philosophy Now* 26: 21–3.

Garrett, Don. 1996. "Spinoza's Ethical Theory". In *The Cambridge Companion to Spinoza*, Don Garrett (ed.), 267–314. New York, NY: Cambridge University Press.

Grossman, Neil. 2003. *Healing the Mind: The Philosophy of Spinoza Adapted for a New Age.* Selinsgrove: Susquehanna University Press; London: Associated University Presses.

Hanegraaff, Wouter J. 1998. *New Age Religion and Western Culture: Esotericism in the Mirror of Secular Thought*. Albany NY: SUNY Press.

Harris, Errol E. 1992. *Spinoza's Philosophy: An Outline*. New Jersey & London: Humanities Press.

Heelas, Peter. 1996. *The New Age Movement: The Celebration of the Self and the Sacralization of Modernity*. Cambridge, MA: Blackwell.

Hessing, Siegfried. 1977. "Prologue with Spinozana". In *Speculum Spinozanum 1677–1977*, Siegfried Hessing (ed.), 1–64. London: Henley; Boston: Routledge & Kegan Paul.

Hu-Shih, 1977. "Spinoza and Chuang-Tzu". In *Speculum Spinozanum 1677–1977*, Siegfried Hessing (ed.), 330–32. London: Henley; Boston: Routledge & Kegan Paul.

Jackson, Jennifer. 1996. *An Introduction to Business Ethics*. Oxford, UK & Cambridge, MA: Blackwell.

James, Simon P. 2004. *Zen Buddhism and Environmental Ethics*. Aldershort: Ashgate.

Kasa, Stephanie and Kenneth Kraft. 2000. (eds.). *Dharma Rain: Sources of Buddhist Environmentalism*. Boston: Shambhala.

Kessler, Clive. 2000. "Globalization: Another False Universalism". *Third World Quarterly* 21, 931–42.

Klever, W. N. A. 1996. "Spinoza's Life and Works". In *The Cambridge Companion to Spinoza*, Don Garrett (ed.), 13–60. New York, NY: Cambridge University Press.

Kraut, Richard. 2007. *What is Good and Why: The Ethics of Well-Being*. Cambridge, MA: Harvard University Press.

Lloyd, Genevieve. 1994. *Part of Nature: Self-knowledge in Spinoza's Ethics*. Ithaca, IL: Cornell University Press.

MacIntyre, Alasdair. 1985. *After Virtue*. Notre Dame, IN: University of Notre Dame Press.

Matthews, Freya. 1991. *The Ecological Self.* London & New York: Routledge.

Mittelman, James H. 2011. *Contesting Global Order: Development, Global Governance, and Globalization*. London & New York: Routledge.

Morris, Thomas V. 1997. *If Aristotle Ran General Motors: The New Soul of Business*. Henry Holt & Company.

Nadler, Steven. 1999. *Spinoza: A Life*. New York, NY: Cambridge University Press.

Nadler, Steven. 2001. *Spinoza's Heresy: Immortality and the Jewish Mind.* Oxford: Clarendon Press.

Naess, Arne. 1973. "The Shallow and the Deep, Long-Range Ecology Movement". *Inquiry* 16: 95–100.

Naess, Arne. 1975. *Freedom, Emotion and Self-Subsistence*: *The Structure of a Central Part of Spinoza's Ethics*. Oslo: Universitetsforlaget.

Naess, Arne. 1977. "Spinoza and Ecology". *Philosophia* 7: 45–54.

Naess, Arne. 1978. "Through Spinoza to Mahayana Buddhism or Through Mahayana Buddhism to Spinoza". In *Spinoza's Philosophy of Man: Proceedings of the Scandinavian Symposium, 1977*, Jon Wetlesen (ed.), 136–58. Oslo: Universitetsforlaget.

Naess, Arne. 1980. "Environmental Ethics and Spinoza's Ethics. Comments on Genevieve Lloyd's Article". *Inquiry* 3: 313–26.

Naess, Arne. 1993. *Spinoza and the Deep Ecology Movement.* Deft: Eburon.

Naess, Arne. 1995. "The Deep Ecology 'Eight Points' Revisited". In *Deep Ecology for the Twenty-First Century*, George Sessions (ed.), 213–21. London: Shambhala.

Naess, Arne. 2001. "Ecosophy T: Deep Versus Shallow Ecology". In *Environmental Ethics: Readings in Theory and Application*, Louis P. Pojman (ed.), 151–7.

Nussbaum, Martha C. 2000. "Aristotle in the Workplace". In *A Parliament of Minds: Philosophy for a New Millennium*, Michel Tobias, J. Patrick Fitzgerald, David Rothenberg (eds.), 30–45. Albany, NY: SUNY Press.

Nussbaum, Martha C. 1988. "Non-Relative Virtues: An Aristotelian Approach". In *Midwest Studies in Philosophy*, Peter A. French, Theodore Uehling and Howard Wettstein (eds.), vol. 13, chapter 3. Notre Dame, IN: University of Notre Dame Press.

Passmore, John. 1980. *Man's Responsibility for Nature: Ecological Problems and Western Tradition.* 2nd ed. London: Duckworth.

Pojman, Louis P. 2001. (ed.). *Environmental Ethics: Readings in Theory and Application.* Belmont, CA: Wadsworth.

Putman, Daniel. 1987. "Virtue and Self-Deception". *Southern Journal of Philosophy* 25: 549–57.

Ramsey, Hayden. 1997. *Beyond Virtue: Integrity and Morality.* London: Macmillan.

Russell, Bertrand. 1979. *A History of Western Philosophy.* London: Unwin Paperbacks.

Saito, Hiroshi. 1977. "Spinozism and Japan". In *Speculum Spinozanum 1677–1977*, Siegfried Hessing (ed.), 442–54. London: Henley; Boston: Routledge & Kegan Paul.

Sessions, George. 1977. "Spinoza and Jeffers on Man in Nature". *Inquiry*, 20, 481–528.

Singer, Peter. 2004. *One World: The Ethics of Globalization.* 2nd edition. New Haven and London: Yale University Press.

Shaw, William H. 1999. *Business Ethics*. 4th ed. Belmont CA: Wadsworth.

Solomon, Robert C. 1992. *Ethics and Excellence: Cooperation and Integrity in Business*. New York, NY: Oxford University Press.

Solomon, Robert C. 1997. "Corporate Roles, Personal Virtues: An Aristotelian Approach to Business Ethics". In *Virtue Ethics: A Critical Reader*, Daniel Statman (ed.), 205–26. Edinburgh: Edinburgh University Press.

Solomon, Robert C. 1999. "Business Ethics and Virtue". In *A Companion to Business Ethics*, R. E. Frederick (ed.), 30–7. Oxford: Blackwell.

Spinoza, Benedict. 1985. *The Collected Works of Spinoza*. Edwin Curley (ed. and trans.). Princeton, NJ: Princeton University Press.

Statment, Daniel. 1997. "Introduction to Virtue Ethics". In *Virtue Ethics: A Critical Reader*, Daniel Statman (ed.), 1–41. Edinburgh: Edinburgh University Press.

Taylor, Richard. 1985. *Ethics, Faith, and Reason*. Englewood-Cliffs, NJ: Prentice-Hall.

Tucker, Mary E. and Ryūnken Williams. 1997. (eds.). *Buddhism and Ecology: The Interconnectedness of Dharma and Deeds*. Cambridge, MA: Harvard University Press.

Van Wensveen, Louke. 2000. *Dirty Virtues: The Emergence of Ecological Virtue Ethics*. New York: Humanity Books.

Velasquez, Manuel G. 1998. *Business Ethics: Concepts and Cases*. 5th ed. New Jersey: Prentice Hall.

Wallace, James. 1978. *Virtues and Vices*. Ithaca, IL: Cornell University Press.

Wetlesen, Jon. 1977. "Body Awareness as a Gateway to Eternity: A Note on the Mysticism of Spinoza and its Affinity to Buddhist Meditation". In *Speculum Spinozanum 1677–1977*, Siegfried Hessing (ed.), 479–94. London: Henley; Boston: Routledge & Kegan Paul.

Wetlesen, Jon. 1979. *The Sage and the Way: Spinoza's Ethics of Freedom*. Assen, The Netherlands: Van Gorcum.

White, Jr, Lynn R. 1967. "The Historical Roots of Our Ecological Crisis". *Science*, 155, 10 March, 1203–07.

Wolfson, Harry Austryn. 1934. *The Philosophy of Spinoza*, 2 Vols. Cambridge, MA: Harvard University Press, 1934.

York, Mark. 1995. *The Emerging Network: A Sociology of the New Age and Neo-Pagan Movement*. Lanham, MD: Rowman & Littlefield.

Yovel, Yirmiyahu. 1988. *Spinoza and Other Heretics*, vol. 1: The Marano of Reason, vol. 2: The Adventures of Immanence. Princeton, NJ: Princeton University Press.

CHAPTER 13

Globalization and the Psychology of the New World Citizen

Henry Venter & Elaine Venter

INTRODUCTION

In recent years globalization has become a driving force connecting the entire globe. Through the transnational transference of economic, political, social and technological ideas, world economies, societies and cultures integrated to form a global network.

Although the term globalization is predominantly used in an economic sense, referring to the worldwide integration of trade and other technological systems, through the global exchange of ideas, language and culture, there is a specific personal characteristic emerging on a transnational scale. This paper will investigate how globalization has sparked the development and evolution of identity and culture in a post-modern world, specifically the role it has played in the emergence of the global citizen. By using the motivational theory of Abraham Maslow and his hierarchy of needs as a framework, this paper will show how the global citizen is emulating the elusive highest level of Maslow's hierarchy of motivation, transcendence, and the corresponding effect on global development.

ABRAHAM MASLOW AND SELF-TRANSCENDENCE

Abraham Maslow, widely considered the founder of humanistic psychology, is best known for his system of personal development, the hierarchy of needs. Traditionally it was believed that Maslow's hierarchy of needs only entailed a five-level hierarchical pyramid to explain a person's motives for development. He organized his different motivational levels in ascending order from lower basic human needs, such as physiological needs, at the bottom of the hierarchy, to higher progressing needs, such as the needs for safety, belongingness and love, esteem and self-actualization, at the top. He identified physiological (survival) needs as those where the person seeks to obtain the basic necessities of life; safety needs involve those where a person seeks security through order and law;

belongingness and love needs entails seeking affiliation with a group; esteem needs are typified by those where a person seeks esteem through recognition or achievement; and lastly, self-actualizing, at the top of the hierarchy, is where a person seeks fulfillment of personal potential (1968; 1971; 1973).

In recent years theorists postulated the notion that before Maslow died, he identified a sixth tier of need, which he believed very few people were capable of achieving in their lifetime – self-transcendence as illustrated in Table 1 (Koltko-Rivera 2006).

During his research, Maslow noted that some individuals have gone beyond the level of self-actualization as a salient motivation. He came to the idea of self-transcendence because he felt that too many theorists defined the Self simply in terms of what other people think or their perception of a person, which Maslow saw as an extreme cultural relativity in which a healthy individuality gets lost altogether. He reasoned that the healthy, fully developed person is characterized by his or her transcendence of other people's opinions. Maslow specifically used the term transcendence to differentiate this kind of person from the dichotomization of self and the environment, stating that it was a person freed from the "dichotomous way of thinking" (Maslow 1968, 180).

Table 1: A Rectified Version of Maslow's Hierarchy of Needs (Koltko-Rivera 2006, 303)

Motivational level	Description of person at this level
Self-transcendence:	Seeks to further a cause beyond the self [a] and to experience a communion beyond the boundaries of the self through peak experience [b].
Self-actualization:	Seeks fulfillment of personal potential.
Esteem Needs:	Seeks esteem through recognition of achievement.
Belongingness and love needs:	Seeks affiliation with a group.
Safety needs:	Seeks security through order and law.
Physiological (survival) needs:	Seeks to obtain the basic necessities of life.

Koltko-Rivera, 2006 Note: The earliest and most widespread version of Maslow's hierarchy (based on Maslow 1943; 1954) includes only the bottom five motivational levels (thus excluding self-transcendence). A more accurate version of the hierarchy, taking into account Maslow's later work (especially Maslow

1969a) and his private journal entries (Maslow 1979; 1982), includes all six motivational levels.

a) This may involve service to others, devotion to an ideal (e.g., truth, art) or a cause (e.g.,social justice, environmentalism, the pursuit of science, a religious faith), and/or a desire to be united with what is perceived as transcendent or divine.
b) This may involve mystical experiences and certain experiences with nature, aesthetic experiences, sexual experiences, and/or other transpersonal experiences, in which the person experiences a sense of identity that transcends or extends beyond the personal self.

According to Maslow (1968; 1973), a healthy personality, while including success in appropriate coping behavior involving mastery, effectance and competence, must also include a point where the individual is freed from the influence of their environment, specifically from the way that environment effects their personal development. One of the main forces inhibiting personal growth he identified was culture. Although culture is important, he reasoned that one needed to reach transcendence of, independence of, or resistance to enculturation, or else such forces could distort the way one sees the world in that such a person only identifies him or herself as the culture prescribes and would eventually perceive the world and people from other cultures only through the prism allowed by their culture. In his seminal interview with Willard Frick, Maslow referred to phenomenon in personality development as the effect of distorting forces in culture (Frick 1989). Maslow reasoned that a person that transcends their culture is not alienated from it, but he or she is no longer grounded or anchored in their own culture alone; they are not exclusively defined by their immediate environment or have an over-identification with one group alone (Frick 1989; Maslow 1968). Without distortion of their own cultural identity or developing crippling insecurity, they can identify and side with other people, different groups, entities, causes and nationalities.

Maslow described self-transcendence as a person's ability to obtain a unitive consciousness with other humans (1964; 1968). The transcended person is therefore able to view the world and his or her purpose in the world in relation to other human beings on a more global scale and is aware that they can have an impact, not just within their own geographical boundaries, but on the whole world. Maslow (1973) postulated that one main characteristic of self-actualized people is autonomy and independence from culture and environment.

They do not need the approval of other people; their opinions are not formed in light of their own immediate circumstances. Maslow held that self-transcendence is reached when a person seeks to further a cause beyond the self and to experience a communion beyond the boundaries of the self (1968). These transcended individuals who reach the top of Maslow's revised hierarchy typically seek a benefit beyond the mere personal, identifying with something greater than the purely individual self, often engaging in selfless service to others (Koltko- Rivera 2006).

The main implication of Maslow's revised model, with the inclusion of self-transcendence, is the effect it has on the worldview of individuals. Worldviews are sets of assumptions held by individuals and cultures about the physical and social universe (Koltko-Rivera 2006). An aspect of worldview specifically affected by Maslow's self-transcendence is one's purpose or meaning of life. Self-transcendence allows for a richer conceptualization of the meaning of- life dimension of worldviews – such a person develops a deeper sense of purpose, a sense of purpose not only focused on the needs of the self, but a sense of purpose anchored in the plight of the whole world. People with a transcended level of perception of the world are less determined by habitual abstraction and are not need-determined, but rather their cause is determined by perceptions of higher unity. They find meaning in life by connecting their life's journey and happiness to the condition of others; not only those from the same culture directly around them, but from others all over the world, regardless of race, sex, country, or religion. The person in a state of transcendence is freed from the practice of categorizing, pre-judging and stereotyping the world and other people in it. They are, therefore, able to view the world differently – not as dichotomous, different, separate, individual, but as a whole, as one interdependent unit (Frick 1989; Maslow 1968). Maslow argued that people at this level of motivation transcended their dichotomous nature and became autonomous, ruled by the laws of their own character rather than by the rules of society (1968). These people, he postulates, "should have less „national character" and that they should be more like each other across cultural lines than they are like the less-developed members of their own culture" (Maslow 1968, 181), becoming members at large of the human species. At one stage he called people like this universal men, not guided by their own culture and external environment, but by the needs and the plight of the whole species – people guided from within, by their inner voices and looking within for the guiding values and rules to live by (Frick 1989). According to Koltko-Rivera (2006), at the level of self-transcendence, the individual's own needs are put aside, to a great extent, in favor of service to others and to some higher force or cause conceived as being outside the personal self, typically the

Mother Theresa's, Albert Schweitzer's, and Gandhi's of the world. While the characteristics of Maslow's level of transcendence were once seen only in the life of a few, changes on a global scale triggered the emergence of the global citizen at large, and this type of transcended person is now becoming commonplace in the world. Increasing numbers of people are displaying this selfless desire to aid others in the world, such as witnessed in the Haiti earthquake disaster, where not only governments and official organizations mobilized to help, but numerous individuals gathered necessities, chartered planes, and flew into the country to aid the people.

GLOBALIZATION AND THE EMERGENCE OF THE SELF-TRANSCENDED WORLD-CITIZEN

Two factors in the process of globalization are now making it possible for people to reach Maslow's previously elusive sixth level of motivational development of self-transcendence – the massive migration of people all over the world and modern technological advances in communication. With rapid globalization, people are now instantly connected to communities all over the world. The world's people were once fragmented, individualized, and isolated from one another. Sovereign nations were distinguished by unique cultures and national identities fiercely protected by strict geographical boundaries (Sassen 2006). This has changed – the world is now a global village, constantly connected and interchanging. Modern technology, such as access to the Internet, has transformed the way of living for the majority of inhabitants on planet Earth. Economies are now intricately and symbiotically connected twenty four hours a day. People are keenly aware of social, political, economic and environmental crises all over the planet, since a crisis in one country can easily affect the global economy (Sassen 2006). This leads to a different way of defining oneself, a change in world view, and the birth of the global or world citizen, and in the process these people becoming clear examples of Maslow's level of self-transcendence where acts of selfless sacrifice are becoming commonplace.

Theorists such as Sassen (2006) confirms the change in the traditional definition of citizenship and what makes up being a citizen is changing, and drastically so. Sassen (2006) states the definitions of citizenship and cultural identification are changing through a process of de-nationalization due to migration and technological and communication progresses caused by globalization. Ever since the first borders were drawn, people have long identified themselves through the nation (Sassen, 2006). Benedict Anderson (2006) defines a nation as a politically imagined community, people who group themselves together based on social and political similarities. As such, Anderson (2006) states that there is more than one imagined community, more than one way through which people can identify themselves, which can affect one's perception of the country and the world in which they live. When in a new nation-state, during the process of naturalization, many immigrants will form new sub-groups or informal social contacts with others, which gradually changes the way they identify themselves and how they view their new world (Anderson 2006). With the formation of these sub- groups, develops a new sense of global thinking and their scope of view transcends national borders and cultures (Anderson 2006). Sassen (2006) refers to these people as the transnationals (Maslow referred to them as universal men), and although still deeply connected to their place of origin (or culture), they are now able to voice concern and bring light to abuses and transgressions of human rights and environmental issues the world over. This connection transcends the typical nationalistic view of today. As social and technological changes continue imagined communities' perceptions of themselves evolve (Anderson 2006). The traditional idea of the imagined community and the idea of nationalism still exist today, but now on a more global scale. Due to the fact that many transnationals now hold political clout, not only in their home country, but in their new country as well, the nation-state listens and can even effect policy change if the outcry is large enough (Sassen 2003). Soysal (1997) indicates that as nation-states are enacting tighter and more restricted immigration and border controls and infusing more nationalistic ideologies among its members in hopes to retain self-identification and loyalty to the nation in an attempt to curb transnational appeals, the numbers of transnational-orientated people are actually growing rapidly at the same time. She states that this paradoxical state is fueled by globalization and its role in helping spread the universal rights movement that claims all people should be afforded the same rights regardless of their land of origin (Soysal 1997). The growth of international markets motivated the massive migration of people from country to country and with this migration developed the new thinking that people's perception of their own citizenship is no longer contained within the borders of the nation, making Maslow's highest level of self-transcendence more commonplace than ever before (Sassen 2006). Being a citizen is no longer merely about associating one's self with a country or nation, but relating instead to other likeminded people across the globe and looking beyond one's own interest to the need of people on a global scale (Sassen 2006). The emergence of these global citizens is a definite step toward Maslow's self-actualization and eventual transcendence of a person.

MASLOW'S SELF-ACTUALIZATION AND EVENTUAL TRANSCENDENCE OF A PERSON

Global citizens are bound together with a common purpose, a global perspective, and joint responsibility for the fate of the planet. They belong to a global community that defines itself not so much by race, religion or region, but by the definition of what it is to be human; they elevate themselves beyond the immanence to which they were previously resigned to by society. They are indeed emulating the level of transcendence Maslow described - a position where one takes responsibility for oneself and the world, a transcended freedom that knows no boundaries. In a world where countries, regions, and different groups of people are increasingly connected and dependent upon each other, world problems and crises cannot be solved in isolation any longer. Narrow minded, distorted and region-bound people are now at more of a disadvantage than ever as they will not be able to understand or empathize with the plight of others in the world and are, therefore, blinded by their isolation and unable to solve their own problems or ensure growth for their people effectively and, in addition, are of little help with problems on a global scale. People that have not reached the level of self-transcendence have what Maslow refers to as an ego-deficiency status and he describes that their dichotomous thinking, due to their isolation, triggers a need to force attributes of security, familiarity and sameness unto others, to create a sort of manageability to alleviate their growing insecurity. Openness to others is for these people threatening and Maslow refers to these people as deficiency motivated personalities that find their solace in an artificially created, simplistic universe, in stereotypes and in a static, polarized world (Frick 1989).

This type of functioning becomes the foundation of the global world conflicts – people unable to perceive the world on a wider plane enter into disputes, conflicts, and war in order to convince or conquer other groups that do not perceive the world as they do. The transcended person embodies the opposite of this destructive rigidity; with a new world consciousness these people are able to transcend their own personal, social, and cultural needs. These are the people best described by Maslow's category of self-transcendents - people that can go beyond themselves and their own needs to embrace the cause of others. Never has there been a time that the transcended person Maslow described has been more necessary than today. Now, in light of the serious challenges of the world, there is a need for the majority of the population of the world to move towards this level to secure lasting peace and sustainability of life on Earth.

CONCLUSION

Transcendence is the means by which to solve global conflicts – citizens all over the world connecting and banding together to make their voice known and support peace and combat social crises such as poverty. Globalization is the impetus that is propelling transcendence to spread across the globe and connecting like-minded transcended people seeking to solve problems on a global scale. Where transcended people were once the exception, it is now more common-place to find everyday heroes all over the world advocating not only for their own needs, but for the needs of others – other's not only in their immediate nation and culture, but people in need all over the world. These people are not merely concerned with human rights and freedoms, but have taken the plight of the environment and global health of the planet up as a cause and a personal responsibility. They realize that without a healthy planet no amount of prosperity or modern advances have any future. Maslow's sixth level of human motivation and development, self-transcendence, is the most accurate description of the new global citizen: people taking responsibility for themselves and the world; people living in a transcended freedom that knows no boundaries. These are the people that are showing that in the modern world of globalization every person, regardless of continent, culture, or region, can be a modern-day Nelson Mandela, Mother Theresa, or Gandhi with the power to shape the future of the world.

REFERENCES

Anderson, B.R. (2006). *Imagined communities: Reflections on the origin and spread of nationalism*. London: Verso Print.

Frick, W.B. (1989). *Humanistic psychology: Conversations with Abraham Moslow, Gardner Murphy, Carl Rogers.* Columbus, Ohio: Wyndham Hall Press.

Koltko-Rivera, M.E. (2006). Rediscovering the later version of Maslow's hierarchy of needs: Self-transcendence and opportunities for theory, research, and unification. *Review of General Psychology,* 10(4), 302-317.

Maslow, A.H. (1959). Psycholigical data and value theory. In A.H. Maslow (Ed.), *New knowledge in human values* (pp. 119-136). New York: Harper & Row.

Maslow, A.H. (1964). Religions, values, and peak-experiences. Harmondsworth, England: Penguin Books.

Maslow, A.H. (1968). *Toward a psychology of being* (2nd ed.). New York: Van Nostrand Reinhold.

Maslow, A.H. (1971). *The farther reaches of human nature.* England: Penguin Books

Maslow, A.H. (1973). Self-actualizing people: A study of psychological health. In R.J. Lowry (Ed.), *Dominance, self-esteem, self-actualization: Germinal papers of A.H. Maslow* (pp. 177-200). Monterey, CA: Brooks/Cole.

Sassen, S. (2003). *Guests and aliens*. New York: New Print.

Sassen, S, (2006). *Territory, authority, rights: from medieval to global assemblages*. Princeton, N.J.: Princeton Print.

Soysal, Y.N. (1997). *Limits of citizenship: Migrants and postnational membership in Europe.* Chicago: University of Chicago.

CHAPTER 14

Evolved Dispositions and the Perspective of the Other

Charles Wright

INTRODUCTION

Reflective human beings have been aware of the role that perspective taking might play in situations of ethical disagreement since at least the time the Golden Rule was first articulated. That versions of this ethical principle are to be found in multiple religious and cultural settings (Wattles 1996) suggests that the basic insight giving rise to it may be fundamental to human moral experience. Given the deep roots that perspective taking has in the ethical life of human beings, it should come as no surprise that scholars from a wide variety of disciplines have endorsed its significance. More recently, though, it has been among theorists concerned with the negotiation of fundamental ethical disagreement in an increasingly pluralistic world that perspective taking seems to have become a kind of sine qua non for ethical reflection and political decision making.

Some prominent advocates of cosmopolitan and deliberative conceptions of normative legitimacy, for example, have suggested that perspective taking among parties to moral and political disagreements is a vehicle that will facilitate the management of chronic moral disagreement characteristic of pluralistic societies. Philosopher Jürgen Habermas (1996; 1998) suggests that elected representatives and members of the judiciary alike will in their deliberations need to take the perspective of the various parties to an issue to best ensure the justice of legally enacted statues and the impartiality of judicial rulings. In a similar vein, political theorists Amy Gutmann and Dennis Thompson (1996; 2004) have proposed that deliberative democratic governance requires citizens and their representatives to cultivate what they "civic integrity" and "civic magnanimity" – an ensemble of moral dispositions that, among other things, requires parties to a moral disagreement to acknowledge and recognize the reasonableness as well as the merits of positions with which they disagree, a practice that could scarcely go forward in the absence of reciprocal perspective taking (Wright 2009).

Scholars of intercultural communication and conflict resolution are similarly concerned with the question of how individuals from different cultural backgrounds might negotiate incompatible social and ethical expectations. In some accounts perspective taking serves as a vehicle that makes possible cross-cultural communication and the development of interethnic identities. Milton J. Bennett (1993; 1998), a leading theorist in this field, has proposed a developmental model which places increasingly sophisticated forms of perspective taking at the heart of advanced stages of "intercultural sensitivity". At the most developed stages of intercultural awareness, an individual is capable of freely moving between a variety of internalized cultural perspectives while deliberating about an appropriate response to a particular situation. Similarly, in his examination of ethical issues arising in contexts of intercultural communication philosopher Richard Evanoff (2004) advances a constructivist theory of ethical judgment built around dialogical principles of mutual agreement and reciprocal perspective-taking. He also investigates the process of integration by which individuals are able to "transcend their own cultures and internalize perspectives gained from a different culture" (Evanoff 2006, 426) as a result of repeated intercultural encounters. Finally, in describing the conditions facilitating the resolution of ethnic conflicts, Wsevolod W. Isajiw (2000) argues on behalf of a principle of identity recognition according to which opposing parties to an ethnic conflict will only be able to achieve the mutual understanding necessary for resolving their disagreements when they are prepared to engage in a kind of reciprocal learning of the basic assumptions of one another's cultural perspective.

As this brief glance at contemporary work in political philosophy and social theory indicates, taking the perspective of another continues to be a central motif of political and ethical reflection. Yet with few exceptions, theorists who endorse perspective taking as a vehicle for managing fundamental cultural and moral disagreement have tended not to subject this capacity itself to careful scrutiny. Perhaps it is just because the notion has been embedded in humanity's ethical traditions for so many centuries that social theorists have not thought it necessary to consider how well equipped human beings might be to undertake such a process. As it happens, though, even as students of moral philosophy and psychology, political theory, and intercultural communication have been building their theories around appeals to perspective taking, scholars in other disciplines have developed theoretical perspectives and obtained empirical insights that offer far reaching insight into how unprepared human beings may be to take the perspective of ethical strangers – by which I mean people with fundamentally different world perspectives. In a word, taking the perspective of such people isn't something that comes naturally to us.

In the remainder of this essay I shall review the biological, sociological and psychological research showing this to be the case. We'll start with explanations for the development of social cooperation based on the theory of evolution by natural selection. These theoretical accounts will together suggest that human beings will possess a basic, innate disposition against engaging in perspective taking with ethical strangers. Subsequent to this review of evolutionary theory, we'll then briefly consider some empirical findings from the social sciences. Here we shall find a wealth of evidence supporting the behavioral tendencies predicted by evolutionary theory. Together, I shall suggest, evolutionary theory and social scientific evidence indicate that philosophical and social scientific theories built around the requirement that people take the perspective of ethical strangers ask human beings to conduct themselves in a manner contrary to species-wide evolved dispositions. But while requiring citizens to engage in perspective taking is requiring them to do something that comes only with difficulty, it is not – I shall finally suggest – to ask the impossible. In the closing remarks of the essay I'll briefly consider some conditions under which humankind's evolved propensities might be counteracted. But before I turn to review of explanations for the origin of social cooperation, it will help if I clarify what I mean by the term "perspective taking".

PERSPECTIVE TAKING

There are a variety of cognitive and affective capacities that have at various times and places been discussed under the rubric of perspective (or "role-") taking. When considering the capacity as a matter of information processing, moral psychologists have distinguished between three different forms of perspective taking: visual (or spatial), cognitive (or communicative), and affective (Eisenberg et al. 1991; Strayer 1987). These consist, respectively, in the abilities to infer what another person situated differently than oneself will or will not have in her visual field, to infer the beliefs and intentions of another person, and to infer another person's emotional states. We should note here that people can and routinely do exercise such cognitive and affective perspective taking capacities in relation to ethical strangers, but not necessarily in pursuit of mutual understanding. American Christian soldiers at Abu Ghraib prison in Iraq, for instance, were exercising these capacities when they inferred that desecrating copies of the Qur'an would outrage and demoralize their Muslim captives.

This example points toward the affective capacities of empathy and sympathy, the first of which is often included under the general heading of perspective taking as well. A conception of empathy widely accepted by moral psychologists holds it to be an affective state in one person elicited by and congruent with an affective state experienced by another (Eisenberg et. al. 1991; Strayer 1987). Sympathy, by contrast, while also an affective state in one person elicited by the feelings or condition of another, is distinguished by sorrow for or concern on behalf of the other (Wispé 1986; 1987). It was these dimensions of perspective taking that were, presumably, absent in Abu Ghraib in particular as well as in most instances of violence against others.

Distinguishing between these cognitive and affective dimensions of perspective taking enables me to specify with more precision the disposition with which I am concerned. The capacity in question can be specified as empathetic responses to ethical strangers that are mediated by culturally informed cognitive and affective perspective taking. The claim I shall be advancing in what follows is that, given the social environment in which the cognitive and affective dispositions of humankind evolved, it is plausible to suppose that people possess an innate disposition not to engage in perspective taking so understood. To see why, let us now turn to evolutionary accounts of human social cooperation.

William Hamilton and Inclusive Fitness

The first account to which we shall turn is William Hamilton's (1964) theory of inclusive fitness (also known as "kin selection") developed in an effort to explain altruistic behavior observed among social animals – warning calls among certain species of birds and ground squirrels, for instance. Conceptions of natural selection current at that time could not explain such behavior because it appeared to be fitness reducing – the benefits provided by alarm calling appeared to come at the cost of an increased risk of predation for alarm calling animals. From the perspective of the prevailing theory, behavioral traits that subject organisms to a relatively greater risk of predation should disappear from the population.

Hamilton's theory of inclusive fitness demonstrated that what matters is not how many offspring any particular organism leaves behind, but how many copies of a particular bit of DNA get left behind. Genes, we must remember, are replicators. Their function is simply to generate more copies of themselves. All the physical and behavioral traits characteristic of living organisms can be regarded as simply so many devices and strategies that have evolved to allow genes to replicate more efficiently – an idea most successfully popularized by the writings of Richard Dawkins. Reproductive success thus depends not simply on how many offspring survive to reproductive age, but also on how many of an organism's siblings, nieces and nephews and their offspring survive and reproduce as well. From the perspective of genes, it is a matter of indifference whether two direct offspring or four nieces and nephews survive to reproductive age. The number of gene copies in the two instances will, on average, be the same. What Hamilton's insight boils down to is that if an organism possesses a behavioral trait that benefits sufficiently close relatives, the probability is that the organisms benefitted will also possess the genes that code for that particular trait. If the inclusive fitness benefits associated with the trait outweigh the costs, it will spread through the population.

For our purposes, the salient feature of Hamilton's theory is that it will account only for cooperative behavior directed toward members of an extended family network. There is reason now to think that this constraint may apply, in part, to perspective taking because one currently influential hypothesis concerning the evolutionary origins of perspective taking (or "mind reading" as it is called in the evolutionary literature) suggests that it was an information processing capacity that conferred fitness enhancing benefits on mothers and infants in populations of cooperatively breeding primates. (Brockway 2003; Hrdy, 2008) Attachments between mothers and infants – evolved dispositions that precede the more complex capacities required for social cooperation – would have provided a preexisting source of affective concern. Capacities for cognitive and affective perspective taking would then have allowed mothers better to interpret and respond to infants' vocal & gestural signals, and would have allowed infants and juveniles better to interpret and predict caretaker responses. If these hypotheses are correct, we should expect that perspective taking capacities that evolved through processes of kin-selection would be preferentially directed toward close kin and not toward ethical strangers. In other words, explanations for the origin of human social cooperation built on Hamilton's model of inclusive fitness predict a nepotistic pattern of empathetic responses to others informed by cognitive and affective capacities for perspective taking. But Hamilton's model is not all there is to the story, so let us turn now to the next.

Robert Trivers and Reciprocal Altruism

While Hamilton's model of inclusive fitness successfully predicts cooperative behavior among closely related organisms, it was Robert Trivers (1971) who offered a convincing theoretical model for cooperation among unrelated organisms. He hypothesized that under certain selective conditions the propensity to engage in simple reciprocal exchanges with unrelated organisms could evolve. In the first instance, the fitness cost to the helping individual would have to be small in comparison to the fitness value of the benefit offered to another. A small price to the helper, in other words, for providing a comparatively larger benefit to the recipient. Further conditions consisted in many opportunities for reciprocal exchanges, repeated interaction with a limited number of individuals, and symmetrically structured reciprocal situations – that is to say, when interacting pairs can offer one another roughly similar benefits at roughly similar costs. In terms of the biological characteristics of organisms, these conditions translate to such features as a relatively long lifespan, a low rate of dispersal, a high degree of mutual dependence, a relatively weak dominance hierarchy, and the availability of benefits made possible only through coalition formation.

Trivers also hypothesized that under such conditions networks of reciprocal relations would most likely be stabilized and sustained through a psychological system built around certain basic emotional responses such as liking and disliking, moralistic aggression, gratitude, sympathy, guilt and reparative altruism. (Trivers 1971, 48-51) According to this account, people do not punish cheats, make amends for misdeeds, and prefer to associate with trustworthy individuals because of some conscious or rational calculation of the fitness advantages of such behavior. Rather, such reactive emotional dispositions evolved simply because getting angry at people who do wrong, feeling guilty about one's own wrongdoing, and being particularly nice to one's friends happened to stabilize networks of reciprocal relations, which in turn ultimately provided a fitness advantage to individuals possessing such dispositions. Evidence from the social dynamics of primates (DeWaal 1996; 2005), from the archaeological record (Aiello, and Dunbar 1993; Dunbar 1996), as well as from existing foraging societies (Boehm 1999) all support Trivers's suggestion that humankind's early hominid ancestors lived in tightly knit social networks in which behavior was regulated by moral emotions such a guilt, anger, empathy, gratitude and a sense of fairness.

Let us consider now what Trivers's model might suggest concerning the capacity for perspective taking. From Hamiltion's (1964) theory of inclusive fitness we learned that the capacities for cognitive and affective perspective taking may have originated as kin selected traits. This would lead us to expect that humans would possess an evolved propensity to exercise these capacities in relation to close relatives, but not ethical strangers. Now we see that networks of reciprocal exchange represent another dimension of the social environment exercising selective pressure in favor of developing these capacities. There would be clear fitness benefits for individuals better able to understand the plans and intentions, and better able to predict the choices, emotional responses, and actions of their partners in reciprocal interaction. The so-called Machiavellian intelligence hypothesis has proposed that humanity's capacities for social cognition evolved for just these kinds of reasons. (Whiten 1997; 1998) It seems, then, that Trivers's model will yield conclusions similar to Hamilton's. We can expect that humans will possess an evolved disposition to engage in perspective taking with others who live in close proximity to themselves and with whom they interact on a regular basis, but not with ethical strangers.

Richard Alexander and Indirect Reciprocity

Trivers' model explained the conditions under which pair wise interactions could be expected to evolve. His model received elaboration by Richard Alexander (1985; 1987), whose concept of indirect reciprocity extended Trivers' model by incorporating social observation and reputation formation, factors enabling stable networks of exchange to develop among relatively larger groups of individuals. Direct reciprocity takes place when an individual who provides a benefit to another receives a benefit in return from the same individual, whereas indirect reciprocity arises when the individual who provides the initial benefit receives repayment from individuals other than the one initially benefitted. One person helps a neighbor to repair damage to his dwelling, for example, and then later receives assistance with a broken tool from the neighbor's brother – where the subsequent assistance is forthcoming only because of the initial offer of assistance. Such patterns are intuitively familiar to us because so intimately woven into the fabric of everyday social life of humans.

Reputation enters into the equation because social observation ensures that an individual's propensity to cooperate, or not, will be known to a wider community. There will be clear fitness benefits for any individual known among members of his immediate community as a reliable partner in cooperation, as well as costs for those known to be unreliable. Alexander thinks that the fitness benefits accruing to an individual generally known as a generous and reliable person can explain the propensity for what he calls indiscriminate social investment in human communities. By this he means a "willingness to risk relatively small expenses in certain kinds of social donations to whomever may be needy – partly because of the prevalence and keenness of observation and [partly because of] the use of such acts by others to identify individuals appropriate for later reciprocal interactions" (Alexander 1987, 97 & 100). In other words, people's readiness to offer low cost assistance to most any member of their local community – charitable contributions, for instance – can be explained by the fitness benefits that accrue indirectly to people with reputations for such helpful dispositions.

Returning now to the question of taking the perspective of ethical strangers, the same conclusions reached in relation to Trivers' model of reciprocity can be seen to proceed fairly directly from Alexander's model of indirect reciprocity as well. Social observation and reputation formation allow for the development of more extended face to face communities of reciprocal cooperators. But the evolved psychological dispositions that ensure the extension of moral concern to members of an individual's own community cannot be expected to move that same individual to show comparable concern to persons outside her community. Alexander (1985) suggests that this difference in attitude towards familiars and strangers can be observed in large urban settings, where the sheer number of inhabitants impedes effective social observation and where the resulting anonymity impedes the successful functioning of reputation formation. The model of indirect reciprocity predicts that under such conditions deviant behavior would increase – a prediction that seems to receive straightforward support in the problems of social order facing large cities.

Let me summarize the discussion so far. Evolutionary biology has provided us with three separate, though related theoretical concepts – kin selection, reciprocity and indirect reciprocity – that together explain how cooperative behavior could evolve among close kin, friends and allies, and small face to face communities. The theories associated with these concepts suggest that the capacity for empathic response mediated by cognitive and affective perspective taking would have evolved because of the selective advantage it offered in an environment marked by prolonged infant dependence, cooperative breeding, and frequent social interaction accompanied by social observation and reputation formation. None of these theories supposes there to have been selective pressure favoring the development of a disposition to engage this kind of perspective taking with ethical strangers. In the next section, we shall see that there are compelling reasons to suppose that the social environment of evolutionary adaptation would have exercised selective pressure against the evolution of such a disposition.

In-group/Out-group Formation

Let us now turn to the matter of intergroup competition. This feature of the social environment of evolutionary adaptation, I want to claim, would have ensured that natural selection would favor the evolution of an innate psychological propensity opposed to taking the perspective of ethical strangers. Paraphrasing social psychologist Jonathan Haidt (2001), from an evolutionary perspective it would be strange (indeed) if humankind's evolved social dispositions encouraged people periodically to side with their community's enemies and against their relatives, friends and neighbors (Haidt 2001, 821).

To find a thinker convinced that dispositions supporting social cooperation evolved in response to the selective pressure exercised by intergroup competition, we need look no farther than Darwin himself. In *The Descent of Man* he articulates this hypothesis with admirable clarity.

> When two tribes of primeval man, living in the same country, came into competition, if the one tribe included (other circumstances being equal) a greater number of courageous, sympathetic and faithful members, who were always ready to warn each other of danger, to aid and defend each other, this tribe would without doubt succeed best and conquer the other...Selfish and contentious people will not cohere, and without coherence nothing can be effected. A tribe possessing the above qualities in a high degree would spread and be victorious over other tribes; but in the course of time it would, judging from all past history, be in its turn overcome by some other and still more highly endowed tribe. Thus the social and moral qualities would tend slowly to advance and be diffused throughout the world. (Darwin 1981/1871, 162-163)

Alexander puts it more bluntly:

> Most of the evolution of human social life, and I will argue the evolution of the human psyche, has occurred in the context of within- and between-group competition, the former resulting from the latter...so far as we know, in no other species do social groups have as their main jeopardy other social groups of the same species – therefore, the unending selective race toward greater social complexity, intelligence, and cleverness in dealing with one another. (Alexander 1987, 79-80)

Social cooperation and morality evolved, in a word, because it gave one group an edge in its competition with others. The "more moral" groups vanquished the less. As a result, Alexander (1985) suggests, the evolutionary function of morality opposes the moral teachings of modern universal and egalitarian moral philosophies.

The evolutionary theories of Hamilton, Trivers and Alexander all suggest, more or less, that human psychology evolved to regulate networks of cooperative interaction among close kin and small face to face communities of friends and neighbors. They suggest also that the propensity to show empathetic concern mediated by cognitive and affective perspective taking evolved in this environment. Now if, as Darwin and Alexander suggest, competition between groups formed a persistent feature of the ancestral social environment, and if, as I am suggesting, this would have fostered the development of a disposition against engaging in perspective taking with ethical strangers, then we should expect to find evidence consistent with this evolutionary story. We have, in a word, now reached the point at which the empirical findings of social scientists become relevant. And as it happens, they have unearthed rather a lot of this sort of thing – compelling evidence that humans are strongly disposed to categorize one another as members of in- and out-groups, to invest these group boundaries with affectively charged symbolic significance, to behave preferentially toward members of the in-group, and so forth. The literature is quite extensive, so I shall limit myself to a quick review of just a few of the best known examples.

During the 1970s Henri Tajfel demonstrated experimentally that people categorized into groups on the basis of factors as trivial as visual judgments or aesthetic preferences were then disposed, when given the opportunity, to behave preferentially toward members of their perceived "in-group". (Billig, and Tajfel 1973; Tajfel, Billig, and Bundy 1971). Philip Zimbardo's Stanford Prison Experiment demonstrated the ease with which normal individuals could be induced to identify with antagonistic roles arbitrarily assigned to them by the experimenter. In this experiment, ordinary young college-age adults were induced to adopt the roles, attitudes and self-concepts of authoritarian guards and subjugated prisoners. The participants' self-identification with these roles became so complete that the experiment had to be ended early out of concern for the participants' well-being. Particularly striking was the student-guards' self-perceived gains in power, social status and in-group identification. (Haney, Banks, and Zimbardo, 1973) Finally, consistent with these findings in social psychology, during the 1950s sociologist Muzafer Sherif and his colleagues reported on the ease with which prepubescent boys with no prior social contact could be induced to form in-groups with differentiated status positions and reciprocal role expectations. In one remarkable experiment they found that just the opportunity to participate in engaging activities over the period of a week fostered in-group cohesion, and that mere knowledge of the existence of another group in the area elicited strong desires for competitive interaction. When on site counselors arranged for a series of intergroup contests, agonistic relations quickly developed, leading to such behavior as name-calling, stereotyping of out-group members, destruction of out-group property and raids on out-group living quarters (Sherif, at al. 1961).

Such evidence is vital for my argument, so the impulse to pile on is strong. But I shall restrain myself in the hope that this gesture toward a large and rapidly growing empirical literature will convince the reader at least of the plausibility of my claim that human beings possess a ubiquitous propensity opposed to an empathic response to ethical strangers mediated by cognitive and affective perspective taking. This propensity, I suggest, represents a fundamental impediment that must be addressed by any theory endorsing perspective taking as a vehicle for managing fundamental cultural and moral disagreement in pluralistic societies.

CONCLUSION

Where does this evolutionary account leave us? Like most arguments appealing to evolutionary processes, this one may seem to have taken on an aura of inevitability. Despite the historical appeal of perspective taking, and despite our tendency to invoke it as an antidote to cultural difference, our evolutionary history as a species, the argument seems to imply, dooms us to perpetual enactment of in-group/out-group hostilities. And since this conclusion is both unpalatable and counterintuitive, critics may wish to take it as a reduction ad absurdum of the evolutionary perspective. But such pessimism is not warranted.

What the evolutionary perspective shows us instead is the magnitude of the challenge. If human communities and individuals are allowed to carry on their day to day business as they always have, as – speaking very loosely – they were designed by nature, then perpetual intergroup conflict is certainly what we can expect. Humankind's response must be to develop institutional orders that foster in people dispositions that counteract the evolved propensity to withhold empathic response mediated by cognitive and affective perspective taking. There are a variety of strategies that could be implemented to foster this end: non-governmental civic organizations that foster interethnic and interreligious cooperation (Varshney 2001); educational programs that foster perspective-taking with ethical strangers (Comunian, and Gielen 2006; Day, 2002); political and religious leaders, like André Trocmé, who endorse and practice perspective taking mediated empathy toward ethical strangers (Hailie, 1979); cross-cultural contact (Commons et al. 2006; Endicott et al. 2003); and possibly even international trade, since those who prosper through business dealings with ethical strangers have a powerful incentive to improve their interethnic understanding. Space constraints do not permit a satisfactory review of the intentional mechanisms that human communities could put in place to foster the development of a disposition toward intercultural perspective taking. But such a review is not necessary to appreciate the force of the lesson at hand. It is only through sustained efforts to develop appropriate institutional structures that the necessary cultural correctives for humankind's innate suspicion of ethical strangers might be implemented.

The remarkable and ironic conclusion to which we seem to be led by this evolutionary history of human cooperation is that while humankind has known of, admired, and recommended perspective taking and empathy as part of its global ethical legacy, it is precisely because these are such difficult and unusual things to do – because these are things that do not come to human beings naturally – that they have acquired their current moral prestige. The evolutionary perspective we have just considered suggests that theorists trying to understand how pluralistic societies can manage chronic moral disagreement and foster intercultural understanding should not simply appeal to the insights to be gained through culturally informed cognitive and affective perspective taking, but should also consider the intentional institutional orders that will support and encourage such practices.

REFERENCES

Aiello, Lesley C. and R. I.M. Dunbar..1993. "Neocortex Size, Group Size, and the Evolution of Language" *Current Anthropology* 34: 184-193.

Alexander, Richard D. 1985. "A Biological Interpretation of Moral Systems" *Zygon* 20: 3 – 20.

Alexander, Richard D. 1987. *The Biology of Moral Systems.* Hawthorne, NY: de Gruyter.

Bennett, Milton J. 1993. "Towards Ethnorelativism: A Developmental Model of Intercultural Sensitivity." *Education for the Intercultural Experience*, edited by R. Michael Paige, 21-71. Yarmouth: Intercultural Press.

Bennett, Milton J. 1998. "Overcoming the Golden Rule: Sympathy and Empathy." *Basic Concepts of Intercultural Communication: Selected Readings*, edited by Milton J. Bennett, 191-214. Yarmouth: Intercultural Press.

Billig, Michael and Henry Tajfel.1973. "Social Categorization and Similarity in Intergroup Behavior" *European Journal of Social Psychology* 3: 27-52.

Boehm, Cristopher. 1999. *Hierarchy in the Forest. The Evolution of Egalitarian Behavior*. Cambridge,: Harvard University Press.

Brockway, Raewyn 2003. "Evolving to be Mentalists. The 'Mind-Reading Mums' Hypothesis." *From Mating to Mentality: Evaluating Evolutionary Psychology*, edited by Kim Sterelny and Julie Fitness, 95-123. New York: Psychology Press.

Commons, Michael.L., Jesus. F. Galaz-Fontes, Stanley J. Morse. 2006." Leadership, Cross-Cultural Contact, Socio-Economic Status, and Formal Operational Reasoning about Moral Dilemmas among Mexican nonliterate Adults and High School Students." *Journal of Moral Education* 35: 247-267.

Comunian, Anna L., and Uwe P. Gielen. 2006. "Promotion of Moral Judgment Maturity through Stimulation of Social Role-Taking and Social Reflection: An Italian Intervention Study." *Journal of Moral Education* 35: 51-69.

Darwin, Charles. 1981/1871. *The Descent of Man, and Selection in Relation to Sex*. Princeton: Princeton University Press.

Day, Laura. 2002. "Putting Yourself in Other People's Shoes': The Use of Forum Theatre to Explore Refugee and Homeless Issues in Schools." *Journal of Moral Education* 31: 21-34.

De Waal, Frans. 1996. *Good Natured. The Origins of Right and Wrong in Humans and Other Animals*. Cambridge: Harvard University Press.

De Waal, Frans. 2005. *Our Inner Ape*. New York: Penguin.

Dunbar, Robin. 1996. *Grooming, Gossip, and the Evolution of Language.* Cambridge: Harvard University Press.

Eisenberg, Nancy., Cyndy .L. Shea, Carlo Gustavo, and George P. Knight. 1991. "Empathy-Related Responding and Cognition: A 'Chicken and the Egg' Dilemma." *Handbook of Moral Behavior and Development, Vol. 2: Research*, edited by William M. Kurtines, and Jacob L. Gewirtz, 63-88. Hillsdale: Lawrence Erlbaum Associates.

Endicott, L., T. Bock, and D. Narvaez. 2003. "Moral Reasoning, Intercultural Development, and Multicultural Experiences: Relations and Cognitive Underpinnings." *International Journal of Intercultural Relations* 27: 403-419.

Evanoff, Richard J. 2004. "Universalist, Relativist, and Constructivist Approaches to Intercultural Ethics." *International Journal of Intercultural Relations* 28: 439-458.

Evanoff, Richard J. 2006. "Integration in Intercultural Ethics." *International Journal of Intercultural Relations* 30: 421-437.

Fiske, Susan T. 1998. "Stereotyping, Prejudice, and Discrimination." *The Handbook of Social Psychology, Vol. 2*, edited by Daniel T. Gilbert, Susan T. Fiske, and Gardner Lindzey, 357-411. New York: Oxford University Press.

Gutmann, Amy and Dennis Thompson, D. 1996. *Democracy and Disagreement.* Cambridge: Harvard University Press.

Gutmann, Amy and Dennis Thompson, D. 2004. *Why Deliberative Democracy?* Princeton: Princeton University Press.

Habermas, Jürgen 1996. *Between Facts & Norms*, translated by William Rehg. Cambridge: MIT Press.

Habermas, Jürgen. 1998. *The Inclusion of the Other*, edited by C. Cronin, and P. De Greiff. Cambridge: MIT Press.

Haidt, Jonathan 2001. "The Emotional Dog and its Rational Tail: A Social Intuitionist Approach to Moral Judgment." *Psychological Review* 108: 814-834.

Hallie, Philip P. 1994. *Lest Innocent Blood Be Shed.* New York: Harper Perennial.

Hamilton, William. 1964. "The Genetical Evolution of Social Behavior II." *Journal of Theoretical Biology* 7: 17-52.

Haney, Craig, Curtis Banks, and Philip Zimbardo. 1973. "Interpersonal Dynamics in a Simulated Prison." *International Journal of Criminology and Penology* 1: 69-97.

Hrdy, S. B. 2008. "Evolutionary Context of Human Development: The Cooperative Breeding Model." *Family Relationships: An Evolutionary Perspective*, edited by C. Salmon and T. K. Shackelford, 39-68. New York: Oxford University Press.

Isajiw, Wesevolot W. 2000. "Approaches to Ethnic Conflict Resolution: Paradigms and Principles," *International Journal of Intercultural Relations* 24: 105-124.

Sherif, Muzafer, O.J. Harvey, B. Jack White, William R. Hood, and Carolyn W. Sherif. 1961. *Intergroup Conflict and Cooperation: The Robbers Cave Experiment*. Norman: Institute of Group Relations.

Strayer, Janet 1987. "Affective and cognitive perspectives on empathy." In *Empathy and its Development*, edited by Nancy Eisenberg and Janet Strayer, 218-244. New York: Cambridge University Press.

Tajfel, Henry, M.G. Billig, and R. P. Bundy. 1971. "Social Categorization and Intergroup Behavior." *European Journal of Social Psychology* 1: 149-178.

Trivers, Robert L. 1971. "The Evolution of Reciprocal Altruism," *Quarterly Review of Biology* 46: 35-57.

Varshney, Ashutosh. 2001. "Ethnic Conflict and Civil Society." *World Politics* 53: 362-98.

Wattles, Jeffrey. 1996. *The Golden Rule*. New York: Oxford University Press.

Whiten, Andrew. 1997. "The Machiavellian Mindreader." *Machiavellian Intelligence II*, edited by Andrew Whiten and Richard W. Byrne, 144-173. New York: Cambridge University Press.

Whiten, Andrew. 1998. "Evolutionary and Developmental Origins of the Mindreading System." *Piaget, Evolution, and Development*, edited by Jonas Langer & Melanie Killen, 73-99. Mahwah: Lawrence Erlbaum Associates.

Wispé, Lauren. 1986. "The Distinction Between Sympathy and Empathy: To Call Forth a Concept, a Word is Needed." *Journal of Personality and Social Psychology* 50 : 314-321.

Wispé, Lauren. 1987. "History of the Concept of Empathy." *Empathy and its Development*, edited by N. Eisenberg and J. Strayer, 17-37. New York: Cambridge University Press.

Wright, Charles. 2009. "Natural Selection and Social Cooperation: Innate Impediments to Taking the Perspective of the Other." Paper presented at the Second Annual Global Studies Conference, Zayed University, Dubai, United Arab Emirates, August 28.

CHAPTER 15

Responsibility and Love: Normative Global Risk Management

Stefan Litz

INTRODUCTION

We humans are dreaming many dreams, and defeating cancer is only one of these dreams. Research focusing on the treatment and prevention of cancer has so far, in fact, resulted in some significant advancement. This progress fuels our hopes to defeat cancer at some point in time[1]. In *I am legend*, a recently screened motion picture featuring Will Smith, scientists seem to have finally developed the ultimate cure for cancer[2]. A genetically manipulated virus seems to have cured all humans with various types of cancer as part of an initial test group. Dr. Krippin, a fictional scientist representing her research team, is pictured smiling into the camera of a fictional news show claiming that, finally, cancer has lost its deadly grip on humankind. But soon afterwards a disaster of previously unknown magnitude starts to unfold: Mysterious behaviour by an increasing number of

---

[1] The idea of continuous progress is an important assumption propelling research and technological development. Progress has been analyzed from a variety of perspectives in an anthology edited by Arnold S. Burgen, Peter McLaughlin, Jürgen Mittelstraß, eds., *The Idea of Progress* (Berlin: Walter de Gruyter, 1996). Christopher Lasch, *The True and Only Heaven: Progress and its Critics* (New York, NY: Norton, 1991) and Athur M. Melzer, Richard Zinman, and Jerry Weinberger, eds., *History and the Idea of Progress* (Ithaka, NY: Cornell University Press, 1995) provide further explorations of this important concept. For more classical works on progress see John B. Bury, *The Idea of Progress: An Inquiry Into its Origin and Growth* (New York, NY: Cosimo Classics, 2008) as well as Robert A. Nisbet, *History of the Idea of Progress* (Rutgers, NJ: Transaction Publishers, 1995).

[2] The novel by Richard Matheson, *I am Legend* (New York, NY: Tom Doherty Associates, 2008), first published in 1954, has so far been adopted for three mainstream movies, that is, *The Last Man on Earth* (dir. Ubaldo Ragona; 1964) starring Vincent Price, *The Omega Man* (dir. Boris Sagal; 1971) starring Charlton Heston, and *I am legend* (dir. Francis Lawrence; 2007) starring Will Smith.

humans is being reported and suspicious deaths begin to occur. Within a few more years, following the declared victory over cancer, according to the narration in the movie, billions of humans everywhere on the planet will have died as a consequence of some unintended side effects of the genetically engineered virus. Only a few million individuals have survived the initial outbreak of a man-made disease characterized by a previously unknown high mortality rate. Most of these survivors eventually changed their physical appearance and behaviour: they start to rest during the day in dark spots and become active during night. The reason for this change seems to be rooted in the fact that the exposure to the ultraviolet rays of the sunlight destroys the molecular integrity of their altered cells and, therefore, exposure to the sunlight causes them to disintegrate quickly. Most survivors of the catastrophe have been transformed, at the same time, into aggressive individuals with exceptional physical strength and capabilities. In a fatal manner they started to hunt and kill the remaining few millions not mutated humans but one, a micro-biologist called Robert Neville. Neville is the main protagonist of the movie and he dedicates henceforth his solitary existence to a desperate search for a treatment which may be able to reverse the mutation of the survivors. He is finally able to find a cure and the spectator discovers that Neville was, contrary to the initial indications in the movie, actually not the only remaining human. The antiserum reverses the mutation process and it reaches, in the hands of a woman Neville has met briefly before being killed by some of the mutants, a fortified enclave in which some other non-mutated human survivors of the catastrophe have created a kind of a gated community[3]. This story illustrates a potential situation which may remind everybody involved in the development of technology and the advancement of knowledge that they may have to ask at some point the fundamental moral question: is the risk involved in some kind of

---

[3] Gated communities are atavisms of ancient times and are designed to exclude unwanted others from entering space featuring next to private properties usually also a quasi-public realm shared by the inhabitants. Walls, fences and electronic surveillance systems may be employed in order to enforce this social exclusion of "the Other". Modern gated communities are omnipresent in many regions around the world and a discussion of contemporary gated communities may be found in Edward J. Blakely and Mary G. Snyder (1997), *Fortress America: Gated and Walled Communities in the United States* (Washington, D.C.: Brookings Institution Press, 1997) and Stefan Litz, "The Fortified Society: Social Exclusion as a Result of Privatization and Fortification of Space", *Berliner Journal für Soziologie* 10 (2000): 535-554.

scientific research and technology simply too high given what could be at stake, that is, the very existence of humankind[4]?

In order to find sound answers to such a question ethical reasoning rooted in moral philosophy may be helpful. Not discounting the potential relevance of older ethical conceptualizations, this paper will focus on two contemporary moral philosophers of significance, namely, Jonas[5] (1984) and Mittelstraß (1992). Unlike earlier moral philosophers both theorists had to consider a new kind of human condition: the possibility that unintended side effects of scientific research and technological actions could result in a self-inflicted elimination of humankind. Jonas was one of the first moral philosophers who have outlined, given such a historically unique context, ethical systems rooted in the assumption that living humans have some kind of responsibility for those humans who are not yet born[6]. Jonas's moral philosophy which is fundamentally discussing how to approach the management of risks in advanced technological civilizations from a philosophical point of view is relatively well known. But Mittelstraß's position,

---

[4] There is a plethora of fiction highlighting the inherent potential dangers of research and technology and, as a matter of fact, a whole genre of dystopian fiction draws on such ideas. This genre is based on the imagination of possible fatal consequences of research and technology and includes, for example, S. D. Perry's, *Resident Evil: The Umbrella Conspiracy* (New York, NY: Pocket Books, 1998) in which an artificial virus created by the "Umbrella Corporation" is animating dead humans to morph into brainless, hungry and cannibalizing zombies. It has also been screened as a motion picture (dir. Paul Anderson; 2002) starring Milla Jovovich. Another recently popular example of fiction of this genre is Michael Crichton's, *Prey* (New York, NY: Harper, 2006) in which the story revolves around organic nanoparticle forming swarms which are hunting and killing humans.

[5] Hans Jonas, *Das Prinzip Verantwortung. Versuch einer Ethik für die technische Zivilisation.* (Frankfurt a.M.: Suhrkamp, 1979). Quotes in this paper are from the English translation: The *Imperative of Responsibility*, transl. Hans Jonas and David Herr (Chicago, IL: University of Chicago Press, 1984).

[6] The idea of "intergenerational responsibility" is closely linked to the notion of "intergenerational justice" made popular by John Rawls, *A Theory of Justice* (Boston, MA: Harvard University Press, 1971). In addition to Hans Jonas, other contributions outlining and refining a theory of responsibility for future generations published after Rawls's seminal work, include D. Clayton Hubin's, "Justice and Future Generations," *Philosophy and Public Affairs* 6 (1976): 70-83; Barry, Jane English's, "Justice between Generations," *Philosophical Studies* 31 (1977): 91-104; Trudy Gorier's, "What should we do about Future People?," *American Philosophical Quarterly* 16 (1979): 105-113; Ernest Partridge's, *Responsibilities to Future Generations* (Buffalo, NY: Prometheus Books, 1981), and Derek Parfit's, "Future Generations: Further Problems," *Philosophy & Public Affairs* 11 (1982): 113-172.

very different if not antithetical to Jonas's point of view, is so far less well known, partly due to the fact that many of his papers and books are not yet translated into English.

Discussing both moral conceptualizations will highlight the different logics of thinking underlying much contemporary philosophical reasoning and political cleavages. It allows to demonstrate that despite the fact that Jonas and Mittelstraß, and many others, may be unanimous when it comes to characterizing the unique quality of the existing modern risks, two very different conclusions may be drawn and promoted from such a diagnosis. The analysis of Jonas's and Mittelstraß's moral positions will also serve to highlight that one important point, which should be part of their argument, seems to be either underdeveloped or non-existing. As a matter of fact, the question of *why* living but mortal humans should actually feel responsible for future generations of humans is not at all addressed by Mittelstraß. It will be furthermore argued that it is very questionable whether or not Jonas's ontological reasoning is providing a sufficient answer to the question. It will be maintained instead that arguments outlined in Fromm's (1947) conceptualization of a humanistic ethics and part of Dawkins's (2006) evolutionary reasoning are, in concert with Rawls's social contract theory, well suited to provide, perhaps, an unexpected rationale for how to approach the management of global risks and to answer the question of why previous generations should feel responsible for future generations. Before this paper embarks upon this task it is important to highlight the key attributes of the aforementioned historically unique modern human situation in some more detail. What sets the modern global risks aside from earlier types of risks and what kind of impact on the experience and conceptualization of human society may these relatively new risks entail?

Global Risks

Human societies were, according to Jonas, for the longest period in time characterized by the fact that technology and research were both, in the context of a relatively hostile natural environment in which humans were struggling for survival, morally quite unproblematic in terms of their impact on nature. As long as technological practices or human action could not fundamentally alter nature, nature itself was not an object of human responsibility. Nature was "taking caring of herself and, with some coaxing and worrying, also of man: not ethics, but cleverness applied to her" (Jonas 1984, 21). But the quest for an ever increasing capability to manipulate the natural world for human purposes, the real essence of the "project of modernity" as Habermas (1992) has emphasized, has changed this situation. Mittelstraß has maintained that technology is increasingly creating a physical world in which human intervention has always had some impact. The modern world we are experiencing, in Heideggers's[7] terminology, as being ("*Dasein*") thrown into the world at some time and place without our consent, is a world which has been shaped over centuries by technological activity of previous generations and continues to be (re)shaped by our current activities. Increasing technological capability, however, does not only increase the possibilities to shape nature in a sense that it will improve human living conditions and enhance the survival chances of the human species while reducing natural dangers. It increases paradoxically at the same time the self-made risks endangering the survival of the human species. The destructive potential of the weapons of mass destruction unleashed at once and, in addition, the unintended negative side effects of industrial action have caused a new problematic quality of human existence. Due to this relatively new eschatological human potential of self-made modern risks, nature must become, according to Jonas, an object of human responsibility.

Beck has outlined an influential social theory based on a systematic analysis of the role of such self-made existential risks in modern societies which distinguish them from traditional societies[8]. He argued that traditional societies were predominantly concerned with the question of how to distribute the produced "goods" (or to increase the production of "goods") while modern societies are predominantly concerned with the challenge of how to distribute human made "bads" (or to decrease the production of "bads")[9]. Beck focused on

---

[7] Martin Heidegger, *Sein und Zeit* (Tübingen: Niemeyer, 1963). English translation: *Being and Time*, transl. John Macquarie and Edward Robinson (Oxford: Blackwell, 1962).

[8] Ulrich Beck, *Risikogesellschaft. Auf dem Weg in eine andere Moderne* (Frankfurt a.M.: Suhrkamp, 1986). English translation: *Risk Society: Towards a New Modernity,* transl. Mark Ritter (London, UK: Sage, 1992). See also Ulrich Beck, *World Risk Society* (Cambridge, MA: Polity, 1999). Risk has also been discussed from a sociological point of view by Niklas Luhmann, *Soziologie des Risikos*. (Berlin: Walter de Gruyter, 1991). English translation: *Risk: A Sociological Theory,* transl. Rhodes Barrett (New Brunswick, NJ: Aldine Transaction, 2005).

[9] Differences between the types of dangers human societies have to deal with have been outlined by Ulrich Beck in, *Gegengifte: Die organisierte Unverantwortlichkeit* (Frankfurt a.M.: Suhrkamp, 1988). English translation: *Ecological Politics in an Age of Risk*, transl. Amos Weisz (Cambridge: Polity, 1995), p. 78. Beck distinguished between 1.) natural hazards endangering and characterizing pre-industrial societies, 2.) limited but self-made risks in the early industrial society, and 3.) existential risks with annihilatory potential characterizing the modern "World Risk Society".

these modern "bads" as materialized or potential risks and stressed that modern industrialization, which brought much material progress or, to employ a different term, more and better "goods", could only unfold since the "bads" it produced at the same time, had been insured. In other words, the potential and manifest costs of the risks of early industrialization, the produced "bads" so to speak, were covered by public or private insurance agreements and, therefore, had been externalized from the economic system. Public and private insurance, in concert with the concept of the limited liability of corporations and investors, and a labour force set free from traditional restrictions of movement and occupational choice as well as career possibilities, provided the socio-legal context for the modernization process and the industrial revolution[10]. But some modern risks are significantly different from pre-modern risks of the early modernization period as the potential harm they may cause if materialized is of such a magnitude which impedes their insurance and therefore externalization. The potential harms of nuclear power, genetically manipulated food and genetically manipulated life, exceed by far the scope of damage an insurance company would be able to compensate for.

Beck highlighted that the potential global impact of such risks and the experience that such risks can in fact materialize, despite their low probability of materialization, as the nuclear accident in Tschernobyl and the currently unfolding events in Fukushima have demonstrated, make us become more and more aware of the fact that we are living in a "World Risk Society". The opportunity to distance oneself physically and mentally from hazards of some modern scientific and technological activities - as there is a chance that the negative consequences, if materialized, will only have an impact on others and not on oneself - has largely vanished. Beck claimed that, as a consequence, the very distinction between oneself and the other has conceptually and, in some forms, also politically and practically disappeared. The very fact that it is

---

[10] James Coleman, *The Asymmetric Society* (Syracuse, NY: Syracuse University Press, 1982) has argued that the emergence and proliferation of large scale modern industrial organizations and corporations, which are often engaged in risky research and technological development, was propelled by the limitation of the owners to their invested capital. Larry A. DiMatteo, "The Transformation of American Business Organizations: The Ascendency of the Limited Liability Company", *Zeitschrift für Vergleichende Rechtswissenschaft*, No. 110 (2011): 37-63, has argued that, at least in the USA, "the corporation-centered focus of business organizations has given way to the limited liability company (LLC) as the dominate form of business organization". Regardless of significant or subtle legal differences the crucial point remains, that is, that the liability of investors is limited to their invested capital in the case of materialized risks ("bads").

impossible to escape some risks, since they are of global magnitude, creates, according to Beck, at various places on the globe an awareness of a common fate of the human species. It is the disappearance of the concept of "the Other" which makes the modern "World Risk Society" so unique and qualitatively different from any of the traditional societies since only an "us" remains being left. In the modern "Word Risk Society", the risk of a self-inflicted catastrophe of large magnitude, potentially resulting in the annihilation of the human species may manifest itself at any time. Lash and Wynne emphasized, like Beck, that the expansion of the adverse impact of harmful events on the human species in time and space must be seen as a consequence of modernization calling for a re-conceptualization of responsibility[11].

Derrida (1995) has pointed out that the development of the concept of responsibility is historically intimately linked to the developing "culture of death" and particularly to the idea of the immortality of the human soul. It is assumed that the idea of the immortal soul resulting in the notion of being held accountable for action not only while being alive but also after death triggered human self-restriction and limitation. Derrida also discussed extensively Patocka who emphasized that the struggle between the archaic concept of the (unlimited) orgiastic behaviour and the ancient concept of (limited) disciplined behaviour has been resolved by the subordination of the orgiastic or ecstatic principle to the disciplining rational principle in the course of the human civilization process[12].

---

[11] Scott Lash and Brian Wynne, *Introduction* in, Ulrich Beck, *Risk Society: Towards a New Modernity*, (London: Sage, 1992) 1-8, stressed this important conclusion as follows: "These dangers can, for example, no longer be limited in time – as future generations are affected. Their spatial consequences are equally not amenable to limitation – as they cross national boundaries. Unlike in an earlier modernity, no one can be held accountable for the hazards of the 'risk society'. Further, it is becoming impossible to compensate those whose lives have been touched by those hazards, as their very calculability becomes problematized.", p. 2.

[12] Jan Patocka, *Is Technological Civilization Decadent, and Why*? in, Jan Patocka, *Heretical Essays in the Philosophy of History*, transl. Erazim Kolak (Peru, IL: Open Court; 1996), 95-118. Friedrich Nietzsche, *Die Geburt der Tragödie (Leipzig: E. W. Fritzsch, 1878)*. English translation: *The Birth of Tragedy*, transl. Douglas Smith (Oxford: Oxford University Press, 2000) has conceptualized the same struggle in terms of a battle between the dionysian principle of ecstatic unrestrained emotional expression and the apollonian principle of the limiting calculative rationality. Norbert Elias in, *Über den Prozeß der Zivilisation: Soziogenetische und Psychogenetische Untersuchungen* (Frankfurt a.M.: Suhrkamp, 1969). English translation: *The Civilization Process. Sociogenetic and Psychogenetic Investigations*, transl. Edmund Jephcott (Oxford: Blackwell, 2000) has discussed this gradual taming of the emotional principle and the resulting predominance of

Derrida highlighted that since everyone must be aware of his or her ultimate death, the only thing in the world that no one else can either "give or take", the freedom of individual choice and action and therefore individual responsibility for these choices and actions becomes undisputable. Heidegger has similarly claimed in his analysis of the "*Man*" (one) that, since nobody can tell another person what to do in the ultimately individual situation of the experience of one's own death, the same principle should apply to the previous life itself. No reference to others and the abstract "one does" will release an individual from the necessity to make decisions based on the idea of individual freedom and, as a consequence, to take responsibility for the decisions. According to Jonas, traditionally only living humans could be held responsible for their actions, and only insofar, as their actions had an immediate or direct negative impact on other concurrently living humans. In light of the collapse of conventional limitations of risks in time and space and the irreversibility of technological activities and scientific discoveries, however, the concept of responsibility must be re-drawn.

Responsibility refers to the fact that not every technologically possible and at a particular point in time in a given society legally not prohibited activity may be justified. Beck (1992, 28) has outlined that responsibility implies that humans must be able to answer questions concerning the legitimacy of their actions in a normative sense and not only the legality of action in a juridical sense and continued to outline important questions to be asked in the context of the new *condito humana*:

> Behind all the objectivications, sooner or later the question of *acceptance* arises and with it anew the old question: *how do we wish to live*? What is the human quality of humankind, the natural quality of nature which is to be preserved? The spreading talk of 'catastrophe' is in this sense an objectivised, pointed, radicalized expression that this development is *not wanted.*

Moral dilemmas may arise for individuals, groups and organizations, for communities and states, as well as for transnational regimes. Moral dilemmas emerge at the "grey zone" characterizing decision-making in a context in which a course of action may be chosen which is not illegal but may be perceived to be illegitimate since the risks are too high. Principles or guidelines are needed in

---

the rational principle in the development of human societies from a historical perspective. Elias's thesis, however, has been challenged by Hans Peter-Duerr in a number of books published under the title *Der Mythos vom Zivilisationsprozeß (The Myth of the Civilization Process)* (Frankfurt a. M.: Suhrkamp, 1988-2005).

order to deal with such dilemmas and to be able to provide arguments for justifying the chosen course of action. Sloterdijk (2011) emphasized that some consequences must be drawn from the diagnosis of a looming catastrophe and stressed that the fundamental absolute imperative must be: "you must change your life". But in which direction do we have to change our lives in order to demonstrate our responsibility? In what kind of sense do we have to self-limit our behaviour as we may be held accountable for our actions?

Pessimism and Fear

Hans Jonas provided answers to these questions and emphasized that the complexity and potential long delay of any negative impact of human technological action in time, and the potential irreversibility of the impact, calls for a particular kind of responsibility. If the consequences of technological action on nature and, in consequence, for the human species are not predictable, special precaution needs to be taken. Due to the eschatological potential of modern technology, it is necessary to cautiously limit our actions. Limitation is necessary since the capabilities of humankind entail self-made dangers for its own existence. Jonas underlined that under no circumstances the possibility of human life may on the whole be bet against something else regardless of its potential benefits in the course of action. But given the fact that predicting the potential negative impact of manifested risks of technological action seems impossible, largely due to the complexity and the long causal chains, how can we possibly come up with a good rationale for decision-making?

According to Jonas, it is not necessary to know exactly what is going to happen in the future in order to have a rationale for decision-making. It is sufficient to be aware of the potential dangers or to be able to imagine the potential risks of some action. He emphasized that such possible negative consequences - which we can imagine - must be always given priority in decision-making. Jonas particularly stressed that the imagination of the possibility of a final and irreversible danger for the very existence of the human species should prevent us from pursuing a certain scientific or technological action. He argued that the predominance of the negative prognosis or the theoretically possible negative consequences can be best explained if we compare the relationship between the probabilities of a positive or a negative result of some kind of scientific and technological experiment with the probabilities of hitting and missing a target. Jonas argued that hitting the target is only one of infinite other alternatives, which are all more or less equivalent to missing the target. Even if we can accept to miss the target when it comes to issues of minor importance, he emphasized, we must never take even the slightest risk to miss the positive imagined outcome of technological action if, at the same time, even just a near miss may endanger the very existence of human life on this planet. In this manner Jonas (1984, 31) wrote:

> It is the rule, stated primitively, that the prophecy of doom is to be given greater heed than the prophecy of bliss. The reasons for this shall be briefly pointed out. [...] First, the mere probability relation between lucky and unlucky results of unknown experiments is generally like that between either hitting or missing a target. The hit is only one of innumerable alternatives which otherwise are more or less wide misses. And although in small matters we may allow many such misses in order to benefit from the rarer chances of success, we may allow but few where greater things are concerned. And in the really great, irreversible ones, which go to the root of the whole human enterprise, we really must allow none.

It is the imagination of negative consequences causing *fear* which must have the prerogative over the imagination of positive consequence causing hope. Fear should therefore guide ethical decision-making and, as a consequence, limit scientific research and technological development in the context of possible existential dangers for the human species which may be inherent in such activities.

According to the earlier sketched narration of the movie "I am legend", a research team had genetically manipulated a virus in order to treat cancer and to free humankind from a terrible disease. The result in this imaginary story was that humankind came very close to its self-inflicted extinction, an idea which may make some of us tremble with fear. The unintended side effects of a well-intended action has caused in this fiction a disaster for the human species. Jonas would argue that if such a consequence is theoretically possible as we manipulate microorganism, if we can reasonably imagine the possibility of such a negative consequence, if we cannot be certain that such a scenario can never happen, and even if it may be just a small chance that this possibility may ever manifest at one point in time, we should rather not engage in such activities. In other words, there are certain things which are an essential part of our existence as human beings which we should simply learn to accept and to live with. Living with the fact that there is cancer, cancer which may turn out to be fatal to individuals who will naturally, if not of cancer, eventually die due to another reason at one point in time may be better - according to Jonas's argument - than living with the risk that a treatment developed and intended to cure cancer may endanger the very existence of the whole human species. Jonas's moral reasoning may demand a stop at a certain point to avoid trespassing an imaginary point of no return in scientific research and technological development. Jonas therefore outlined the following imperative which should be considered to be the fundamental moral guideline for researchers and politicians alike:

> Act so that the effects of your action are compatible with the permanence of genuine human life; or expressed negatively: Act so that the effects of your action are not destructive of the future possibility of such life; or simply: Do not compromise the conditions for an indefinite continuation of humanity on earth; or, again turned positive: In your present choices, include the future wholeness of Man among the objects of your will. (Jonas 1984, 11)

Any scientific or technological research and action backed or not backed by political will must not be undertaken, even though we may be able to do so, if this action could possibly endanger the very existence of humankind.

It should be highlighted that Jonas does not argue that we should not try to find ways to treat cancer or that there should not be research or technological development taking place. We should, however, be careful with developing techniques which theoretically may contain dangers for the very existence of the human species. On one hand, for example, pharmaceutical drug treatment or nuclear medicine is quite limited in their possible impact to the various individual cancer patients. Manipulated micro-organisms on the other hand are subject to natural evolutionary processes which humans cannot control. Nobody will be able to guarantee that human engineered microorganisms may not eventually become a fatal danger to the existence of the human species at some point in the future.

In the light of Jonas's argument, genetic manipulation may be completely banned due to the potential inherent existential risks for the human species. In fact, scientists should have never been allowed to find out about it. Upon discovery, based on their moral reasoning predicting possible negative fatal consequences, they perhaps should have destroyed their findings. For the better or worse, scientists discovered the genetic code and the fundamental building blocks of life. Meanwhile not only the whole human genome and the genome of other species have been decoded but scientists have developed technological means to manipulate the genetic structure of cells, to manipulate genetically human *Dasein* itself[13]. We currently living humans and the following generations somehow must

[13] The fundamental achievement enabling this possibility of genetic manipulation was the discovery of the DNA structure by Francis Crick and James Watson in 1953 who both became Nobel Laureates in 1962. The discovery of the code of life may be - according to

live and cope with the fact that we have already created such knowledge and made such technological developments.

It is important to keep in mind: genetic manipulation is merely one of many scientific and technological developments which may be theoretically capable to destroy human existence as a consequence of some unintended side effects. Given such apocalyptic possibilities, shall we perhaps at least stop, prohibit and control strictly further research in this field? If so, how likely would it be the case that all scientists in all countries in the world would comply? Moreover, would this be the proper course of action if one considers carefully the de facto existing human situation?

Optimism and Hope

In fact, Mittelstraß emphasized that *not* further engaging in scientific research or into technological development could, contrary to Jonas's argument, turn out to be fatal for the human species. He agreed with Jonas's assumption that we are confronted with many problems and being not willing to accept living with these problems may have negative consequences for our experience of our human existence. In some instances we may be just too quickly and too much engaged with the struggle to eliminate some perceived problems rather than accepting them as a part of our existence as genuine human beings. In this manner, Heidegger (2008, 332) pointed out that the human species may, given all the technology being developed and at its command, at the end forget to consider the ends to which it has developed this technology and warned:

---

the differentiation between phases of radical and incremental scientific progress by Kuhn, *The Structure of Scientific Revolution* (Chicago, IL: University of Chicago Press, 1996) - described as revolutionary scientific progress. Likely positive and negative consequences of this revolutionary developments and its challenges have been discussed, for example, by Jeremy Rifkin and Ted Howard, *Who should Play God? The Artificial Creation of Life and What it Means for the Future of the Human* (New York, NY: Dell Publishing, 1977) and Jeremy Rifkin, *The Biotech Century: Harnessing the Gene and Remaking the World* (Los Angeles, CA: J.P Tarcher, 1998). Peter Sloterdijk's, *Regeln für den Menschenpark* (*Regulations for the Human Zoo*) (Frankfurt a.M.: Suhrkamp) discussed possibilities of deliberate human engineering in order to improve human capabilities and stirred a hot debate and controversy in Germany. How such a future may look like has been demonstrated in *Gattaca* (dir. Andrew Niccol, 1997) starring Ethan Hawke, Uma Thurman, and Jude Law.

> In truth, however, precisely nowhere does man today any longer encounter himself, i.e., his essence. Man stands so decisively in subservience to on the challenging-forth of enframing that he does not grasp enframing as a claim, that he fails to see himself as the one spoken to, and hence also fails in every way to hear in what respect he ek-sists, in terms of his essence, in a realm where he is addressed, so that he can never encounter only himself.

But regardless of such warning words by Heidegger and apocalyptic possibilities inherent in modern research and technology, Mittelstraß is challenging Jonas's conservative attitude to scientific progress and technological development since, for example, genetic manipulation may give us not only the opportunity to deal with some problems much better than we have ever been able to cope with. It may turn out one day to be the only reason that human life remains to be possible on this planet. Mittelstraß pointed out that the decoding of the human genome by research and the development of technical possibilities enabling humans to engage in genetic engineering may turn out at one point in time to be in fact the *conditio sine qua non* for safeguarding further genuine human existence on this planet. For example, should someday a new or so far not virulent naturally evolved microorganism endanger the existence of the human species, humankind may be saved only because of the capability of genetic engineering. It may enable us to create vaccinations or to alter some component of the human genome eliminating the fatal impact of some kind of microorganism on humans. Mittelstraß emphasized that self-limitation may bring us into "a situation in which we may not know enough and we may not be able to deal with the problems the future will bring to this world. The problems will not suddenly stop developing and remain the same, if we stop developing [knowledge and technology]"[14]. In fact, voluntarily stagnating at the current level of scientific and technological capability may – given the already existing scientific and technological development and their impact on humankind – in fact not reduce but rather

[14] Jürgen Mittelstraß, *Die Angst und das Wissen (Fear and Knowledge)* in, Annemarie Gethmann-Siefert and Carl Friedrich Gethmann, eds., *Philosophie und Technik (Philosophy and Technology)* (München: Wilhelm Fink, 2000) wrote in German: "…in eine Situation führen, in der wir zu wenig wissen und zu wenig können, um mit den Problemen fertig zu werden, die die Welt noch bringen wird. Denn die Probleme bleiben nicht stehen, wenn wir stehen bleiben." p. 34, my translation.

increase existential risks. Mittelstraß emphasized this important conclusion as follows[15]:

> The [scientifically informed and technically stabilized rationalities] have their own problems, particularly in the form of unintended side effects, which cannot be disputed. But – I would like to repeat this here – the solution is not less scientific and technological intelligence but in many cases, though in a cautious manner, more scientific and technological intelligence.

He stressed that we must not only approach the issue of risks involved in scientific research and technological development asking what kind of risks such actions may entail. In addition, we must also consider the potential risks of *not* further engaging in scientific research and technological development for the human species. Mittelstraß reasoned that only continuing scientific research and technological development may be the hope for the human species to improve, in the long run, the conditions of its existence and to increase the chances for its survival. It may therefore be argued that imagining possible existential risks for the human species resulting from self-limiting research and technological development provide an argument for propelling further activities and efforts in scientific research and technological development.

As a matter of fact, the mutations of the humans are in Matheson's trendsetting novel "I am legend" originally portrayed as the results of a naturally emerged disease. They are neither described as the result of a metaphysical phenomenon or the result of human activity. The cause for the mutation of the human species into blood consuming and zombie like creatures and the death of billions is being attributed to a naturally evolved microorganism. It is suggested in the novel that the microorganism causing the mutation had been active many centuries ago. But at that time only a few humans were infected and it is indicated that the infection spread only via direct blood contact. Due to the low numbers of infected and the limitations containing the spread of the microorganism in the

---

[15] Jürgen Mittelstraß, *Die Angst und das Wissen (Fear and Knowledge)* in, Annemarie Gethmann-Siefert and Carl Friedrich Gethmann, eds., *Philosophie und Technik (Philosophy and Technology)*, wrote in German: "Daß diese [wissenschaftlich informierte und technisch stabilisierte Rationalitäten] ihre eigenen Probleme, vor allem in Form von unerwünschten Nebenfolgen, haben, ist unbestreitbar. Nur lautet – und auch das sei hier noch einmal wiederholt – die Lösung nicht weniger wissenschaftlicher und technischer Verstand, sondern, allerdings auf besonnenen Wegen, in vielen Fällen sogar Steigerung des wissenschaftlichen und technischen Verstandes", p. 39, my translation.

human population, the disease was not an existential danger for the human species. Given the very limited scientific knowledge of biological phenomena and microorganisms, as well as technical capabilities at that time in human history, so Matheson's novel, the confrontation with mutated humans resulted in the creation of legends and myths about vampires and zombies. Robert Neville, the last surviving non-mutated human in Matheson's novel, reflects the horrible situation he is confronted with many centuries after the initial outbreak of the disease as follows[16]:

> Something black and of the night had come crawling out of the Middle Ages. Something with no framework or credulity, something that had been consigned, fact and figure, to the pages of imaginative literature [...] A tenuous legend passed from century to century. Well, it was true. [...] True, he thought, but no one ever got the chance to know it. Oh they knew it was something, but it couldn't be that – not *that*. *That* was imagination. *That* was superstition, there was no such thing as *that*. And, before science had caught up with the legend, the legend had swallowed science and everything. (Matheson 1954, 28)

Matheson's novel in fact makes, in stark contrast to the narrative being told in the latest screen adaptation of the story for the motion picture "I am legend", an argument *for* further scientific and technological progress and not against it. In fact, it seems that humankind is permanently confronted with the natural emergence of new diseases which could cause, as a pandemic unfolds, the death of millions or billions, the collapse of modern economies and societies, and perhaps the elimination of the very kind of genuine human life on the planet. SARs and the worries concerning the emergence of an Influenza virus characterized by a mortality rate comparable to the "Great-Flu"[17] caused in 2010 the WHO to issue an alert and to initiate concerted efforts to develop and produce very quickly large amounts of vaccinations which were administered to a large amount of people within a very short time. The outbreak of a newly evolved stem of the virulent EHEC germ in Germany and in some other European countries also illustrates the fact that humankind seems to be in a permanent "war" with naturally emerging new diseases. EBOLA or a similar naturally evolved disease may turn out to cause a global disaster. Without the scientific discoveries and

---

[16] Richard Matheson, *I am Legend*, p. 28.

[17] Gina Colata, *Flu: The Story of the Great Influenza Pandemic of 1918 and the Search for the Virus that has Caused it* (Toronto: Touchstone, 2010).

technological capabilities we have now at hand our reaction to those dangers would have been very different.

But even though Mittelstraß emphasized the necessity to continue with scientific research and technological development it does not automatically follow that there should be no restrictions in place. There is the possibility for misuse and the abuse of science and technology by individuals, organizations and regimes. But as a matter of fact: there are no technical instruments which cannot be used with negative consequences for human life. The intention of those humans using the technology is of crucial relevance and the intention reflects their moral individual ethos. There is, as Mittelstraß stressed, some good reason to be afraid of purposeful misuse of science and technology. He pointed out that limiting research is always necessary when it is intended to deform genuine human life instead on improving human living conditions. Mittelstraß's categorical imperative is therefore phrased as follows[18]:

> Make sure that [technological] construction and [scientific] development are instrumental for maintaining and improving the living conditions and for life in a Leonardo-World!

In addition to institutional control mechanisms which are designed to minimize the possibility of intentional abuse of scientific research and technology, we need to ensure the development of a strong moral ethos of responsible action among individuals, not only in science and politics but also in business. But how can we create a strong ethos of individual responsibility? What would be the rationale for this moral ethos of responsible behaviour limiting action and the driving force behind behaviour directed by the categorical imperative outlined above? What is the very reason why humans are actually able to experience responsibility and what may cause humans to voluntarily limit their activities in the first instance or, to phrase it differently, from an axiomatic perspective?

Love and Care

Fromm's conceptualization of a humanistic ethics, which may hold the key to the question of why such an ethos of responsibility exists or can be deliberately

---

[18] Jürgen Mittelstraß, *Die Angst und das Wissen (Fear and Knowledge)* in, Annemarie Gethmann-Siefert and Carl Friedrich Gethmann (eds), *Philosophie und Technik Philosophie und Technik (Philosophy and Technology)*, wrote in German: "Stelle Konstruktion und Entwicklung in den Dienst der Erhaltung und der Verbesserung der Lebensgrundlagen und des Lebens in einer Leonardo-Welt", p. 40, my translation.

generated, begins with challenging an idea deeply rooted in many religions and societal behavioural expectations, namely, that being selfish is something wrong or sinful. In this respect Fromm's point of view is similar to Nietzsche's (1976) position who strongly objected the demonization of egoistic behaviour[19]. But while moral values are in Nietzsche's conceptualization necessarily generated by strong "aristocratic" individuals who are later on imposed on the masses and mimicked by the submissive subjects ("*Untertanen*")[20], this kind of authoritarian morality has been rejected by Fromm[21]. In contrast to Nietzsches' authoritarian approach Fromm (1947, 162) emphasized that moral values must be derived individually by each human being and a humanistic conscience is therefore "not the internalized voice of an authority whom we are eager to please and afraid of displeasing; it is our own voice, present in every human being and independent of external sanctions and rewards". Fromm (1947) continues to ask the important question of what the nature of this inner voice may be. The answer to this question may help us to understand what triggers an ethos of responsibility in individuals and how it may be strengthened.

Fromm argued that, as a matter of fact, being concerned with oneself is an inherent ontological feature (instinct) of human existence and a "biological programme" humans are naturally born with. In fact, Freud (1961, 42) maintained that the capability to love oneself or that, to employ more technical terms, "*narcissm* is the universal original condition, out of which object-love develops later without thereby necessarily causing a disappearance of the narcissism". Fromm (1947, 124) emphasized that narcissistic love for oneself is an important characteristic feature of a healthy human being. He also highlighted that the social or cultural expectations that individuals should demonstrate altruistic behaviour

---

[19] Friedrich Nietzsche, *Genealogie der Moral (Leipzig: C. G. Neumann, 1887).* English translation*: On the Genealogy of Morals and Ecce Homo*, transl. Walter Kaufmann and Reginald J. Hollingdale (New York, NY: Random House, 1967).

[20] Heinrich Mann, *Der Untertan* (Frankfurt a. M.: Fischer, 2008). English translation: *Man of Straw* (London: Penguin, 1984) which has also been screened as a motion picture (dir. Wolfgang Staudte; 1951) starring Werner Peters. Theodor Adorno, Else Fraenkel-Brunswick, Daniel Levinson, and Nevitt Sanford, *The Authoritarian Personality* (New York: Harper and Row, 1950) have outlined the psychosocial determinants (characteristic features) of the submissive personality.

[21] A discussion of various suggestions of how moral values emerge, including the propositions of Nietzsche, James, Durkheim, Simmel, Scheler, Dewey, and Taylor may be found in Hans Joas, *Die Entstehung der Werte.* (Frankfurt a.M.: Suhrkamp, 1997). English translation: *The Genesis of Values,* transl. Gregory Moore (Chicago, IL and Cambridge, MA: The University of Chicago Press & Polity Press, 2000).

stands in stark contrast to the idea that the most "powerful and legitimate drive in man is selfishness and that by following this imperative drive the individual makes his best contribution to the common good". As a consequence, Fromm asked to accept the existence of a natural and healthy narcissism or love for oneself. Love is for Fromm (1947, 134) "an expression of productiveness and implies care, respect, responsibility, and knowledge. It is not an 'affect' in the sense of being affected by somebody, but an active striving for the growth and happiness of the loved person, rooted in one's capacity to love". Fromm claimed that this naturally given ability to love is crucial for the development of a feeling of responsibility for oneself and others[22].

Not fear of the punishment of an immortal soul in some kind of imagined afterlife or fear from punishment by legal or other punitive institutions but the very selfish yet healthy capability to feel and experience love for oneself and others implies, according to Fromm, an ethos of self-limiting responsible behaviour. Love may, therefore, be considered as the basic rationale or natural human capability on which to build a strong ethics of responsibility. Fromm (1947, 143) wrote in that manner that not the "fact that people are too much concerned with their self-interest, but that they are not concerned enough with the interest of their real self; not in the fact that they are too selfish, but that they do not love themselves" and significant others, I would like to add, seems to be the reason for irresponsible behaviour[23]. It is therefore necessary to reformulate the

---

[22] Erich Fromm, *For Man Himself*, p. 135 explained this important idea as follows: "*The affirmation of one's own life, happiness, growth, freedom, is rooted in one's capacity to love*, i.e., in care, respect, responsibility, and knowledge. If an individual is able to love productively, he loves himself too; if he can love *only* others, he can not love at all". Fromm, *For Man Himself*, p. 131 emphasized, discussing Nietzsche's, *Thus Spoke Zarathustra,* transl. Reginald J. Hollingdale (London, UK: Penguin Books, 1969), further: "The essence of this view is this: Love is a phenomenon of abundance; its premise is the strength of the individual who can give. Love is affirmation and productiveness, 'It seeketh to create what is loved'! To love another person is only a virtue if it springs from this inner strength, but it is a vice if it is the expression of the basic inability to be oneself."

[23] Jacques Derrida, *The Gift of Death and Literature in Secret,* has illustrated that, for example, if humans love a deity more than themselves and other humans, they are more prone to display irresponsible behavior. Derrida illustrated this phenomenon by discussing a narrative reported in the bible. Abraham was willing to sacrifice his son to the god who has asked for this in order to test his love for him. In this case, fortunately, Abraham was prevented from murdering his own son in the last moment but he has passed the test and demonstrated that he loves god more than anybody else. Individuals full of love for themselves and their significant others are unlikely to engage in such behavior violating

fundamental ethical imperative for the modern "World Risk Society", perhaps surprisingly, in the following words:

> Make sure that humans are enabled to love themselves as much as they are taught to love others as this will prevent them from engaging in behaviour which could existentially endanger themselves and others they love!

Generating a strong ethos of responsibility by enabling and teaching love to all but particularly to leaders in science, politics and business may be a crucial "insurance mechanism" for the survival of the human species, in addition to the implementation of various institutional control mechanisms. But some questions remain: Why has nature enabled or programmed humans to be able to experience the feeling of love? Why is the capability of love an inherent "natural voice" in human beings? And why may we have to expand the notion of love for significant others from containing only those who live concurrently to include those who may live in the future?

According to Dawkins (2006), loving oneself and loving others may, from an evolutionary perspective, be essentially linked with the struggle for survival. In general terms, this concern for survival may be rooted in the natural program inherent in individuals to ensure that their, in principle, immortal genes will continue to survive long after they are dead. In other words: the ethos of responsibility may not require the belief in the existence of an immortal soul but in the existence of immortal genes. Dawkins (2006) discussed human behaviour in the context of the idea that the individual human *Dasein* is merely a survival machine for the genes its body contains. According to Dawkins's argument humans are therefore normally programmed by nature – if they are aware of it or not – to be concerned with the survival of their genes in a gene pool. From the perspective of the genes, so to speak, individual humans should in the first

---

the principle of care inherent in love. Michael Reiter, *Opferordnung. Philosophisches Unbehagen in der modernen Kultur und Faszination der Gewalt im Ersten Weltkrieg. (The Structure of Sacrifice: Philosophical Discomfort in the Modern Culture and the Fascination of Violence in World War I)* Berlin: Dissertation Freie Universität Berlin, 1997, p. 180) explained the dedication to sacrifice (oneself and others) to some kind of abstract idea as follows: "The willingness to sacrifice is the subjective signal that some absolute value is being accepted, the sacrifice itself is the objective signal underlining the absolute imperative of a value. In this sense, the act of sacrifice transcends itself into the practical form of value generation". Quoted in Hans Joas, *Die Entstehung der Werte* (Frankfurt a.M.: Suhrkamp; 1997), p. 120, my translation.

instance be concerned with their survival. Secondly, they should be concerned with the survival of other individuals with whom they share their genes, that is, their close relatives or kin and in particular their children. As genes are carried forward from one generation to another generation they become – in principle – immortal. Dawkins (2006, 99) highlighted that the general rule "be nice to your relations" promoted in human societies may, from an evolutionary point of view, be a logical consequence of "genemanship". The notion of "genemanship" translates into a concern for the survival of one's own genes in the gene pool of the human species. Each individual *Dasein* holds accordning to Dawkins (2006, 66) "its immortal genes in trust for the future" as the predecessors did for those who are born afterwards[24]. According to this bioevolutionary perspective, humans should have and usually do have a naturally programmed interest in enhancing the survival chances for themselves and for significant others, particularly their offspring[25]. If we selfishly care for ourselves and others whom we may love we may develop a strong ethos of responsibility. We will be less likely to intentionally engage in actions which may endanger our own survival or the survival of loved ones. As a consequence, individuals are unlikely to deliberately engage in activities which may result in the extinction of the human species as this would necessarily include their own and their significant others or loved ones or, to be more precisely, the extinction of their genes. But what about individuals who do not have offspring or significant others to care for? What if there is nobody who may carry their genes into the future and, hence, may make their genes in principle immortal? Why should such individuals nevertheless limit their behaviour and demonstrate responsibility? Why should they agree or be assumed and asked to restrict their behaviour for the good of the coming generations if nothing of them remains to be part of the future?

---

[24] Moreover, Richard Dawkins, *Selfish Gene*, p. 95 wrote: "To extend the actuarial analogy, individuals can be thought of as life-insurance underwriters. An individual can be expected to invest or risk a certain proportion of his own assets in the life of another individual. He takes into account his relatedness to the other individual, and also whether the individual is a 'good risk' in terms of his life expectancy compared with the insurer's own. Strictly we should say 'reproductive expectancy' rather than 'life expectancy' or to be even more strict, 'general capacity to benefit own genes in the future expectancy'." It is interesting to highlight that Dawkins employs the notion of *risk* and *insurance* to discuss the survival of genes. While Dawkins' argument is discussing risk and insurance in the context of ensuring the survival of one's genes, Beck focused on risks and insurance for the survival of the human genome and, therefore, the survival of our species on this planet.

[25] Hans Jonas (1984, p. 130) discussed accordingly the parent-child relation as an archetype of responsibility.

Ignorance and Contract

Rawls's theory of justice as fairness may provide some answers to such questions. Every *Dasein* who has been granted the gift of life could, in principle, have been also born in the past – a possibility we need not to consider further at this point – or could theoretically have been born in the future. But if we would be born in the future and we selfishly love ourselves, we would be inherently interested in finding an inhabitable nature for ourselves. It is the construct of the hypothetical "veil of ignorance", i.e. the assumption of not knowing the individual situation before consenting to particular norms determining a social order, which is the bedrock of social contract theory, and which comes into play in order to provide an argument for voluntary self-limitation. According to Rawls's dictum, we have to assume the existence of a hypothetical "veil of ignorance" concerning the time at which we could have been born or, in Heidegger's terminology, being thrown into our existence as *Dasein* at a particular place and time without our consent. Rawls (1971, 137) outlined the basic idea of the "veil of ignorance" in his version of the social contract theory as follows[26]:

> …I assume that the parties do not know the particular circumstances of their own society. That is, they do not know its economic or political situation, or the level of civilization and culture it has been able to achieve. The persons in the original position have no information as to which generation they belong. These broader restrictions on knowledge are appropriate in part because questions of social justice arise between generations as well as within them, for example, the question of the appropriate rate of capital saving and of the conservation of natural resources and the environment of nature […] They must choose principles the consequences of which they are prepared to live with whatever generation they turn out to belong to.

We can assume that in the hypothetical "original position", to which Rawls and other social contract theorists like Hobbes[27] grant so much theoretical importance,

---

[26] Rawls, however, assumed in his assumptions and discussion that the very succession of generations itself or, to put it into other words, the existence of the human species is not in question.

[27] Fromm's assumptions concerning the human nature as intrinsically programmed to love stands in stark contrast to the opposing assumption characterizing human nature intrinsically as hostile or programmed to hate unless disciplined and checked which, perhaps, has been most popularly heralded by Thomas Hobbes, *Leviathan* (Oxford: Oxford University Press; 1998).

all human beings (inherently programmed by nature to be able to love themselves and significant others) would agree that under no circumstance any previous generation of humans may endanger the existence of the following generation(s). In other words, humans, who have learned to love themselves and furthermore to love others they care for, would agree not to engage in deliberate action which may endanger the existence of future generations as they theoretically could have been part of these future generations. Moreover, individuals in the theoretical original position would not know if they may have offspring capable of carrying their immortal genes further into the future or not. But if they would have offspring, they would be interested in an inhabitable nature and would give their consent to necessary limitations. Finally, they would reasonably be expected not to intentionally engage in activities which may endanger the existence of the human species. But the risk of creating unintentionally existential risks by research and technology remains as an inherent chance the human species is taking and must take - balanced carefully against the chance of existential dangers which may emerge if scientific and technological opportunities are not further pursued.

Conclusion

Jonas and Mittelstraß may be considered to represent two streams or opposing poles of moral philosophy and *eo ipso* also political camps. Both camps have good arguments for their very different answers when it comes to the central question in the context of the emergence of a "World Risk Society": shall we allow whatever we could technologically do regardless of the potential unintended existential risks for humankind theoretically inherent in such activities?

Jonas suggested that we should accept in some cases self-imposed limitations and remain humble. We must never risk the existence of the human species in our quest for scientific and technological progress. For this purpose, Jonas has proposed a heuristic of fear in which pessimism has priority. Jonas stressed that we may be allowed to put our own individual existence at risk, but never the existence of the whole human species. In doubt, we must let go the possibilities certain technological developments may bear in the light of the potential risks. It has been demonstrated in this paper that one may imagine scenarios in which research and technological development may unintentionally endanger the very existence of the human species. But, at the same time, one may easily imagine situations which will underline that only further research and technological development may save the human species from existential threats in the future.

Different versions of Matheson's "I am legend" have vividly illustrated this phenomenon.

Mittelstraß has argued that a conservative attitude and practice could lead us into a situation in which we may not know enough and we may not be able to deal with human made problems and naturally occurring problems the future may bring. He claimed that setting limits to the quest for knowledge development by pointing out imagined negative effects of some technology could in fact lead to a situation in which the existence of humankind may be endangered. Mittelstraß's ethical imperative is based on a "heuristic of hope" in which optimism dominates [28]. He proposed to accept the unintended existential risks the development of some scientific knowledge and technology may entail. In fact, Mittelstraß stressed that our civilization is likely to be doomed due to the already existing human made dangers unless we continue to engage in research and technological development. In addition, unknown natural dangers may lurk hidden in some ecological niches or may emerge in the future threatening the human species. Not placing limitations is therefore the appropriate course of action in order to enhance the survival chances of our species, particularly in the context of the modern "World Risk Society", but engaging further into scientific and technological development.

But some kind of limitation is necessary in order to reduce the chance of intentional abuse of scientific research and technological development. Developing a strong ethos of responsibility characterizing those individuals who conduct scientific research and command technology is pivotal. But how can we ensure such a strong ethos of responsibility guiding research and technological development? Fromm suggested that part of the human nature is our naturally given potential to love. Based on Dawkin's biological evolutionary point of view, this love may be a natural program inherited by human beings in order to ensure that individual humans who may be considered to be mere replication machines for genes may act according to the principles of "genemanship". According to this principle, activities and investments or, to put it more generally, human behaviour should always be directed towards enhancing the survival chances of one's own genes[29]. The fundamental ethical imperative which will ensure that

---

[28] Ernst Bloch, *Prinzip Hoffnung* (Frankfurt a.M.: Suhrkamp, 1982). English translation: *Principle of Hope*, transl. Neville Plaice, Stephen Plaice and Paul Knight (Boston, MA: MIT Press, 1995) analyzed some classic utopian ideas and discussed the creative potential of alternative utopian ideas for a better human life.

[29] Nigel Nicholson and Wendy de Waal-Andrews (2005) have argued that career success, which usually grants the successful individual a high social status and material wealth, is

humans are less likely to intentionally engage into activities which may endanger the very existence of humankind calls therefore to help humans to retain their capability for love or to (re)learn it. Promoting an ethics of love may reduce the chances that individuals are willing to intentionally engage into existential dangerous activities. Love is fundamental for the development of an individual ethos of responsibility. It may be the best kind of "insurance" against the existential risks a deliberate misuse of modern science and technology may entail, next to institutional arrangements imposing restrictions and exerting control, we may be able to think of. The best "insurance" for the human species in terms of reducing the possibility that some of its members may engage into some kind of intentional activities entailing existential dangers for the human species, in addition to institutional control mechanisms as I would like to repeat, may read perhaps, surprisingly: Make sure that humans maintain or (re)learn the naturally given ability to love themselves and others more than anything else!

References

Beck, Ulrich. 1992. Risk *Society: Towards a New Modernity*. London Sage, UK.

Beck, Ulrich. 1995. *Ecological Politics in an Age of Risk*. Cambridge: Polity.

Beck, Ulrich. 1999. *World Risk Society*. Cambridge, MA: Polity.

Blakely, Edward, and Snyder, Mary. 1997. *Fortress America: Gated and Walled Communities in the United States.* Washington, D.C.: Brookings Institution Press.

Burgen, Arnold, and Peter McLaughlin. 1996. *The Idea of Progress*. Berlin: Walter de Gruyter.

Bury, John. 2008. The *Idea of Progress: An Inquiry Into its Origin and Growth.* New York, NY: Cosimo Classics.

Colata, Gina. 2010. *Flu: The Story of the Great Influenza Pandemic of 1918 and the Search for the Virus that has Caused it*. Toronto: Touchstone.

Coleman, James. 1982. *The Asymmetric Society*. Syracuse, NY: Syracuse University Press.

Crichton, Michael. 2006. *Prey.* New York, NY: Harper.

Dawkins, Richard. 2006. *The Selfish Gene.* Oxford: Oxford University Press.

Derrida, Jaques. 1995. *The Gift of Death and Literature in Secret*. Chicago: University of Chicago Press.

---

basically driven by the implicit struggle of individuals to enhance their reproduction chances and the survival chances of their offspring.

DiMatteo, Larry. 2011. "The Transformation of American Business Organizations: The Ascendency of the Limited Liability Company", *Zeitschrift für Vergleichende Rechtswissenschaft* 110: 37-64.

Elias, Norbert. 1969. *The Civilization Process, Sociogenetic and Psychogenetic Investigations*. Oxford: Blackwell.

Freud, Sigmund. 1961. *A General Introduction to Psychoanalysis.* New York, NY: Washington Square Press.

Fromm, Erich. 1947. *Man for Himself: An Inquiry into the Psychology of Ethics.* Fawcett, CT: Greenwich.

Gorier, Trudy. 1979. *What Should we do about Future People?*. American Philosophical Quarterly 16. 105-113.

Heidegger, Martin. 1962. *Being and Time*. Oxford: Blackwell.

Hobbes, Thomas. 1998. *Leviathan.* Oxford: Oxford University Press.

Hubin, D. Clayton. 1976. "Justice and Future Generations." *Philosophy and Public Affairs* 6: 70-83.

Jane, Barry. 1977. "Justice between Generations." *Philosophical Studies* 31: 91-104.

Jonas, Hans. 1984. *The Imperative of Responsibility*. Chicago: University of Chicago Press.

Kuhn, Thomas S. 1996. *The Structure of Scientific Revolution*. Chicago: University of Chicago Press.

Lasch, Christopher. 1991. *The True and Only Heaven: Progress and its Critics*. New York, NY: Norton.

Lash, Scott, and Brian Wynne. 1992. *Introduction in, Ulrich Beck, Risk Society: Towards a New Modernity*. London: Sage.

Litz, Stefan. 2000. "The Fortified Society: Social Exclusion as a Result of Privatization and Fortification of Space". *Berliner Journal für Soziologie* 10: 535-554.

Luhmann, Niklas. 2005. *Risk: A Sociological Theory*. Aldine Transaction.

Mann, Heinrich. 1984. *Man of Straw.* London: Penguin.

Martin Heidegger. 2008. "The Question concerning Technology" In *Basic Writings*, edited by David Krell, 311-341. New York, NY: Harper Perennial.

Matheson, Richard. 1954. *I am Legend.* New York, NY: Tom Doherty Associates.

Melzer, Arthur, Richard Zinman, and Jerry Weinberger. 1995. *History and the Idea of Progress*: Cornell University Press.

Nicholson, Nigel, and Wendy de Waal-Andrews. 2005. "Playing to Win: Biological Imperatives, Self-regulation, and Trade-offs in the Game of Career Success" *Journal of Organizational Behavior* 26: 137-154.

Nietzsche, Friedrich. 1967. On *the Genealogy of Morals and Ecce Homo*, translated by Walter Kaufmann, and Reginald J. Hollingdale. New York: Random House.

Nietzsche, Friedrich. 2000. *The Birth of Tragedy*. Oxford: Oxford University Press.

Nisbet, Robert. 1995. *History of the Idea of Progress*. Rutgers: Transaction Publishers.

Parfit, Derek. 1982. "Future Generations: Further Problems." *Philosophy & Public Affairs* 11: 113-172.

Partridge, Ernest. 1981. *Responsibilities to Future Generations.* Buffalo: Prometheus Books.

Patocka, Jan. 1996. *Is Technological Civilization Decadent, and Why?* Peru: Open Court.

Perry, S.D. 1998. *Resident Evil: The Umbrella Conspiracy.* New York: Pocket Books.

Rawls, John. 1971. *A Theory of Justice.* Boston: Harvard University Press.

Rifkin, Jeremy, and Ted Howard. 1977. *Who should Play God? The Artificial Creation of Life and What it Means for the Future of the Human.* New York: Dell Publishing.

Rifkin, Jeremy. 1998. *The Biotech Century: Harnessing the Gene and Remaking the World.* Los Angeles: J.P Tarcher.

Contributors

Dr. Lydia Amir, Senior Lecturer, The College of Management Academic Studies (Israel). Research Interests: Ethics, History of Philosophy, Practical Philosophy, Humor.

Dr. Elizabeth Edmonton, Senior Lecturer, Federation University (Australia). Research Interests: Globalization, Collective Responsibility, Climate Change, International Governance.

Dr. Pedro Geiger, Professor, State University of Rio de Janeiro (Brasil). Research Interests: Political and Economic Geography.

Randall Horton, PhD, Ethicist and Ethics Trainer, Ethics beyond Compliance (USA). Research Interests: Social Justice, Globalization, Grief.

Dr. S A Hamed Hosseini, Lecturer and Associated Researcher, School of Humanities and Social Sciences, The University of Newcastle (Australia). Research Interests: Transnational Social Movements, Global Ideologies, Transnational Identities, Global Social Change.

Dr. M Raymond Izarali, Associate Professor, Department of Criminology, Wilfrid Laurier University, Brantford Campus (Canada). Research Interests: International Crime and Justice, Globalization, Theories of Human Rights.

Dr. John Janzekovic, Lecturer, Faculty of Arts and Business, University of the Sunshine Coast (Australia). Research Interests: International Relations, Humanitarian Interventionism, International Law, Peace and Conflict, Democratic Development.

Dr. Stefan Litz, Associate Professor of Management, Schwartz School of Business, St. Francis Xavier University (Canada). Research Interests: Globalization, Corporate Social Responsibility, Business Ethics, Human Resource Management, Career Management, Organizational Theory.

Dr. Edwin Mares, Professor of Philosophy, School of History, Philosophy and Political Science, Victoria University (New Zealand). Research Interests: Logic and Probability.

Dr. Teodor Negru, Post-Doctoral Fellow, Faculty of Philosophy and Socio-Political Sciences, Alexandru Ioan University (Romania). Research Interests: Continental Philosophy, Philosophy of Mind, Autopoiesis, Philosophy of Cognitive Sciences.

Dr. Alessandra Sarquis, Research Associate, Institute of International Relations, University of Brasilia (Brasil) and Centre de Rationalites Contemporaines, University Paris VI-Pavillon Sorbonne (France). Research Interests: Contemporary Political Philosophy, Theories of Justice, Globalization and Human Rights.

Dr. Henry Venter, Associate Professor in Psychology, College of Letters and Sciences, National University, Fresno (USA). Research Interests: Leadership performance; Anxiety Disorders, Grief, Post-Traumatic Stress Disorder (PTSD).

Elaine Venter, Graduate Student, Claremont Graduate University, Claremont (USA). Research Interests: Globalization, Culture, Identity, Social Media, Digital Media and Learning.

Dr. Susan Wild, Senior Lecturer, School of Business and Economics, University of Canterbury (New Zealand). Research Interests: Accounting Theory, Human Rights and Corporate Accountability, Sustainability Reporting, Applied Ethics, Integrated Reporting.

Dr. Charles Wright, Associate Professor of Philosophy, Department of Philosophy, St. John's University (USA). Research Interests: Social and Political Philosophy, Moral Psychology and Evolutionary Ethics, Environmental Ethics, Asian Philosophy.

www.ingramcontent.com/pod-product-compliance
Lightning Source LLC
Chambersburg PA
CBHW032130020426
42334CB00016B/1107

* 9 7 8 1 6 1 2 2 9 7 9 3 4 *